BUILT-INS, STORAGE AND SPACEMAKING

BUILT-INS, STORAGE AND SPACEMAKING

an Allen D. Bragdon book

ARCO PUBLISHING, INC.
New York

An Allen D. Bragdon Book

Published by Arco Publishing, Inc.
215 Park Avenue South, New York, NY 10003

Library of Congress Catalog Card Number: 83-71279
ISBN 0-668-05919-2 (Cloth Edition)
ISBN 0-668-05923-0 (Paper Edition)

Printed in the United States of America

10 9 8 7 6 5 4 3 2 1

TECHNICAL CONSULTANTS

Tim Snyder, who prepared the material in sections I and III, is Associate Editor of *Fine Homebuilding* magazine and the author of Adding Storage Space, Petersen Publishing Company, 1978. He has been a carpenter, a cabinetmaker and, for fun, he builds guitars from scratch. Currently, he is reconstructing the space in a Connecticut hunting lodge to make it his year-round home.

The expertise for section II was provided by Seymour Minkin and John V. Vanderwende. Their editor was James Wykoff.

Seymour Minkin comes from a long line of skilled carpenters. A licensed Master Carpenter who has worked at his trade for more than 30 years, Mr. Minkin is an instructor in woodworking at Alfred E. Smith Vocational High School and teaches Apprentice and Journeyman Retraining at Labor Technical College, both in New York City. During the summer months he takes on home remodeling and other carpentry jobs to keep his skills sharp.

John V. Vanderwende holds several Master Plumber licenses, and has 32 years' trade experience in remodeling and construction work. Since 1962 he has taught plumbing and related technical subjects at Alfred E. Smith Vocational High School. For 14 years he has served as instructor and consultant to local plumbing apprentice training programs. He works every summer as a plumber to keep in touch with new trade technology and materials.

EDITORIAL PRODUCTION

The contents of this book were created, designed, and produced by the staff of Allen D. Bragdon Publishers, Inc., 153 West 82nd Street, New York, N.Y. 10024.

Most of the material in sections I-IV of this book has appeared in two other works that were given limited distribution by the Petersen Publishing Company. Their titles were Adding Storage Space and Remodeling Kitchens and Baths.

The following people helped to build this book:

Editors: Allen Bragdon, Nancy Jackson, Eileen Martines, Laura Palmer, Erwin Rosen, Hannah Selby, James Wykoff
Designers: Vivian Chin, John Miller, Clara Rosenbaum
Photographers: Jack Abraham, Monte Burch, Tim Snyder
Artists: Pat Lee, Gary Monteferante, Chuck Pitaro, Jerry Zimmerman
Production: Ellen Dichner, Eleanore Fahey, Dana Sephton, Chon Vinson

ACKNOWLEDGEMENTS

The Editors wish to thank the following individuals and firms for their help in the preparation of this book: S. F. Bailey & Sons; Creative Woodworking; Evans Products Co., Riviera Division; Excel Wood Products Co., Guildmark Furniture Division; Haas Cabinets; John Jackson; Minolta Corp.; National Recessed Cabinets; Poggenpohl USA Corp.; Rockwell International, Power Tool Division; Rubbermaid Corp.; Schulte Corp.; the Stanley Works, Tool and Hardware Divisions; U.S. Gypsum; Allmilmo Corporation; American Institute of Kitchen Dealers; American Olean Tile Company; American Standard, Inc.; Argus Kitchens Incorporated; Aristocrat Kitchens Ltd.; Armstrong Cork Co.; Peter Bleckman; Celotex Division, Jim Walter Corp.; Champion Building Products, Division Champion International; Delta Faucet Company; E. I. du Pont de Nemours & Co. Inc.; Eljer Plumbingware, Division Wallace-Murray Corp.; Ernesto Tile Supply; Excel Wood Products Co., Inc.; General Electric Company; Georgia-Pacific Corp.; Goodyear Tire & Rubber Company; Kohler Co.; Lloyd Lumber Company; Kert Lundell; Mario Manstrandrea; Masonite Corporation; National Kitchen Cabinet Association; Nemo Tile Company Inc.; Owens-Corning Fiberglas Corp.; John Richmond; Robert Sosa; Tile Council of America; U.S. Plywood, Division of U.S. Plywood-Champion Papers, Inc.; Western Wood Products Association; Westinghouse Electric Corp.; Tom Yee.

Table of Contents

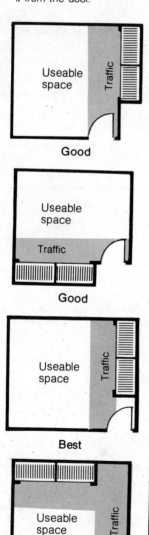

Using space wisely

In these four examples, all floor plans have the same outer dimensions and closet space. They illustrate that once you have established the maximum dimensions of the room and the amount of closet space you require it is possible to increase usable space within given room sizes by making a scale drawing that takes traffic patterns and the swing of doors into account. Locating a closet near the door requires less space that needs to be left open for movement of traffic and it takes fewer steps to reach it from the door.

Useable space

Traffic

Good

Useable space

Traffic

Good

Useable space

Traffic

Best

Useable space

Traffic

Poor

Introduction

This book is designed to show home-owners how to convert wasted or unusable interior space into attractive, accessible living and storage spaces. Most specifically, it provides design options and construction techniques to organize the accumulated clutter of, for example, a growing family living in a house or apartment that cannot grow with it. Adding to the *total* available space is expensive, often impossible, and the work usually cannot be done by the owners themselves. They are forced to find ways to make better use of the space they do have, which is where this book comes in.

Reorganizing storage areas or creating new and successful living spaces depends not only on careful planning, but on good craftsmanship and an open-minded reconsideration of how one wants to live. Is it time for a tag sale? a wedding? a baby? to make over a room so a lonely, aging relative can come to your house to live? Inconvenient, cluttered interior space is one of those irritations that often comes to be taken for granted, but can usually be at least partly cured. Creating convenient, visually pleasing storage doesn't happen without planning and attention to detail. When you have pulled off an effective coordination of those two elements of organization and construction, it is an unusually satisfying accomplishment.

The main body of this book is divided into four sections. The first, "Adding Storage Space" shows how to construct and attach shelving, closets, cabinets, rough storage, and custom-designed possession-organizers for all the different living and utility parts of the house. Light carpentry and some cabinetry skills are all that is required.

Section Two, "Space Modeling" shows how you go about changing the shapes of rooms, removing old fixtures, relocating electrical and plumbing fixtures, installing cabinets and counters, and finishing details for floors, walls and mouldings. To handle space modeling jobs like these, no load-bearing construction is involved. A knowledge of within-room wiring and simple, finish-plumbing connections may be required, so those basic techniques are covered in this section.

Since constructing storage units and revising living areas require some basic carpentry know-how, Section Three, "Carpentry Techniques" is a short course in the tools, materials and techniques required to handle the jobs described in the first two sections.

Section Four, "Case Studies," presents four photo-documentaries that show the "before," "during," and "after" of four real-life spacemaking projects. The reader is able to "watch" the workmen as they go about making old spaces more efficient and attractive to live in. They tear down walls and ceilings; relocate electrical outlets; put in base and overhead cabinets, counters and shelving; install sinks, tubs and toilets; lay new floors; even take on such custom exotica as a sunken tub, a stone wall, and a cathedral ceiling.

Editorially, the book tries to act as a good teacher would, as well as work as an effective reference tool. All important steps are illustrated with photos or diagrams. Color helps clarify the working parts in the illustrations. The facts and advice comes from people who not only do this kind of work for a living but also *teach* it. The instructions are the down-to-earth stuff the reader will encounter when he or she actually does the work. (See "Dust control" on page 72, for example.) Yet both the technical consultant and editors made an effort to include the steps that a pro may have forgotten that he knows, but a first-time do-it-yourselfer needs to be told about. The cartoon feature, "Practical Pete" pops up in the margins every few pages for that reason. He is there to flag pitfalls that the pros have identified as traps that anyone can easily stumble into. Pete tells how he fell in or almost did, and how to avoid that particular trap. See the opposite page for a diagrammatic review of the different kinds of editorial features you will find in the pages of this book. May your work go smoothly and be well completed in good time.

How to "read" a page. These pages show examples of most of the tips, guides and other helps that you will find in the pages of how-to instructions that follow.

Exploded Diagrams show how to assemble a unit.

"New wrinkles" tell about new materials or tools that may make the job easier.

Callouts identify parts referred to in the text.

"Practical Pete" warns you about common mistakes and how to avoid them.

Color clarifies important parts of diagrams.

This describes the specific job.

Professional "TIP"

"What it takes" helps you plan time enough to do the job; lists the tools and materials needed for it.

"Stopgaps & copouts" suggest useful shortcuts and temporary repairs.

Photos that show exactly how each step should be done.

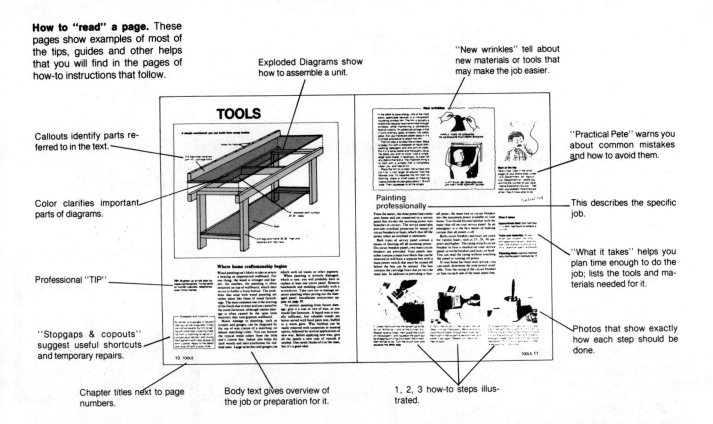

Chapter titles next to page numbers.

Body text gives overview of the job or preparation for it.

1, 2, 3 how-to steps illustrated.

The human dimension

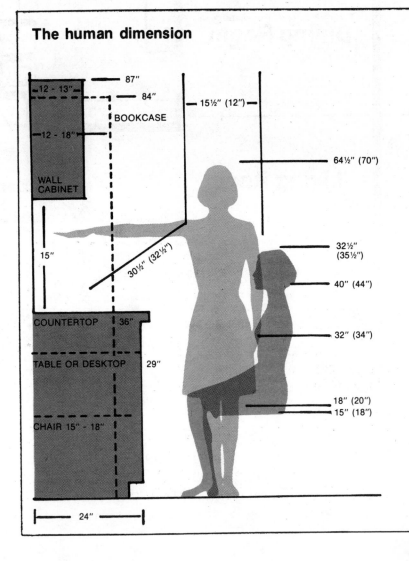

When deciding on specifications for length, width, and depth of shelves, cabinets, or other new storage space, there are two important factors to consider: (1) the size of the items to be stored and, (2) how convenient it will be to reach these items. Measuring articles is an easy job; usually you need only concern yourself with the larger things that will be taking up a substantial amount of space.

Building convenience into new storage space largely involves human dimensions: how far you can stretch or bend comfortably to reach stored goods. The standard width for kitchen counters is 24 inches because it is 6 or 8 inches less than the maximum reach of an outstretched arm. Goods stored in the cabinet space underneath the counter can be reached easily. The 36-inch standard for counter height allows the average man or woman to work conveniently. Wall-hung cabinets usually aren't deeper than 13 inches because items at the back of deeper cabinets would be difficult to identify and reach. There may also be some items that you'll prefer to store safely out of reach of children or pets.

Human dimensions. The dimensions of the typical female figure shown above are followed in parentheses by typical dimensions for a 6-foot male. Adjust the standard dimensions given here for shelves, cabinets, etc., to fit the convenience of the people who will be using them most.

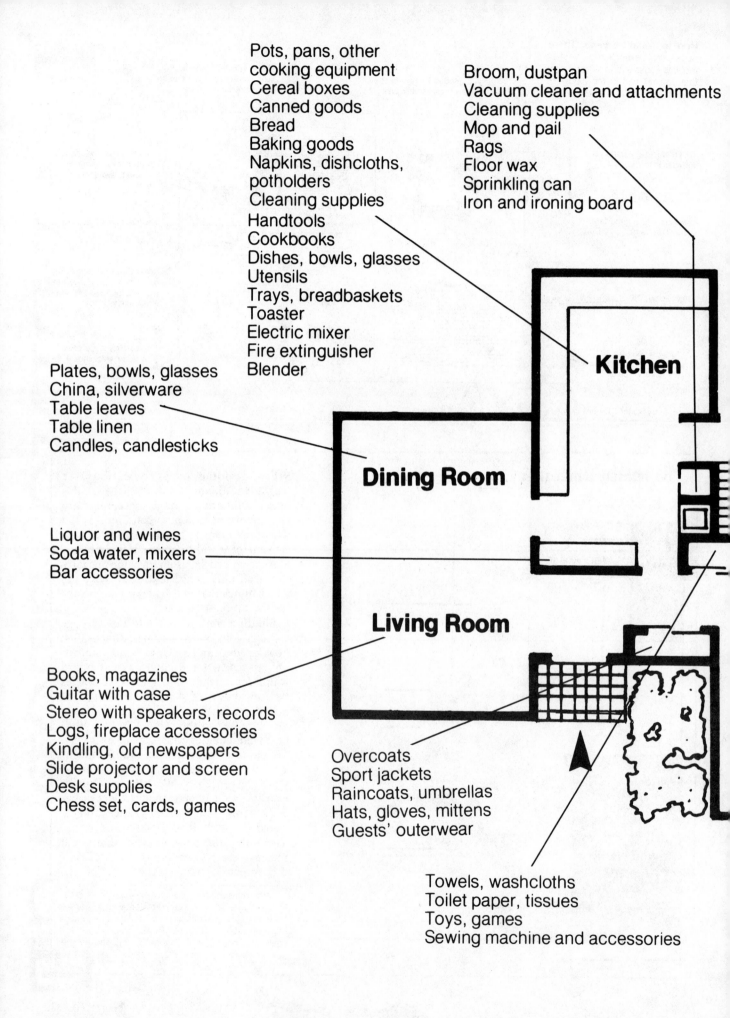

Pots, pans, other
cooking equipment
Cereal boxes
Canned goods
Bread
Baking goods
Napkins, dishcloths,
potholders
Cleaning supplies
Handtools
Cookbooks
Dishes, bowls, glasses
Utensils
Trays, breadbaskets
Toaster
Electric mixer
Fire extinguisher
Blender

Broom, dustpan
Vacuum cleaner and attachments
Cleaning supplies
Mop and pail
Rags
Floor wax
Sprinkling can
Iron and ironing board

Kitchen

Plates, bowls, glasses
China, silverware
Table leaves
Table linen
Candles, candlesticks

Dining Room

Liquor and wines
Soda water, mixers
Bar accessories

Living Room

Books, magazines
Guitar with case
Stereo with speakers, records
Logs, fireplace accessories
Kindling, old newspapers
Slide projector and screen
Desk supplies
Chess set, cards, games

Overcoats
Sport jackets
Raincoats, umbrellas
Hats, gloves, mittens
Guests' outerwear

Towels, washcloths
Toilet paper, tissues
Toys, games
Sewing machine and accessories

Medicine
Vitamins, makeup, cosmetics
Hair dryer
Laundry
Scale
Electric razor
Toiletries
Towels, washcloths

Shirts, shoes, socks
Dresses, skirts, blouses, sweaters
Jackets, ties
Sneakers, golf shoes
Tennis racquets, golf bag
Warm-up suit

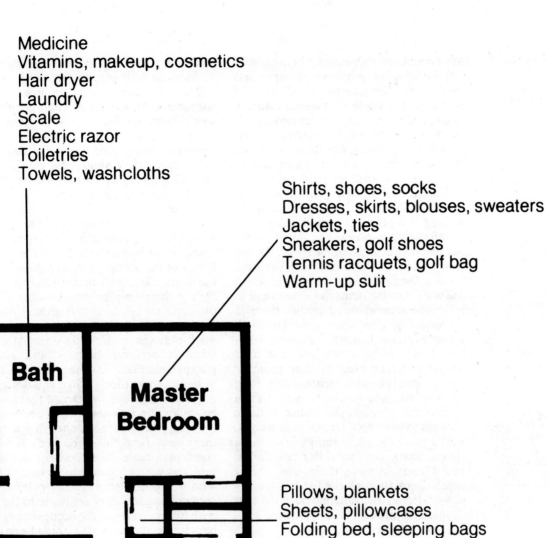

Bath

Master Bedroom

Pillows, blankets
Sheets, pillowcases
Folding bed, sleeping bags

Bedroom

Bedroom

Clothes
Dollhouse, toys
Radio, hi-fi

Clothes
Football, basketball, tennis racquet
Textbooks, magazines
Typewriter
Tools, hobby equipment
Trophies
Radio

Evaluating storage needs

Minimum shelf depths	
Item	**Inches**
Books	8-14
Business papers	12-16
Cleaning supplies	4-10
Dinnerware	12-16
Glasses and cups	4-6
Infant supplies	20-24
Luggage	20-24
Magazines	8-12
Radios	8-12
Sheets and blankets	20-24
Toiletries	4-8
Tools (hand-held)	4-10
Towels and bath supplies	16-18
Trays and bowls	16-18
Turntable, records	16-18
Typewriters	16-18

Most problems with existing living spaces can be divided into two groups, and consequently are usually solved in one of two ways: (1) There isn't enough storage space, and more must be created, or (2) existing space is used inefficiently, and must be reorganized. Use these guidelines to evaluate your present spaces and to help plan new areas or redo old ones.

Take a trip around your living spaces—including attic, cellar and garage—looking for places it would be easy to install shelving, closets or cabinets without spoiling the looks of the space. Return to the parts of the house that have the greatest congestion and clutter problems. Make a list of the items there that need to be stored somewhere. Number them in the order of how often they are used, giving items used together the same number. First, assign items that are used rarely or never used in that room to storage space elsewhere without upsetting the way you live in either space. Then isolate the objects you think will be difficult to store because of size or weight; find a place for these things first. Put a special mark next to children's things; you'll want to store these within easy reach. Look through the list for dangerous, delicate, or valuable articles that should be confined to limited-access storage and safekeeping.

Let the location of your planned storage units help to determine their design and construction. The study or living room is a good place for built-ins. Storage needs will change little in these rooms, so flexibility is not as important as a well-made, nicely-finished structure. Display cases or cabinets which provide glass-enclosed, dust-free, storage space work well in the hallway or dining room, or in a den.

Cases, cabinets, or closets in the basement or attic can be built inexpensively from rough lumber, with less attention to detail and joinery than a kitchen cabinet would require. Remember, though, that if you plan to remodel your basement or attic within the next few years these units will probably have to be taken down.

In the kitchen or workshop, convenience is the primary consideration. Tools, utensils, ingredients, and other specialized items are used on a day-to-day basis, and should be especially easy to locate, identify, and replace. High traffic storage areas like these must be well constructed in addition to being well planned.

The bathroom is another area where convenience is important. There are many small items to keep track of here, so storage space must be arranged on a correspondingly smaller scale. Bear in mind that safety should be considered here. Certain medicines must be inaccessible to children, for example.

More than any other single room in the house, the bedrooms are the places where uniquely tailored, personalized spaces must be planned. There the living habits of the occupant, or occupants, call the shots. Children's bedrooms, especially, are their only private havens. They usually want *all* their stuff around them, so storage is a major consideration, as is work-play space. A child's physical size, sense of personal modesty, and work-play paraphernalia all change dramatically as he or she matures. When you design a room for an infant, be warned that it will be walking in two years. Only overnight, it seems, the space planned for a crib must now fit a full-sized bed. A low-sized play table must be torn out and replaced with a "grownup's" study desk with a reading lamp. Closet poles keep creeping higher; drawers begin to fill up with bulky sweaters; the occupant begins hanging on the walls everything he or she can buy or borrow.

When you plan a child's space, allow room for the child to grow inside it. Otherwise you will find yourself having to tear it apart and reconstruct it every two or three years, to keep pace with that child's physical growth, maturing interests and changing image of itself as a private person. This last point hits home dramatically when two young children start out sharing a bedroom. Suddenly that arrangement does not work. At the very least, you will need a tall room-dividing wall with storage in it. If the room is large enough, you can make two rooms out of that space with a permanent partition-wall, another closet, and a separate entrance. You may even have to convert some other low-traffic space in the house into a bedroom, perhaps with another bathroom to handle the increased traffic. The second section of this book shows how to handle spacemaking jobs like those.

Drawing plans

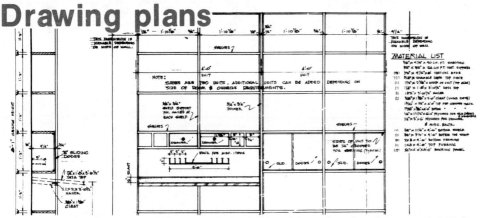

MATERIAL LIST

Tools

1. Make a scale drawing of the *area* you will be redesigning. You may want to draw a side view or a floor plan in addition to a front view in order to show the proper depth. Ink it in when you have it right. 2. Sketch in lightly, in pencil, your ideas for location and scaled size of the storage units you would consider building or installing now, *or later*. Erase and relocate until you have a plan that works in *time* as well as space (see pages 8 and 9). 3. Take the exact measurements of the area in the room where each storage unit will fit. Use a level and a square on walls and corners to be sure they are both plumb

and at right angles; often they are not. 4. Make a rough drawing of the unit that will fit there and add its exact dimensions: height, width, depth. Then rule up an exact-scale, construction drawing with a ruler and triangle (see below). 1 inch equals 1 foot is a comfortable scale to use. Graph paper helps. Watch out for *inside* vs. *outside* dimensions. 5. Finally, make a list of materials, including quantities and sizes, that you will need to assemble before you start. Remember that plywood is sold in 4-foot by 8-foot sheets (see pages 140-143).

An **architect's scale** is a time-saver if you like to "blueprint" your ideas or if you find yourself making many scale drawings. Triangular in shape, it contains over 11 scales from $1/16'' = 1'$ to $3'' = 1'$, and each scale has exact calibrations for feet and inches.

You'll also need a **right triangle** to square up your drawings. Both instruments are available at office supply outlets or art supply stores, along with mechanical pencils, graph paper, drawing boards, and other helpful drafting supplies.

Inside and outside dimensions

The inside and outside dimensions for all 3 plans are identical, but the width of the horizontal piece changes according to the joint detail.

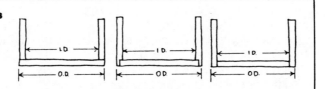

How to make a construction drawing

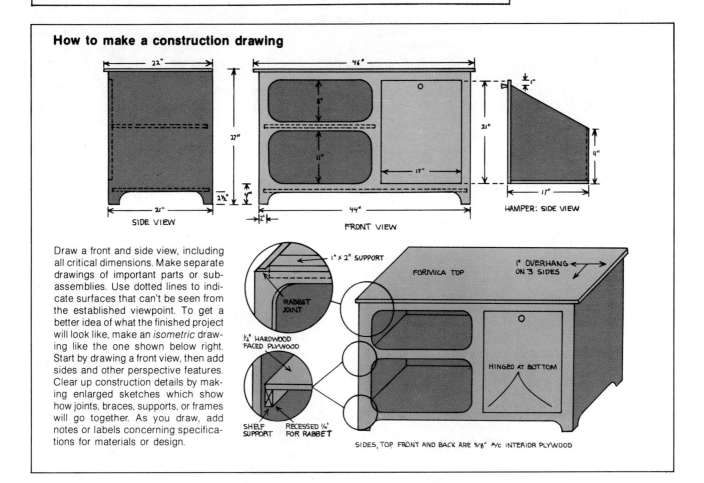

SIDE VIEW

FRONT VIEW

HAMPER: SIDE VIEW

Draw a front and side view, including all critical dimensions. Make separate drawings of important parts or sub-assemblies. Use dotted lines to indicate surfaces that can't be seen from the established viewpoint. To get a better idea of what the finished project will look like, make an *isometric* drawing like the one shown below right. Start by drawing a front view, then add sides and other perspective features. Clear up construction details by making enlarged sketches which show how joints, braces, supports, or frames will go together. As you draw, add notes or labels concerning specifications for materials or design.

SHELVES & CLOSETS

Simple solutions

What it takes

Approximate time: One hour or less, to cut and hang a 3x6 foot panel.

Tools and materials: Crosscut saw or power saw with fine-toothed blade, drill with bits, screwdriver, plus: 2-inch or 2½-inch round-head screws with washers, rubber pegboard spacers or furring strips.

Sad sag story
You wouldn't believe how fast I put up a sheet of pegboard in my T.V. room. From bare wall to beautiful storage area took just half an hour. A couple of weeks later though, things didn't look so good. Because I had only put in screws around the edges, the pegboard was starting to bow and sag. Luckily I spotted the bend just in time and managed to save the board. Next time I'll space my screws at more frequent intervals and I won't forget that middle sections need support too.

Practical Pete

Pegboard

With just a few tools and perhaps an hour of work time, you can transform an empty wall into an impressive storage area with the help of pegboard. Pegboard, technically called perforated hardboard, is easy to work with, inexpensive, and offers flexible, quick-change storage space. The vast array of pegboard fixtures on the market can handle all kinds of storage chores and can be removed or rearranged for changing storage needs. Pre-finished pegboard, available in several colors and wood tones, lends a fine decorative look.

Pegboard is sold in standard 4x8-foot sheets, though you may be able to find 4x4 sheets at some home decorating centers. Standard thicknesses are ⅛- and ¼-inch. The ¼-inch pegboard, which has larger holes and requires heavier-gauge fixtures, is only necessary if you have very weighty implements to hang. For storing most hand tools and general household items, ⅛-inch pegboard will work fine.

Pegboard is easy to cut but tends to fray at cut-line edges. To prevent this, use a fine-toothed plywood or finish cut blade with your power saw. If you're cutting by hand, use a crosscut saw. An equally important preventive measure is to support the board very securely along the cut line. Don't let it flop or vibrate while sawing.

When hanging pegboard, be sure to allow clearance for fixtures, at least ⅜-inch airspace is required between the pegboard and the wall. This means that if you are putting up pegboard over paneling, sheetrock, plaster, or masonry, you will have to use special rubber spacers or furring strips to get the proper clearance. If you're covering exposed studs, clearance behind the pegboard is built-in.

When fastening pegboard to any wall, it is important to give the board all-over support. Without a screw to secure it every 16 to 24 inches, sooner or later your pegboard will bow out from the wall—not a happy prospect. Use 2-inch round-head screws with washers to secure it.

An alternate anchoring method is to construct a sturdy frame on the back of your pegboard panel, using wood strips at least ½-inch thick. Once the frame has been glued and nailed in place, you can fasten it to the wall in several places along the top and bottom edges. This method is good for working on masonry or any hollow wall with irregularly spaced studs.

It's a good idea to round pegboard edges slightly with medium-grit sandpaper. Pegboard can be painted or clear-finished just like wood. It isn't waterproof and has a tendency to deform and weaken when wet. A protective finish is advisable if the board will be exposed to moisture.

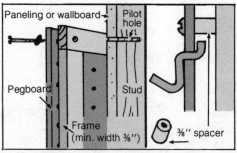

Mount rubber spacers, or build a frame between pegboard and wall to provide clearance for fixtures and good support.

You can give pegboard a finished appearance to complement the decor of your den, kitchen or bedroom. Here the addition of molding strips will frame new hang up space nicely.

Buying unfinished furniture

An unfinished cabinet or bookcase can be a very attractive readymade solution to storage problems. With a little creativity and as much elbow grease as you are prepared to supply, your own finishing work can give any piece of raw furniture a custom-built look.

Before you go to a raw furniture store, write down the minimum and maximum dimensions for the bookshelf or cabinet you want to buy. While shopping, pay attention to construction. There should be no cracks, discolorations, or loose joints in the piece you're thinking of. You should also know in advance whether you want to stain or paint the piece. The same unit is generally available in two or three grades of lumber. Clear lumber will cost a bit more, but may be worth the price if a smooth finish is desirable.

Highlighting: for a light, clean look that doubles as a wood sealer. Working on one surface at a time, brush on white pigmented stain in a full, flowing coat. Allow the stain to stand for ten minutes. Then use a soft cloth to wipe it down, moving against the grain. Wipe the stain off evenly and as completely as you can. The look you want is a white luster only. Allow 24 hours before using the piece.

Louvered doors, purchased separately, can be attached to the front of an unfinished bookcase. Mortise the hinges to the doors and bookcase frame, then hold temporarily in place while screw holes are pre-drilled. Position each hinge exactly square with both the bookcase and the door frame and drill the holes exactly on center. Add magnetic catches and handles after finishing the piece.

TIP: Most raw furniture stores offer lists of their factory-standard dimensions. If one store does not have the exact dimensions you want, check another store. Custom built raw furniture is not cheap, and each manufacturer's standard dimensions list will vary slightly. You may find the additional shelf inch you need on someone else's standard sheet.

Molding strips added to a cabinet door give the piece a finished look. Select your favorite half-molding. Measure and mark molding and door, aligning carefully. Use a miter box to angle the corner cuts for perfect fit. Nail the molding to the door using brads at 4-inch intervals. Set and putty nail holes before finishing the piece. (Molding can dress up a plain pre-finished piece too. If you can't match the finish exactly, try an accent tone.)

Antiquing your unfinished readymade will give it the look of a valuable heirloom. This process involves applying an accenting *glaze* over an enamel finish. (The glaze should always be darker than the base enamel.) Give the wood an enamel finish and let it dry overnight. Then brush on a generous coat of glaze, let it sit for a few minutes, and wipe it off with a piece of cheesecloth. The effect is enhanced if a little extra glaze remains in cracks and corners.

Attaching
to walls

Before you hang something on a wall or ceiling, from a picture hook to a cabinet, you have to find out what the surface covering on the wall or ceiling is made of; what, if anything, is behind it; how much weight the fastener must support fully loaded; and what type of fastener can support that weight without pulling out. See page 152 for a description of standard wall fasteners and how they work.

Fasten to a stud or a joist if you can

The easiest reliable way to attach anything weighing over five pounds per square foot to an interior wall is to nail or screw it into one of the wood or metal studs behind the wall surface. Studs are 1½-inches wide and run from floor to ceiling every 16 inches. Since they are spaced exactly 16 inches apart (unless your house is very old), you will always find one within eight inches of the spot at which you wanted to hang something anyway.

Wooden joists that support the floor above are usually spaced 16 (sometimes 12, 20 or 24) inches apart and are two inches wide. They generally run across the width, not the length, of the house.

Fasten light objects (up to five pounds per square foot) into wood studs with a 4d finishing nail, 6d common nail, or No. 6 wood screw driven at least one inch into the wood. Increase the nail sizes by 50 percent to support objects weighing about 10 pounds per square foot. Objects weighing much over that should be held by No. 8 wood screws or ¼-inch lag bolts driven at least 1½ inches into the wood.

If you cannot locate a stud where you want to hang something on wallboard, you can use a 4 to 8d finishing nail or ⅞-inch plastic anchor with a No. 4 to 8 sheet metal screw to fasten objects weighing up to five pounds per square foot. Over that, use a molly hollow wall anchor, or stronger still, a ¼-inch diameter toggle bolt. Beware of attaching very heavy objects only to hollow wallboard or thin plaster because they can collapse. If you make a cross of sticky tape over the mark on the plaster or wallboard before you drive or drill a hole for the fastener, the tape will keep the surface from chipping or crumbling around the hole.

I made more holes than a woodpecker—and with less result!

My exploratory holes near the bottom of the wall brought out solid wood, but when I drilled on a plumb line farther up, all I got was hollow wall. Frustration! Then I realized I was drilling into the horizontal sole plate instead of the vertical stud. Every exploratory hole was bound to be in solid wood, regardless of actual stud location. Now I do my stud searching at least 4 inches above the floor, and when I hit solid wood, I'm sure it's the real thing.

Practical Pete

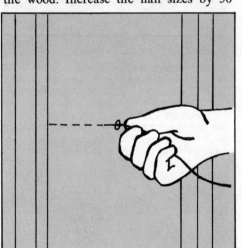

To find the nearest stud, tap with your knuckles lightly along the wall until you hit a dead-sounding spot, and tap up and down floor to ceiling to be sure it is a stud. Drill a tiny hole where you want to hang the fastener. If you hit wood shavings, it's a wood stud; hard resistance and metal shavings indicate a metal stud (usually hollow). If you can't locate a stud by tapping, drill a small hole through the wall covering at an extreme angle. Push a straight length of coathanger wire along the inside of the wall until you hit something. Pinch the wire at the hole with your fingers and pull it out of the wall, Measure the distance between the end of the wire and your fingers. Add ¾-inch and mark that total distance from the hole. The mark will be pretty close to the center of the stud, but drill a tiny pilot hole to be sure.

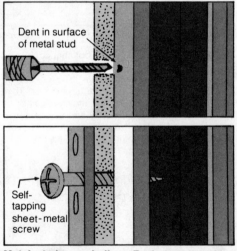

Metal studs are hollow. To fasten something through a wall and into a metal stud, drill a small hole through the wall covering, but not into the metal. Make a dent in the metal by tapping a finishing nail or center punch so the drill tip won't slip around (top). Drill a hole one half the thickness of a No. 4 self-tapping sheet-metal screw for light objects; No. 8 for heavy objects over 10 pounds per square foot. Drill a hole almost the same thickness as the screw in the object you are hanging, and drive the screw through the object, through the wall, and through the metal side of the hollow stud (bottom).

How to find out what the wall is made of

When you drill a test hole into	You will find . . . .
Wallcoverings:	
Wallboard or plaster only	White dust, little resistance, quick breakthrough
Thick plaster	White dust, some resistance, no breakthrough
Thin plaster over wood lath	White dust, then gray powder, then breakthrough
Behind-wall materials:	
Wood stud	Moderate resistance, light wood shavings
Metal stud	Heavy resistance, silver shavings
Cinder block or concrete	Very heavy resistance, gray-brown dust
Brick or hollow tiles	Heavy resistance, red dust
Mortar between bricks/blocks	Moderate resistance, gray dust

Attaching things to solid concrete, brick, etc.

If you want to hang something heavy on a solid brick, concrete or cinder block surface, you generally have to drill a hole in it to receive an insert that you can then drive a screw or other fastener into. For light, rough work masonry nails and cut nails can be driven directly into concrete with a hammer. (These and inserts for wall fasteners are shown on page 152.) Whatever type of insert you use, be sure that the screw or bolt you drive into it is long enough to pass through both the thickness of the object you are attaching to the wall and the insert in the wall. Check before making any holes.

When you drill holes in concrete, blocks, brick or stone, wear goggles and gloves because chips and powder will fly around.

The mortar between cement blocks and bricks is easier to nail or drill into, but it is more likely to crumble, so the fastener is more likely to pull out if you hang something heavy from it.

How to drill the holes

Power

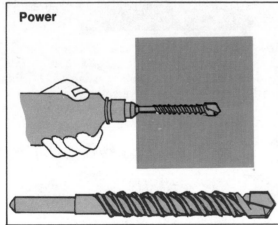

A **power drill** with a carbide-tipped bit is the easiest and fastest tool. Most home-shop electric drills have ¼-inch or ⅜-inch chucks. These spin too fast and may not have enough power to drive a big bit into solid concrete or brick. A drill with a ½-inch chuck is ideal. If you don't have one, try drilling a small hole first, then a larger one.

Carbide-tipped bits range in size up to one inch in diameter. If your drill has a variable-speed trigger, use a low speed and stop if it begins to stall so you won't burn out the motor in your drill. Slide the drill bit back and forth in the hole as it rotates rather than pushing hard continuously.

Hand

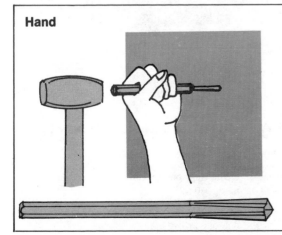

A **hand Rawl drill** has interchangeable bits that make holes up to ¼-inch in diameter. The bit fits into one end of a steel shaft. Place the tip of the bit against the wall surface and hit the drill with a hammer, rotating the drill slightly between blows.

A **Star drill** makes larger holes, ¼- to one inch in diameter. It is a heavy duty tool and needs a strong arm wielding a light sledge to drive it into solid concrete or brick. Rotate it after each blow and blow out the dust from time to time.

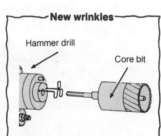

Hammer drill

Core bit

Electric hammer drill
These pound a carbide-tipped bit into concrete, brick or stone at the rate of about 3000 blows a minute. For holes over one inch in diameter, use a core bit that cuts a plug out of the masonry.

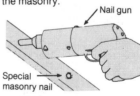

Nail gun

Special masonry nail

Masonry nail gun
Specially hardened masonry nails can be loaded into a gun that fires them, with .22-caliber blank cartridges, into cement blocks and concrete. This is a quick way to put up 1x3 furring for example, so you can attach rough shelving to it. Rent these gadgets if you can. They are too expensive to buy for a one-time project.

Wall-mounted shelving

The quickest, easiest, and least messy way to convert unused wall space into useful shelf storage is to put up individual shelf brackets or track-and-bracket shelving (technically called "standards"). Hardware for both is widely distributed in a variety of styles, sizes, and materials which makes it easy to fit them into the space you have available. The following pages provide some of the most popular options and instructions for easy installation.

If you're putting up only a few shelves, it's practical to buy them pre-cut and pre-finished. Ready-to-use shelves are available in different widths and finishes at most hardware stores, lumber suppliers, and home decorating centers. For larger projects, you'll save money by buying unfinished lumber in standard dimensions and cutting it to size yourself.

Shelf brackets, left, are made in sizes ranging from three inches to eighteen inches. They are usually packaged in pairs and range in decorative appeal (and price) from flat angle irons to handmade wrought iron or finely finished wood. Track-and-bracket "standards," right, are equally easy to put up and preferable if you need more than one or two adjustable shelves.

Individual angle brackets

The quickest way to put up built-in shelves is to use metal angle brackets. These shelf supports have been around for a long time and are great in places where only one or two shelves are needed. Their only limitations are that they're permanent and non-adjustable, and they must be securely anchored to the wall. This means you usually have to locate studs to fasten into.

Shelf brackets in a variety of styles can be found at any hardware store or home decorating center. Wrought iron brackets go well with paneling or an antique decor, while brushed aluminum supports give a more modern appearance. You'll also find inexpensive angle irons which can be used in the workshop, garage, basement, and other parts of your home where storage space needn't be stylish.

In addition to appearance, you'll also have to select brackets according to the load you want to support and the shelf width you want to use. The longer side of the bracket should be installed vertically, against the wall. The shorter, or horizontal support should be at least three-fourths as long as the width of the shelf. The heavier the load on the shelf, the longer the vertical side of the bracket should be.

What it takes

Approximate time: Only a few minutes per bracket after you have located and marked the studs.

Tools and materials: Drill with bits to pre-drill screw holes, screwdriver, carpenter's level, pencil, crosscut saw and combination square for cutting shelf lengths, shelving lumber, bracket hardware.

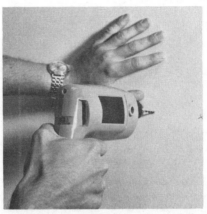

1. Locate and mark the centers of the studs (usually spaced 16 or 24 inches apart) by tapping the wall and drilling a row of ⅛-inch holes until you hit one. Use a level to draw vertical guidelines for attaching the brackets.

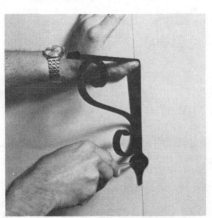

2. Determine the best height for your bracket, and anchor it through the wall and into the stud with screws. Remember that at least ⅔ of the screw's length should be in the stud.

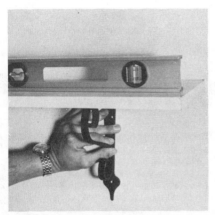

3. Use the level as shown to line up accompanying brackets, then anchor brackets as in step 2. Now you're all set to lay down the shelving itself.

Shelving hardware

Pilasters and clips. These slotted metal tracks are used in groups of four inside cabinets and bookcases. They are screwed in place (sometimes dadoed flush), and accept metal clips which act as corner supports for the shelves.

Pins are used in groups of four, with each pin supporting one corner of the shelf. Available in either *spade* or *angle bracket* styles, they fit into holes drilled in the side shelf supports.

Shelving standards are the most popular type of shelving hardware, mainly because they are versatile, easy to install (see page 20), give a weightless, contemporary effect, and can accommodate heavy loads. The shelf brackets that fit into the slotted tracks are made in several sizes so you can install shelves of different widths. The tracks themselves are available in different lengths and styles, from plain aluminum to enameled or wood-grain vinyl. Shelving standards should be fastened through the wall surface into studs for maximum holding power.

Angle brackets are attached to the wall in a horizontal row with screws that pass through the wall and into studs. They are available in a wide range of sizes and styles and are commonly used where only one or two shelves are needed.

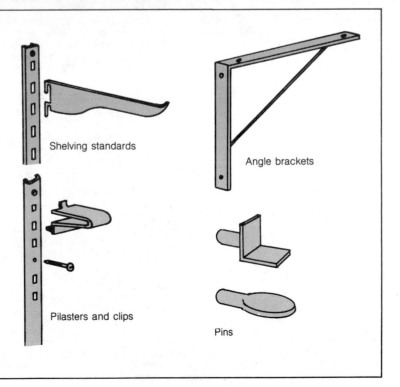

Shelving standards

Angle brackets

Pilasters and clips

Pins

Track-and-bracket shelving standards

Upside down and bowlegged

There are at least three ways to foul up the job when you install track-and-bracket shelving standards—and I managed to combine all three in one go. First, a lot of those wall-mounted metal tracks are made with no holes for the brackets at one end. *That* end should be at the *top* so you can put the last shelf at the very bottom of the track. Second, don't cut corners by skipping screwholes on those metal tracks. With any weight at all on the shelves, the track will bow away from the wall where it isn't held by a screw. Third, shelves full of books will sag in the middle unless you have a bracket for every two feet of shelf length. The studs inside most interior walls are spaced 24 inches apart anyway.

Practical Pete

Since conventional shelving standards are relatively inexpensive, easy to install, and able to support heavy loads, they can readily solve storage problems all around the house. Here an entire wall has been converted to shelf storage with the track and bracket system.

Here's an unusual track and bracket system that's elegant enough for your finest room. Made from teak, it is designed so that the slanted pegs in each bracket fit precisely into the holes in the teak track.

For a little extra money, you can buy a shelf standard system with a wood-grain vinyl finish. *Cranmere* shelves by Kirsch Co. (Sturgis, Mich.) feature decorative standards and shelf brackets, along with shelves of different widths, as shown.

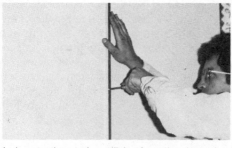

1. Locate the stud you'll be fastening into, then sink a screw through a hole near the middle of the standard, into both the wall and the stud behind it. Drill a pilot hole out as usual before sinking any screw. If you're not fastening into a stud, use a wall fastener that's suited for your type of wall (see page 152). Don't tighten the screw completely.

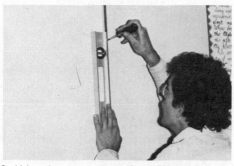

2. Using the screw as a pivot point, plumb the standard with your level, mark locations for pilot holes with a pencil or awl, as shown here, and sink screws through the remaining holes.

3. Use your level to mark a vertical line for the adjacent standard. For maximum shelf strength, fasten through the wall and into a stud, as you did for the other standard.

4. Insert brackets in corresponding slots on both standards, then use your level and a shelf as shown to position the adjacent standard. Fasten the standard to the wall as in steps 1 and 2. Insert brackets as desired and lay down shelves.

Get fancy with the shelves themselves

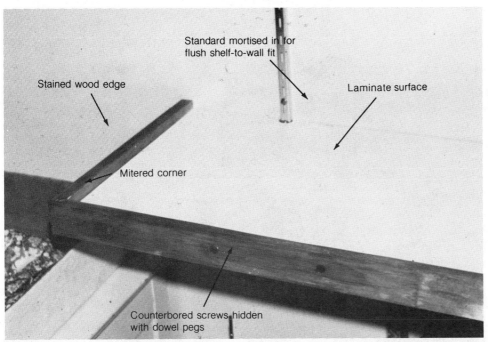

Stained wood edge

Standard mortised in for flush shelf-to-wall fit

Laminate surface

Mitered corner

Counterbored screws hidden with dowel pegs

You don't have to be satisfied with conventional shelves when using standards. Here are some ideas that will give your new shelf storage space a unique, eye-catching appearance.

Off the wall ideas
Most shelving standards are made to be used on the wall, but you make a free-standing unit by mortising the standards into upright supports which are secured to the floor and ceiling. Use angle brackets or screw-in casters as shown below to secure the supports.

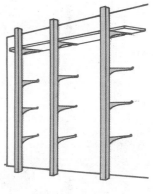

The easiest way to give your shelves a fancy look is to buy them pre-cut and pre-finished at your hardware store or home decorating center. You'll find them in a variety of sizes and surfaces.

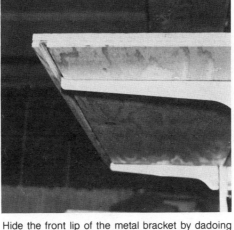

Hide the front lip of the metal bracket by dadoing a groove or making a depression to fit with your drill—but don't drill all the way through!

Screw-in caster adjust to ceiling height

Standard track mortised in

Standard bracket

2''x2'' upright

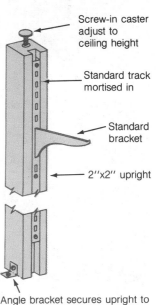

Angle bracket secures upright to floor.

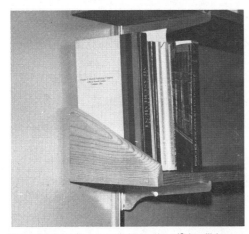

How about adding a built-in bookend? It will keep books from falling off the end of the shelf.

Give your shelf a special edge treatment with half-round molding. Miter the corners as shown.

Stereo shelf-wall

What it takes

Approximate time: Plan on spreading the work out over two or three days. Taking and transferring measurements is time consuming, especially where an odd angle or contour copying is involved.

Tools and materials: Basic cutting and joining tools, sliding bevel, level, plus the following materials: 2 sheets ¾″ A/C interior plywood, 16 shelf supports (optional), 10d common nails, 10d finishing nails.

This stereo/record shelf-wall was built in three evenings. Notice how the side support at left was angled to give the small adjacent window a better chance to brighten up the room.

These are the important points to remember when you're working on new shelf space for your stereo components: Give your set room to breathe. The fit of the enclosing shelves and side supports should allow for at least 1″ of airspace on all sides. If possible, cut component-supporting shelves so that there's an inch of open space between the back shelf edge and the wall. If you intend to replace your present system or any part of it at some point in the future, don't nail or glue the shelves for these units. Use pilasters and clips or shelf supports so you can make adjustments for any size discrepancy.

1. Measure, mark, and cut three side supports, then fasten them to the wall and floor, starting with the corner support. Nail the left support to window molding. Notice how the back edge of the support has been cut out to accommodate the molding.

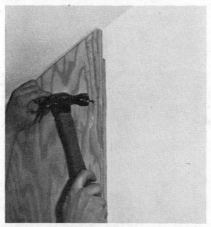

2. Because of floor molding or an out-of-plumb wall, you may have to slip *shims* between the corner support and the wall, as shown above. Drive a 10d nail in at an angle to catch the nearby stud.

3. Use cleats as shown to secure the two remaining supports to the floor; then install a kick-plate along the bottom front as shown. Don't worry if the center support is slightly shaky; it will firm up as you nail shelves in place. Nail a cleat to the molding to support the back edge of the bottom shelf.

4. Mark locations for shelf support holes, then drill them out. Start each hole with an awl to keep your bit exactly on center.

5. Press the shelf supports into holes, then cut and install the shelves. For this project, shelf supports are used for corner shelves; the longer center shelves will be glued and nailed in.

6. Cut the longer shelves to size, then glue and nail them in place. Angled window support means you'll have to custom-fit the shelves, so measure carefully.

7. Even with expert measuring and cutting, you may get an imperfect fit. Use a plane, file, or surform tool to trim all edges flush.

8. Cut and install trim along the front edge as shown.

9. Set all nails, fill holes with wood dough, sand your work smooth, remove the sawdust, and apply finish. Don't skimp on finishing touches; they make a big difference.

Construction guidelines

When creating wall storage, your design is limited only by the dimensions of the empty wall you have to work with. As the step-by-step instructions for the design on these pages suggest, your wall-work can be as simple or as complex as your needs and abilities allow—given the dimensions of your wall. Here are a few guidelines that apply to all built-in wall storage projects:

1. Before you start building, locate and mark all studs along the section of wall where you'll be working. Fastening into a stud is *always* better than just fastening into the wall. If possible, plan your design so that at least a few shelves or supports will be secured to studs.

2. Establish your vertical supports before you decide on definite shelf lengths and locations. The stability of the uprights will determine the steadiness of the entire wall unit.

3. It's usually best to begin in the corner and work out toward the middle of the wall. Your corner shelves and supports are the easiest to square, plumb, and join firmly. Remember that you don't always have to work *on* the wall. It's easier to construct the bulk of the framing on the floor, then tilt it up and fasten it to the wall.

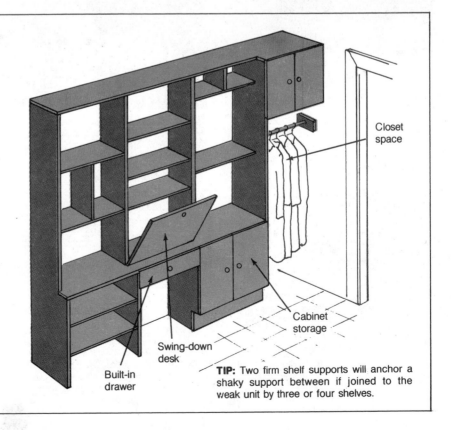

Closet space

Cabinet storage

Swing-down desk

Built-in drawer

TIP: Two firm shelf supports will anchor a shaky support between if joined to the weak unit by three or four shelves.

Free-standing shelves

Take-apart book shelves

What it takes

Approximate time: 1-2 hours, not including finishing.

Tools and materials: 1 4'x4' sheet ¾-inch A/A plywood, crosscut saw, table or saber saw, and ½- or ¾-inch chisel.

If you're a frequent mover, you've probably had to leave plenty of shelves, cabinets, or bookcases behind because they've been too bulky, built-in, or just too inconvenient to take along. Here's a project for pull-apart shelves that will enable you to take some storage space with you when you move. You can take them apart in a minute or less, carry them easily under one arm, and put them back together just as fast.

Plywood is the best building material to use for this project, since the slotted design demands strength in all directions. For extra stability, attach a diagonal brace to the back of your shelves, using screws on both sides and on at least two shelves (see step 7).

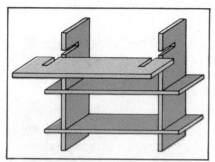

1. Start with a simple design labeled with dimensions and specifications for materials and construction details. Make sure the depth of the slots can be reached with your saw.

2. Cut out all shelf pieces. Here's where a table saw comes in handy, since the rip guide sets the width and eliminates the need for repetitive measurements.

3. Join shelf pieces together with finishing nails (don't hammer them all the way in). Measure and mark slot locations, then saw out slots as shown. Use a back saw or a saber saw with a long blade.

4. If you're using a handsaw or saber saw to cut slots, saw all the way to both corners first. Then square up the slot to make two curved cuts to opposite corners. Chisel away any remaining waste.

5. Cut both sides in the same way you cut the shelves. Joining sides together before marking and cutting the slots makes the job go twice as fast.

6. Assemble your new shelves. The slotted parts should have a snug, but not forced fit; use a file to smooth out any tight joints.

7. Adding a mortised-in, diagonal brace not only makes these slide-together shelves steadier, it gives your project a unique appearance. Screws can easily be removed for quick take-apart.

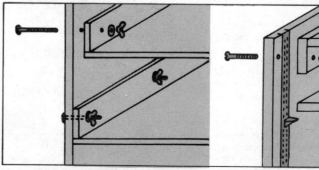
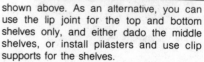

More take-apart ideas Build your shelves with a lip on both ends so they can be fastened to the side supports with two bolts and a couple of wing nuts. For extra stability, dado the lips into the sides as shown above. As an alternative, you can use the lip joint for the top and bottom shelves only, and either dado the middle shelves, or install pilasters and use clip supports for the shelves.

Build yourself a bookcase

What it takes

Approximate time: 3-4 hours.

Tools and materials: Basic cutting and joining tools plus the following materials: 3 8'x1''x8'' pine boards, 16 shelf supports, 4d finishing nails, 8 No. 6 gauge flat-head screws (1½'' long), 4'x4' paneling, plywood, or hardboard for back.

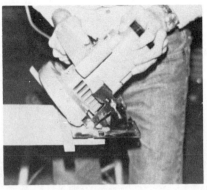

1. Cut sides, top, and bottom pieces to finished size. Mitered corners must be cut precisely, so use a saw guide. Set the blade for a 45° angle cut.

2. Mark sides for shelf support insert holes, then drill them out. Use a depth gauge on your bit (here a piece of adhesive tape) so you don't drill all the way through the board.

3. Join sides, top, and bottom, using two 4d finishing nails in each corner (and glue, of course). Corner clamps make the job easier. Set all nails, then fill holes with wood dough and sand it smooth.

4. Miter joints should be reinforced with metal angle braces and screws. Counterbore screws and fill holes with dowel plugs. Glue plugs in place, then cut and sand them flush when glue dries.

5. Put the back on. Here paneling is used for appearance, but you can also use wallboard or ¼'' plywood.

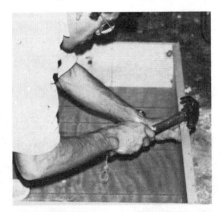

6. Glue and nail molding to front of bookcase, using number 18 gauge ¾-inch nails. Miter the top corner joints.

7. Cut shelves to size, push shelf support inserts into their holes, slide shelves into place, and it is ready to be finished.

Divide a room with shelves

What it takes

Approximate time: 2 hours, not including finishing.

Tools and materials: Basic cutting and joining tools plus the following materials: Five 1″x12″x8′ #1 common pine boards, one 4′x8′ sheet pegboard.

Here's an idea for new storage space that doubles as a room divider. The divider is nothing more than a set of free-standing shelves backed with pegboard. It can be built in the proportions that best fit the area. The drawing, far right, gives the dimensions of the unit pictured here.

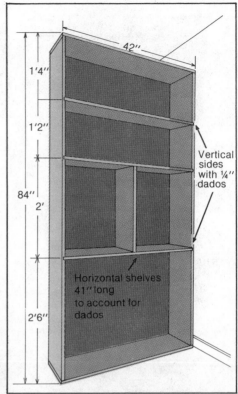

Vertical sides with ¼″ dados

Horizontal shelves 41″ long to account for dados

42″

1′4″

1′2″

84″

2′

2′6″

1. Cut sides, top, and bottom to size. Then mark locations for dados as shown, using a tape measure and combination square.

2. When cutting dados, be sure to groove the supporting shelf board no more than half its thickness. A dado does not have to be deep to make a strong joint.

3. Assemble the outer frame with 8d finishing nails. Then glue and fit shelves into the dado grooves. Use a scrap of wood between the hammer and the shelf when you're tapping in.

4. Add vertical dividers and other shelves according to your design for shelf size and location.

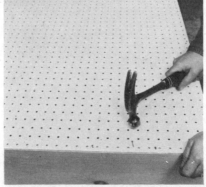

5. The true edges of the pegboard backing will help you align the sides of the cabinet. Fractional adjustment of the cabinet edges can be done by hand. Don't drive nails home until the frame is aligned with the pegboard all the way around.

6. Countersink the nails and fill all holes prior to giving the assembly the finish you have selected.

7. Fasten the completed divider to the floor with lag screws and washers. One screw in each corner will do the job.

8. Two separate units, bolted across the top, will divide larger rooms and offer extensive storage. You can get a combination of shelf and hang up storage on both sides by bolting them front to back.

Building a wall to divide a room

1. Measure and mark the location for the 2x4 sole plate, then nail it in place. If you're nailing through linoleum or asphalt tile into cement, you'll have to use masonry nails, as shown above.

2. Cut the first stud to size (the distance from the sole plate to the ceiling), then nail it to the wall, using a level as shown to make sure it's plumb.

3. Nail the 2x4 top plate to the ceiling, making sure it aligns with the sole plate. Then start toe-nailing the studs in place. Studs should be spaced 16 inches on center.

4. Cut the sheetrock to size and nail it to the studs. After the sheetrock is in place, install molding along the floor, wall, and ceiling.

5. Spackle the nail depressions, and tape the joints as shown above. When the spackle has dried, sand the new wall smooth. For more details on sheetrock work, see page 30

6. A couple of coats of paint, some track and bracket shelves, and a table complete the job. Good work!

Don't fuss with it!
You should see a professional wallboard seam taper zip around a room after the wallboard panels have been nailed up. One 8-foot seam after another—plaster-tape-plaster—zap! Fifteen seconds each, smooth as paper.
It's enough to make you cry.
  When I try to smooth taped wallboard seams, it's like trying to keep my checkbook balanced. The more I fuss with the compound after a point, the worse it gets. I learned to leave it rough after the first couple of tries and sand it smooth after it dries.

Practical Pete

Closet storage

Before

Cutting wallboard

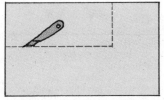

1. When cutting sheetrock or any other gypsum-core wallboard, first score the face paper along your measured cut line, using a utility knife.

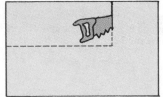

2. Use a saw to cut all the way through the panel along the shorter line.

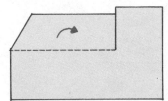

3. Fold along the second score, snapping through the core. Then cut through the back paper with the utility knife.

Building a closet from scratch is a big job involving careful measuring, designing, and planning, large amounts of expensive building materials, and lots of time. If your proposed closet site looks something like the room-end pictured above left, you've got your work cut out for you. This site was plagued with a curved, slanting ceiling, out-of-plumb walls, and irregularly-spaced studs. A heating vent located on the left meant the closet could not extend all the way across the wall. In spite of such problems, a major project like this is fun to undertake. You'll want to spend time considering designs and materials (door types, paneling vs. sheetrock, shelf and clothes-pole locations) before you begin building. The reward is a closet that's custom-built to fit your needs.

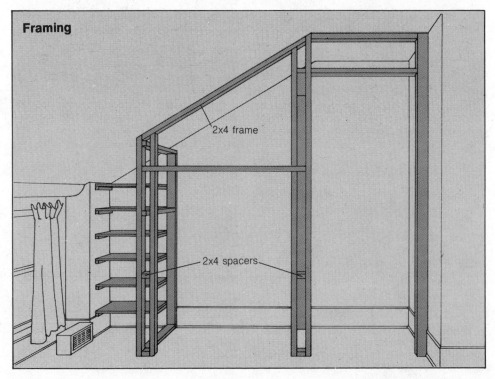

Framing

2x4 frame

2x4 spacers

Step-by-step construction

1. The first step is to pull up the wall-to-wall carpet and expose the bare floor where the new closet will go. Carpeting can be refitted after the closet is complete.

2. Working from the wall out, frame in the closet door. Installation instructions for this bi-fold door call for an opening 2″ higher and 3″ wider than the door dimensions.

3. Continue framing in the closet front. A curved, slanted ceiling and out-of-plumb walls mean you'll have to spend extra time measuring and custom-fitting.

4. Here's the completed front frame. For additional stability, vertical studs should be toe-nailed to the floor.

5. Because this closet doesn't extend all the way across the room, the end must be framed in. Here molly bolts are used to fasten the stud to the wall.

6. Cut door jambs to size and nail them in place. The front edge of the jamb should extend ½″ out from the rough frame to allow for the width of the sheetrock.

7. Jambs for the bi-fold door must be *shimmed* as shown so that they're plumb and the finished width of the doorway matches the width of the door. This is a job where patience and precision pay off.

8. Cut sheetrock to size (see margin opposite), then nail it to the studs with sheetrock nails. For this particular project, it's best to install the vertical panels first.

9. Horizontal sections require careful measuring and cutting. **TIP:** Don't put in more nails than you need: you'll make your spackling job harder that way.

10. Measure, mark, and cut molding to fit over the front edge of the door jamb and the sheetrock. To assure a good fit at mitered corners, cut joints on a miterbox with the saw guide set at 45°.

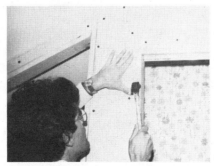

11. Nail the molding in place. Use 1¼″ *brads* (small finishing nails) and nail through the thickest part of the molding to minimize the chance of splitting the wood.

12. Use a block plane to smooth the edge of the molding flush with the jamb where necessary.

Spackling

A paint job is only as good as the spackling job it covers. Depressions in the sheetrock around nailheads, corners and other areas where the gypsum edges of the sheetrock are exposed, and joints between separate pieces of sheetrock, must all be filled with spackling compound and sanded smooth before painting.

If you haven't used spackling compound before, don't worry. It doesn't take long to get acquainted with this special preparation. Spackle, or spackling compound, is a dough-like substance which adheres readily to gypsum wallboard, plaster, wood, and other porous materials. It dries in 1-3 hours, becoming hard and brittle, but is easily shaped and smoothed with sandpaper.

The real art to spackling is learning how to use your putty knife as quickly and effectively as possible. For dishing out spackle, filling small depressions, and working in narrow areas, you'll need a 1-1½-inch-wide putty knife. For taping, corner work, and wide areas, use a knife at least 3 inches wide.

TIP: Deep or extensive depressions should be filled in stages; apply a layer of spackle, let it dry, then apply another layer until the hole is filled. Once a can of spackle has been opened, its shelf life is shortened considerably. Keep this in mind when you're buying and using it. Don't open a large can for a small job. Spackle is also fine for filling holes in wood. It can be stained and clear-finished, but won't blend in with the wood as well as wood dough.

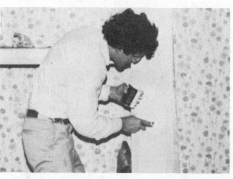

1. Using a putty knife to apply spackling compound, fill the depressions around nailheads and smooth the filled area flat.

2. Cut corner bead to length and nail it in place as shown. Angle the nails slightly to get a good hold in the corner stud.

3. Spread spackle generously along the edge, covering both metal and sheetrock.

4. Use a wide putty knife as shown to smooth spackle and create a uniform edge. Keep one edge of the knife on the metal bead and use firm pressure, working from top to bottom.

5. Joints where two pieces of sheetrock meet should be taped as well as spackled. Spread spackle over the joint, press the tape in place over the joint line, then cover the tape liberally with spackle.

6. Using a wide putty knife, force the tape firmly against the joint, work the surface flat, and remove excess. When the compound has dried, go over the spackled areas with medium-grit sandpaper until the surface is smooth enough to paint.

The door

When the closet door goes on, the job is nearly done. Actually, the door should be removed before you paint the rest of the closet, finished separately, and then re-attached. It's a good idea to temporarily install the door before you start painting, since you may have to make some small adjustments for a better fit (planing down a jamb or door edge, for instance).

You may decide that a sliding door or simple hinged door is better for your closet. Modern hardware for both folding and sliding doors makes installation easy. The door used in this closet came completely assembled, with hinges and pivots already attached. Lumber retailers and builders' supply outlets have different models to choose from. These ready-to-install doors come in standard dimensions.

The crucial factor in hanging a door is the doorway itself. Are the jambs plumb and square? Does the width of the doorway equal the width of the door? Is the doorway high enough to accommodate the track? The manufacturer's instructions that accompany each set of doors or door hardware contain specifics regarding dimensions, construction, and installation, so your best bet is to be guided by them while planning, measuring, and building.

1. Screw the track for the folding door in place. Follow the manufacturer's instructions concerning the position of the track on the top jamb.

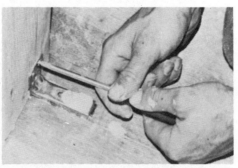

2. Align and screw the bottom pivot in place according to installation instructions.

3. Lift the door into place. For most doors, whether they are sliding or folding, the top edge of the door is positioned first, then the bottom.

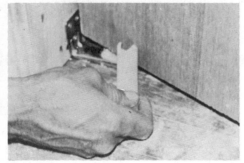

4. Adjusting a threaded peg attached to the bottom edge of the door locks the door in the pivot assembly. A special wrench for this job is enclosed with other door hardware.

Other options

Sliding doors are easy to install. Most sliding door hardware consists of an aluminum track, rollers that are attached to the top door edge, and a simple plastic guide assembly that screws to the floor.

Louvered doors are more expensive than flat or raised panel doors. Use them where ventilation is important, or where you want to have a distinctive appearance.

Refitting the closet

There's no need to despair over a closet that defies all attempts at organization (see below left). A little imagination combined with the basic cutting and joining tools and some lumber can result in an attractive storage area that uses the available space well and meets your particular storage needs (below right).

Before. The stuff-stack-and-cram look

After. Same space, same gear, but what a difference!

First steps: cleaning out, measuring, planning

The first and most dramatic part of the job is the complete cleanout. Remove the old clothes pole and the shelf, but leave the pole-holding cleat; you can use it as a shelf support later. Once everything is out, take measurements and make final plans. For this refitting job, the limited space in a single closet is to be divided and reorganized for two people.

You'll be surprised at how much space you have to work with once you've completely emptied out your closet. The clothes pole and single shelf arrangement found in most clothes-storing closets leaves a great deal of space unused and makes the storage situation haphazard. Shoes, bags, boxes, and other closet items are all left on the floor, and the shelf above the pole is almost always overcrowded.

A more practical way of organizing closet space for clothes is to remove the single eye-level pole and replace it with one or more shorter poles at different locations in the closet. The object is to confine hang-up storage for shirts, pants, or dresses to smaller, well-defined areas of the closet in order to gain space for new shelves, dividers, or even additional poles.

After you've gutted your closet and have started measuring and planning, take a moment to locate a few studs in the closet wall. You can always count on studs in corners, but finding one or two in the back wall will make it easier to nail in new cleats, shelves, and upright supports.

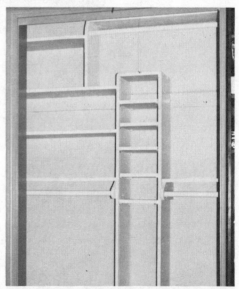

The finished job, before refilling, is used here to illustrate construction sequence. The center unit, which acts as a divider, was installed first, after being completely assembled in the workshop. With the divider in place, both lower clothes poles were installed, then new shelves were added between the divider unit and the side walls. Construction was completed with the addition of the upper clothes pole.

Relocating the clothes pole

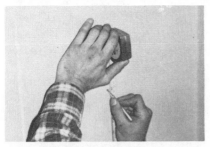

1. The lowered clothes pole should be about 40 inches above the floor, but you can adjust this height according to how much hanging room your clothes need.

2. Since the pole holder will also serve as a shelf support, make sure it's level. Use your two-foot level to mark a horizontal guideline for installing the holder.

3. Use stock one inch thick and 4 to 6 inches wide for the pole holder. Cut the stock to fit the depth of the closet, then drill out a hole for the clothes pole. (Here two identical pieces are being drilled out together to save time.)

4. When the hole is made, saw out a slot in the top of one holder so the pole can slide into place.

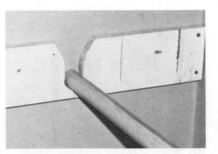

5. Nail the holder in place, using 8d-10d common nails. The top edge can be used to support a shelf.

6. The companion pole-holder should remain closed to reduce wobbling. If a closet pole isn't going to extend all the way across, as is the case here, a custom-built holder like this one adds a nice touch.

Building in more shelves

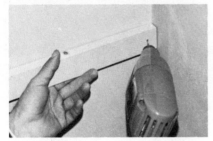

1. Cut the cleats for new shelves from one-inch stock, then pre-drill holes for 10d nails in corners as shown. Drill in at a slight angle so you're sure to nail into a corner stud.

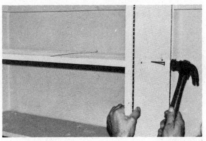

2. Cut new shelves to size, position them with a level, then nail through the center upright into the shelf edge as shown here to complete installation.

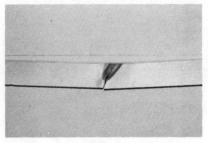

Caution: Don't use a knotted cleat; it's bound to split sooner or later. Knots are structurally weak, especially in narrow pieces like this one.

Finishing touches

Once the construction is over, the only job left is applying a finish. Before you apply stain or finish, however, take some time to soften sharp edges, round corners, and give all shelf surfaces a once-over with medium-grit sandpaper.

If you're going to paint, use a quick-drying primer, followed by a gloss or semi-gloss enamel. A flat coat won't stand up to everyday use like enamel, and can't be dusted or wiped clean as easily. **Note:** Your finishing plans should include a new coat of paint for the inside of the closet; now's the best time to do it.

No matter what finish you use on your closet, make sure you allow *more* than enough time for the final coat to dry before moving your stuff back in. Let the closet air out completely; otherwise, your favorite shirt may pick up the odor of the finish—a not too desirable cologne.

Before you paint, stain, or finish your work, remove sharp edges with a plane or surform tool. For this refitting job, lumber from some dismantled shelving was recycled to make new shelves and supports.

Because previously painted lumber was used in this project, new shelves will have to be painted rather than stained or clear-finished. Use a quick-drying primer, followed by a gloss or semi-gloss enamel.

Refitting tips and ideas

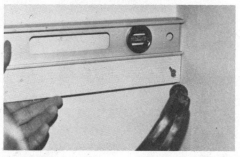

The quickest way to put up shelf supports in a closet is to hammer your nail just part way in, hold the support in place, and use your level as shown while nailing the support to the wall. The nail is hammered in at an angle to catch the corner stud.

The uppermost shelves in your converted closet may have to be made narrower, like this one, so you can reach up and in easily.

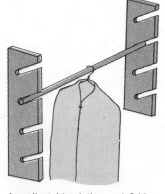

An adjustable clothes pole? It's a great idea if you've got a fast-growing child or if a change in seasons demands a higher (or lower) pole. To make this unit, drill out holes first, then use a saber or crosscut saw to cut slots at an angle, as shown above.

Hammer a few nails into a shelf support and you can convert an empty closet corner into storage space for belts.

How about refitting your closet with a tie rack? This one slides in and out; ties hang on a double row of ¼-inch dowels.

Special closet hardware

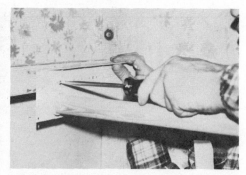

Refitting a clothes closet usually involves relocating the clothes pole and combining multiple pole locations with new shelf space, as shown in the photo above.

You can buy plastic clothes pole holders like these at most hardware stores. They are screwed in place as shown, and one holder is open so the pole can be removed.

Stanley Hardware makes a metal *Pin Strip* which serves as both a pole holder and shelf support. The strip is fastened to the closet side-wall by driving screws through two or more holes in the strip.

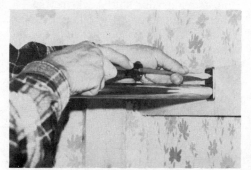

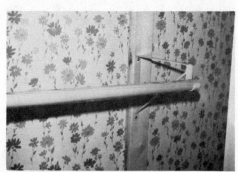

Your hardware store may also have adjustable metal clothes poles like the one shown above. Available in different extendable lengths, these poles are sturdy and easy to install.

A combination shelf bracket/pole holder is made by Stanley Hardware and can make your refitting job easier. The bracket is fastened into a wall stud.

Old-fashioned clothes pegs

Here's a project that can do a handsome job of converting an unused entryway wall into storage space for hats and coats. It's simple in design, easy to build, and attractive as well. Adjust the length and number of dowel pegs to suit your wall space, but keep the pegs at least 6 inches apart. They should also be at least 65 inches from the floor to hold long coats.

For this project, you'll need a drill guide so all the dowels will go in at the same angle. Many hardware stores carry both 90 degree and adjustable drill guides, but it's very easy to make your own.

Select a small, thick piece of scrap wood such as a 2x4. Then drill out a hole at the angle you want your dowels to incline, using the same bit you'll use for sinking the dowels (¾''). The drill guide is then clamped over the rack back at pre-measured locations.

What it takes

Approximate time: 1-2 hours, not including finish.

Tools and materials: Hammer, back or crosscut saw, drill with ⅜'' and ¾'' bits, plus the following materials: pine board 1¼'' x 8'' x 6', pine board ¾'' x 8.'' x 4', 3' length of ¾'' dowel rod, 1' length of ⅜'' dowel rod, 7d finishing nails, white or yellow glue.

1. After the rack back has been cut to size, mark the locations for dowel centers. Then align your drill guide over each spot, clamp it in place, and drill out the dowel holes.

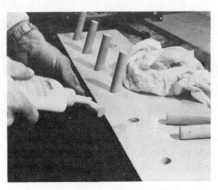

2. Coat the dowels and holes lightly with glue, then hammer the dowels in place. Tap them in gently, bit by bit, until the dowels protrude 2-3 inches.

3. Join the top to the rack back. Keep a rag nearby so you can wipe off any excess glue immediately.

4. Cut angled side braces to size and join them to the top and back of the rack. Use a couple of finishing nails in each side, followed by one or two dowel pegs for decoration.

5. Round off the dowels with a file and medium-grit sandpaper, then soften the corners and edges of the rack. Sand the surface smooth before finishing.

6. Apply a penetrating oil stain to the wood. When the stain dries (24 hours), give the wood extra protection with an oil or satin style varnish finish. Fasten the coatrack to the wall by screwing it into three studs.

ORGANIZING IDLE SPACE

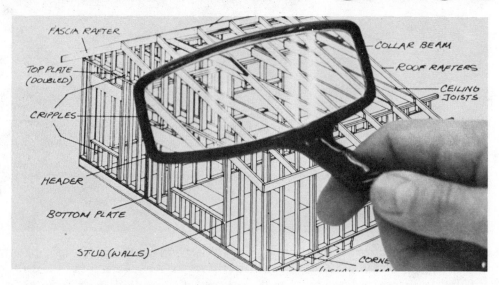

Out-of-the-way storage

It's not always easy to find room in your home for new storage space. If you already have a lion's share of storage space and can't find room for more, don't give up. A closer look around your house or apartment is sure to unearth potential storage areas that haven't yet been taken advantage of. (See the illustration above.) The projects and ideas on the next twelve pages can help you make use of these hidden storage areas.

Between-stud storage: a readymade solution

Readymade cabinets of metal and wood are available in various lengths but built to a standard width that fits exactly between the studs (usually 16 inches apart) in interior walls. The readymade model shown below is metal.

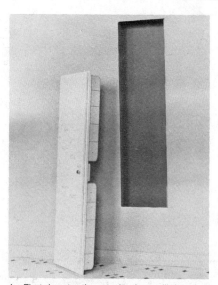

1. First locate the studs that will bracket your installation. Measure the exact dimensions of the recessed cabinet frame, not the facing. Determine the desired wall height of the cabinet, then cut away the wallboard to the studs on each side.

2. The recessed part of the cabinet will probably be a little narrower than the distance between the studs. If so, cut spacers out of scrap wallboard and nail them to one of the studs so the cabinet will slide in snugly.

3. Lift the cabinet into place and screw it to the studs on both sides through holes on the inside. The molding around the face of the cabinet will cover the edges of the cut wallboard even if the cuts are a little ragged.

Doing the job yourself

1. Cut out and remove wallboard or paneling between the studs as shown on page 131, using a keyhole or saber saw. Then nail cleats for the bottom shelf in place; they should be flush with the bottom edge of the wallboard.

2. Cut a sheet of hardboard, paneling, or ¼" plywood to the dimensions of the opening, then glue and nail it into place, using cleats to support the bottom corners, as shown above.

Push-pull click-click
Oops! I got a bit too enthusiastic with my keyhole saw when cutting out the wallboard between a couple of studs, and ended up cutting through two walls instead of one. Luckily I caught the mistake before the cutout was complete, but the subsequent repair could have been avoided if I'd kept my sawstrokes shorter.

Practical Pete

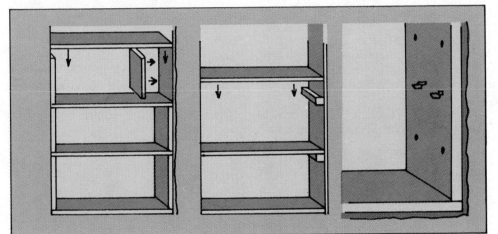

3. Install shelves, following one of the designs shown above. Be sure to cut and fit all shelves so that the front edge of each shelf is flush with the wall surface, not the stud behind it.

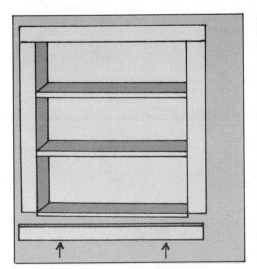

4. Measure, cut, and nail the trim in place. You can use either straight lumber or casing molding.

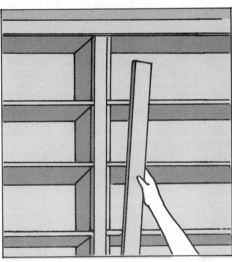

Note: For more extensive between-stud storage, remove the wallboard between several adjacent studs and build in new shelves as shown above. Install molding over the center studs to hide both the studs and the shelf support cleats.

Frame a window with shelves

What it takes

Approximate time: 3-4 hours, for the set of shelves and size of window shown. Larger windows or more extensive shelving will take longer.

Tools and materials: Basic cutting and joining tools plus these materials: 4 eight-foot pine boards (1"x8"), 6d finishing nails, 6d box nails.

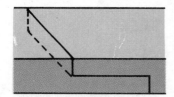

TIP: You may not be able to find a piece of lumber long enough for the top shelf. If this is the case, *splice* two boards together with a lap joint, as shown above, to get your shelf the right length.

Don't bypass the space around windows in your search for more storage area. Framing a window with shelves will give both the room and the view a new personality.

If you've got room and really need to make as much shelf space as possible, frame the window completely instead of just part way, as was done here. Extend your side supports all the way down to the floor and build shelves in below the window sill. You can also increase the length of the shelves all around the window area.

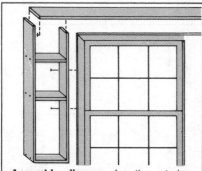

Assembly diagram for the window shelf unit. Note that the side shelves, shown here in color, are constructed before they are mounted on the wall.

1. Assemble both side shelf units completely before attaching them to the wall. Leave the upper sections open, as shown, to accommodate the top shelf. Use screws or 6d finishing nails to assemble the pieces.

2. Drive screws or 6d box nails through the vertical side supports into the window molding. The top edge of each inner side must be flush with the top edge of the window molding.

3. Measure and cut the top shelf, then fasten it to the top window molding and side shelf units. Glue all bare wood joints.

4. Nail or screw through the outer shelf sides into the top shelf as shown. Set all the nails, fill holes with wood dough, and sand before finishing.

5. For extra stability, or to keep the outer edges of the shelf securely on the wall, use small angle braces or toe-nail into a stud, as shown.

Build a window seat with storage space underneath

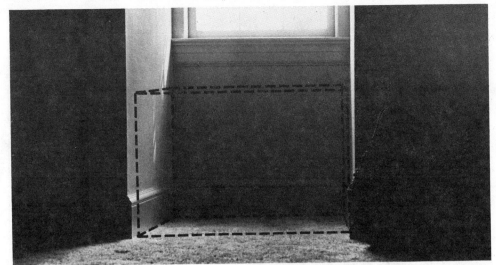

What it takes

Approximate time: 4 hours.

Tools and materials: Basic cutting and joining tools, plus the following materials: 3 eight-foot 2x4s, 1 sheet ⅝″ A/C interior plywood, 1 pair ⅝″ butt hinges, 6d finishing nails, 10d common nails.

Here's a plan for a sturdy window seat that doubles as a storage area. If your window isn't recessed from the wall like the one above, you can still use the same design and just add sides. Putting a bottom on is optional.

Constructing the seat is a simple but satisfying job that can be done in an afternoon. The first step is to measure, mark, and cut the front panel, top, and framing pieces. **Note:** Make your seat ¼″ narrower than the width of the alcove. The drafts and temperature changes common to window areas can cause the wood to swell, making it difficult to open the seat.

Assemble the frame first, using 10d common nails and beginning with the top. The lap joints will give extra strength and make nailing easier. (Toenailing gives a much weaker joint and often splits the wood.)

When the frame is together and you've tested it for fit, glue and nail the front in place. Here you'll want to use 6d finishing nails, since they can be easily set and hidden with wood dough. The front should be high enough to hide the seat or top and provide a slight lip to keep the cushion from slipping off.

Installing the top is the last step. Fasten the hinges to the back edge of the plywood, position the top, then screw the free wings of the hinges to the back frame member. Make sure the back edge of the top is at least an inch from the back edge of the frame (see design detail below).

Now all you need to do is finish your project and give it a cushion.

TIP: If you don't want to take the trouble to apply a finish to the front, use a piece of pre-finished paneling instead of regular plywood.

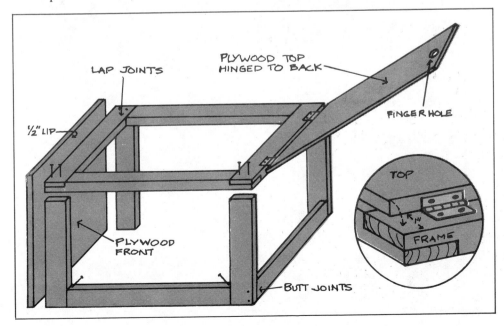

Build a bed with drawers underneath

What it takes

Approximate time: The bed shown took one long afternoon and a couple of evenings to complete, not including the finish; you should allow at least 6 hours.

Tools and materials: Basic cutting and joining tools, plus the following materials: 2 6' 2x6s, 6 3' 2x4s, 2 6' 2x4s, 1 sheet ⅝'' or ¾'' A/C exterior plywood, 1 sheet roughsawn plywood or other siding and drawer front material, drawer pulls (2), 8 rollers for drawer bottoms, 12 4-inch bolts, with nuts and washers, 10d common nails.

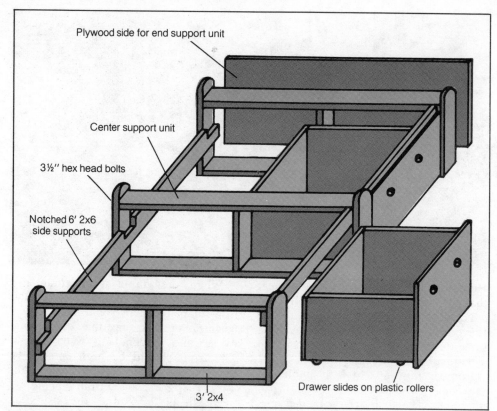

- Plywood side for end support unit
- Center support unit
- 3½'' hex head bolts
- Notched 6' 2x6 side supports
- 3' 2x4
- Drawer slides on plastic rollers

Assembling the frame. Here's a super design for a bed with loads of storage space built in underneath. The entire bed can be taken apart and put back together easily so you can build it in your workshop instead of on the spot. Construction-grade lumber keeps materials cost down and gives the bed a rugged, rustic look. (When buying your lumber, choose 2x4s and 2x6s that are straight and as free of cracks and knots as possible.) The drawers slide out completely for maximum accessibility. **Note:** Because this bed had to go against the wall, drawers were built into one side only. If your bed is going to be in the middle of the room, you can build an identical set of drawers for the other side. (Each drawer must be no more than 17'' in length.)

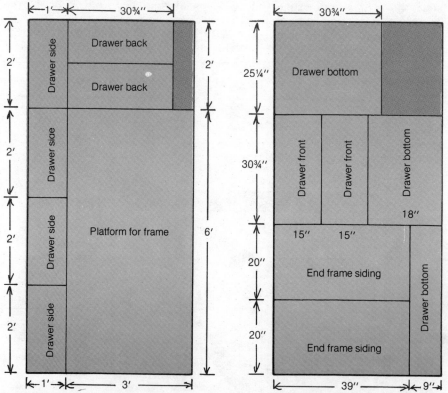

Cutting diagrams. To get the most from your plywood and siding sheets, use these cutting diagrams.

Building the frame

1. Build end and center support units, working from the design opposite. Glue all joints, and use 10d common nails for fastening.

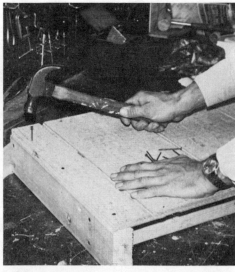

2. Glue and nail sides to end support units. Here you can use plywood, paneling, or rough lumber, depending on the style and appearance you want.

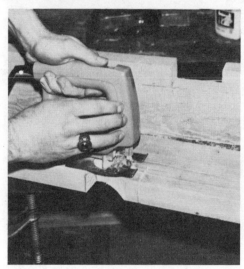

3. Cut 2x6 sidepieces to correct length (6', in this case), then measure, mark, and cut notches as shown. File or chisel notches to final dimensions.

4. Temporarily secure completed 2x6 side supports to the three frame units with clamps as shown, then drill out bolt holes and install bolts.

5. Cut and fit platform in place.

6. Round off the six upright frame members. Use a saber or coping saw to cut curves and a file or surform tool to soften edges.

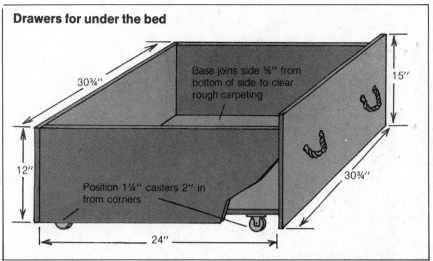

Drawers for under the bed

30¾"

Base joins side ⅝" from bottom of side to clear rough carpeting

15"

12"

Position 1¼" casters 2" in from corners

30¾"

24"

1. Measure, mark, and cut the back, bottom, sides, and front for each drawer according to the design above. If the finished bed is to go against a wall, as is the case here, then only two drawers are needed. If the bed is to be located in the middle of the room and both sides are accessible, you can build four drawers. But each drawer should be no deeper than 18 inches.

2. Join the sides to the bottom. Here a rabbet joint is used for extra strength.

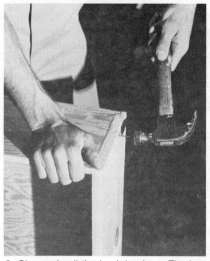

3. Glue and nail the back in place. The bar clamp forces the back against the bottom.

4. Join the front to side and bottom edges. Position the front panel so that roller clearance is at least ¼" for bare floor; ⅝" if the drawer must roll on a thick pile carpet.

5. Screw one caster into each corner of the bottom as shown. Make sure your screws don't stick through to the opposite side. If they do, file them flush.

TIP: When you've got the bed frame assembled, label the joints where the different parts meet, using either a permanent felt-tipped marker or a soldering iron, as shown above. Since holes for the bolts are slightly different for each joint, labeling will make it easy to realign parts when you reassemble the bed.

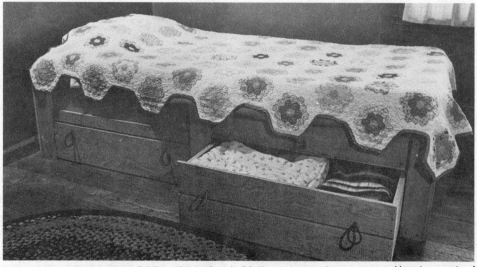

6. Now you are ready to put a finish on the bed and slide in your new storage space. Here two coats of polyurethane varnish (satin-style) were applied, to protect the wood and accent its natural beauty.

Storage under the stairs

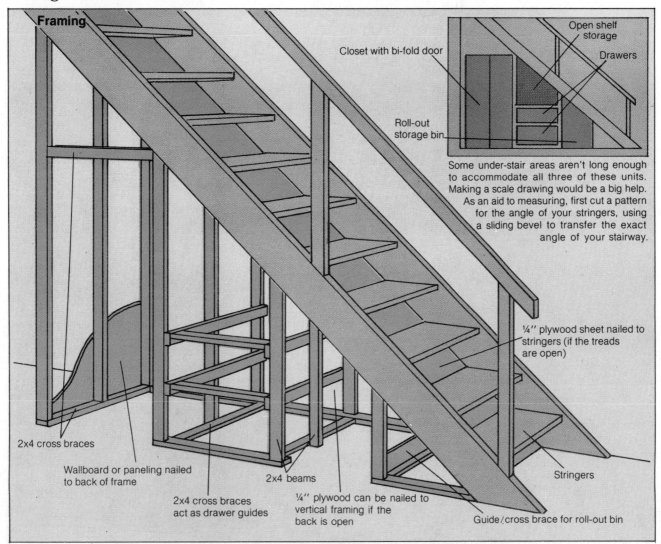

Framing

Closet with bi-fold door

Roll-out storage bin

Open shelf storage

Drawers

Some under-stair areas aren't long enough to accommodate all three of these units. Making a scale drawing would be a big help. As an aid to measuring, first cut a pattern for the angle of your stringers, using a sliding bevel to transfer the exact angle of your stairway.

¼″ plywood sheet nailed to stringers (if the treads are open)

2x4 cross braces

Wallboard or paneling nailed to back of frame

2x4 cross braces act as drawer guides

2x4 beams

¼″ plywood can be nailed to vertical framing if the back is open

Stringers

Guide/cross brace for roll-out bin

Nail ¼-inch plywood to the stringers if necessary (see **TIP:** this page). For framing, begin by nailing the 2x4 vertical frame members to the stringers. Then complete framing with 2x4 horizontal crossmembers both front to back and side to side between verticals.

Nail front to back supports for the drawer/ shelf verticals at a height that they can be used for runner guides. Should your stairs be accessible from both sides, you will want to close in the back side of your storage space. Fit ¼-inch plywood or sheetrock in

under the stringer on that side and nail it to the vertical supports. Then nail on your precut and measured front paneling (⅜-inch plywood or sheetrock), including a small triangular piece at the low end. (For more information on framing, see page 29.)

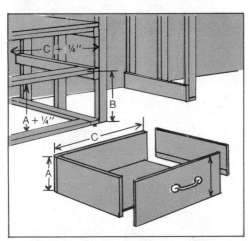

Drawer and shelf framing detail. For the shelf, nail a sheet of ¾-inch plywood over cross braces measured for the top drawer height. The cross braces serving as runner guides must be level.

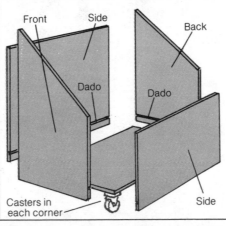

Front   Side   Back

Dado   Dado

Casters in each corner   Side

Roll-out storage bin detail. When measuring for the roll-out bin, be sure to leave clearance of about one inch on both sides to allow for easy sliding. The bin bottom should be inset 3″ to make room for the 3½″ casters.

TIP: If your flight of stairs is openbacked (just treads, no risers), dirt will fall down into the storage area unless it is protected. Nail a fitted sheet of ¼-inch plywood across the underside of the stairs, from stringer to stringer, to eliminate the problem.

Claim that empty corner

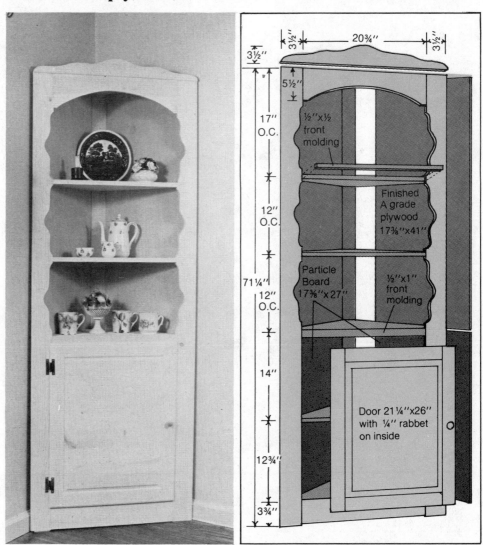

Here's a handsome cabinet which will make good use of an available corner in any living space. The assembly diagram above and the photo sequence below will help you build it yourself. This same cabinet is available preassembled from S.F. Bailey and Sons, Clarks Summit, PA. Other styles are also available from the same manufacturer.

1. After making dados for the sides and shelves, assemble the decorative front frame, using glue and wood braces as shown to secure joints.

2. Fasten triangular shelves to the front frame. Dados in the frame combined with glue and screws anchor shelves firmly.

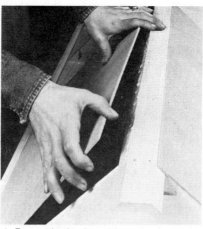

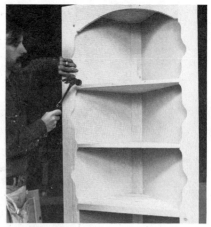

3. Glue and nail the back support to the shelves, using 2 nails per shelf as shown. Dadoing these joints isn't necessary, but does make the cabinet stronger.

4. Fasten the back panels to the back support, shelves, and front. Use glue generously, but be sure to wipe off the excess as soon as the joint is closed.

5. Nail molding to the top three shelves to bring the front edge of each shelf flush with the front frame. Wide molding goes on the third shelf from the top.

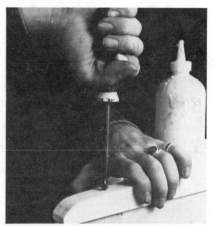

6. Screw hinges to the door first, then position it squarely in the front frame opening and fasten the hinges to the cabinet.

7. Fasten the two-part magnetic catch assembly to the door and front frame.

8. After rabbeting the decorative top piece, glue and screw it to the top of the cabinet as shown. Now you're ready to show off your work with a good finish. (For finishing suggestions, see page 15.)

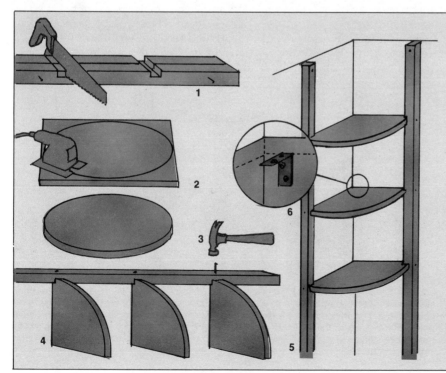

Stopgaps and copouts

1. Temporarily join the side supports together with finishing nails, then measure, mark, and cut out dados as shown above.

2. Use a saber or coping saw to cut out a circle from ¾-inch A/C plywood.

3. Cut the circle into quarters.

4. Join the shelves to side supports, using white or yellow glue and 8d finishing nails.

5. Install assembled shelves by fastening side supports to wall as shown. If you can't screw into a stud, use the wall fastener designed for your wall type (see page 16).

6. Check shelves to make sure they're level, then join back corner of each shelf to wall corner with an angle brace. Keep angle brace close to wall corner so you can fasten into corner stud.

Rough storage

This chapter contains ideas and how-to information on rough storage projects. Every house or apartment has some garage, attic, basement, or utility room space that is unfinished or in some way not usable as living space. Studs and framing are usually exposed; the area is unheated, not easily accessible, or poorly lighted. Until you decide to remodel these areas, you might as well exploit their storage potential. Here there's no need to get fancy; materials should be economical and easy to work with. Use C/D plywood, particle board, and cheap grades of lumber whenever possible. If you do plan to remodel in the future, make sure your rough storage project can be dismantled or removed without much trouble.

There are quite a few ready-made rough storage ideas. If you're working with exposed studs, using pegboard is hard to beat. It's inexpensive, and you don't need to build a frame or use spacers to install the board; just fasten it directly to the studs. Heavy-duty shelf brackets work well too, and you'll also find a variety of specialized hardware "hang-ups" for garden hose, bicycles, rakes, shovels.

A 6" plastic-sheathed hook for each wheel safely supports a bicycle hanging frame down on a garage wall. A hole for the hook threads (which are about 2" long) is drilled into the joist, using a drill bit slightly smaller in diameter than the hook. The hook is then handscrewed into the joist.

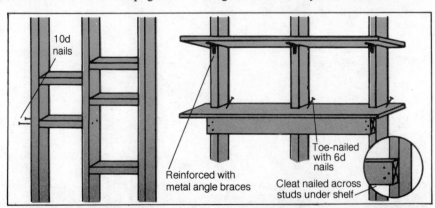

Shelving between the studs: Utilize between-stud space by putting up shelves as shown above. Nailing short lengths of 2x4 stock between the studs is the quickest way to make more storage space in exposed framing. If you need wider shelf space, slot your shelves to fit over studs, as shown at right. Toe-nailing alone won't make the shelf strong enough, so get extra support by using metal angle braces or nailing into a cleat that's been fastened firmly across the front of the studs.

Putting up rough shelving

In general, rough shelving should be inexpensive, easy to install, and very sturdy. The shelves you see here were put up in the corner of a garage, but they would work equally well in the basement, attic, or utility room. Because they're held together with bolts (use finishing nails just to position the supports for drilling and bolting), you can relocate them if you decide to remodel. **Note:** If your shelves are going to be exposed to outdoor conditions, treat the lumber with wood preservative.

1. Join the horizontal crosspieces to the vertical supports as shown, using just one finishing nail. Don't put the nail in the center of the crosspiece; that's where bolt will go.

2. Use a level to position the crosspieces on the wall framing, then nail them in place. Allow 16″ between the wall stud and the vertical support to accommodate the shelf.

3. Once you've positioned the support with finishing nails, secure each joint with a matching bolt as shown. Drill out holes for the bolts with a slightly larger bit.

4. Repeat steps 1-3 for each support. Four supports, positioned 32 inches apart (skip 1 stud, for 16-inch center framing), will make a shelf 8 feet long.

5. Cut and install plywood shelves.

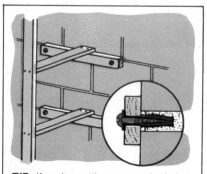

TIP: If you're putting up rough shelves against a cement wall, fasten 2x4 cleats to the wall with bolts and expansion shield anchors made for masonry walls. You can also use 2x4 stock for vertical supports and crosspieces, as shown above.

Ideas for the attic

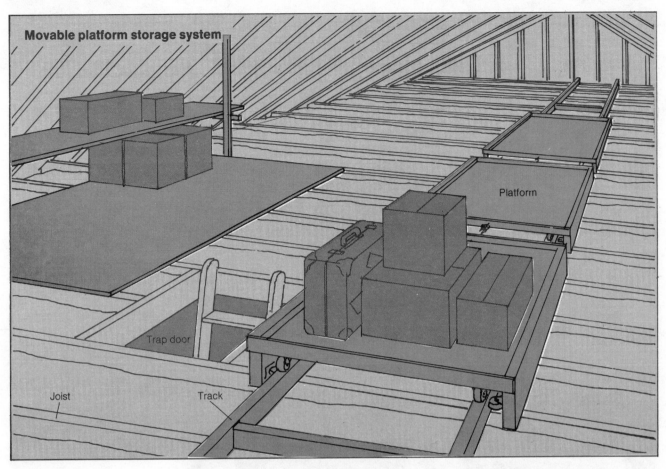

Movable platform storage system

Platform

Trap door

Joist

Track

Building storage space into an unused attic or crawlspace can substantially reduce the storage load in other parts of your home. Out-of-season clothes, sleds, suitcases, folding beds, camping equipment, any articles that are used on a sporadic or seasonal basis, are candidates for attic storage. Storing such items in the attic keeps them out of the way but accessible, so they're not taking up valuable space in the main living areas of the house.

If there's room to stand up in your attic, lay down a rough plywood floor before you start building new shelf or closet space. Use C/D exterior grade plywood to keep costs down. Over joists spaced 16″ apart, ½″ thickness is good; use ¾″ thick plywood over joists set on 32″ centers.

If your attic or crawlspace has no room to stand, building a movable platform storage system like the one detailed here is an excellent way to squeeze space out of this otherwise useless area. **Note:** A movable platform system will only work in crawlspaces where the access door is centrally located, as shown above.

I put my best foot forward—and look what happened.

I was up in the attic taking measurements for some shelves I planned to build, and the next thing I knew my foot was sticking through the living room ceiling. I was so intent on my tape measure that I lost my footing on the ceiling joist and stepped through the sheetrock. Calling on my constantly reliable hindsight, I realized that the first step should have been to lay down a rough plywood floor in the area around my planned shelf space.

Practical Pete

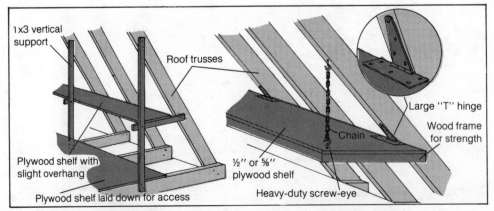

1x3 vertical support

Roof trusses

Plywood shelf with slight overhang

Plywood shelf laid down for access

Large "T" hinge

Wood frame for strength

Chain

½″ or ⅝″ plywood shelf

Heavy-duty screw-eye

Shelves and the slanted ceiling. You can build shelves in your cramped, slant-roofed attic with one of the designs illustrated above. Cut a sheet of ½″ or ¾″ plywood lengthwise for long shelves. The slope of the roof and the amount of headroom in the attic will determine the size of your shelves.

Building the platform

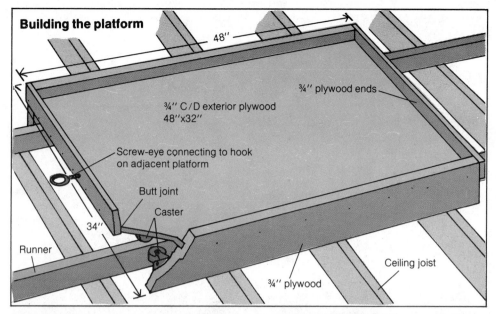

48''

¾'' C/D exterior plywood 48''x32''

¾'' plywood ends

Screw-eye connecting to hook on adjacent platform

Butt joint

Caster

34''

Runner

¾'' plywood

Ceiling joist

What it takes

Approximate time: 4-5 hours, for building and installing 3 platforms and two 16' runners.

Tools and materials: Router with ¾'' dado bit, crosscut saw, hammer, screwdriver, plus the following materials: one sheet ¾''x4'x8' C/D exterior plywood, 6 4' 2x6s, 2 heavy-duty screw-eyes, with matching hooks, 24 small-wheel (1''), screw-on casters, 32' of straight 2x4s for runner assembly.

1. Working from the drawing shown above, build the platform/runner assembly from ¾'' C/D exteri- or plywood and 2x6 lumber. Cut three 48x32-inch platforms from one 4x8-foot sheet of plywood.

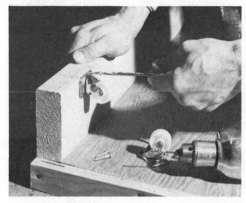

2. Attach the side casters to the 2x6 platform supports as shown. Locate each caster several inches from the corner, and place it high enough to allow for good runner contact.

3. With a length of 2x4 stock held against the side casters and the platform bottom (top photo), mark the runner outlines. Then screw the top casters in place, making sure that the caster wheel is centered between runner outlines (bottom photo).

Installing the runner assembly

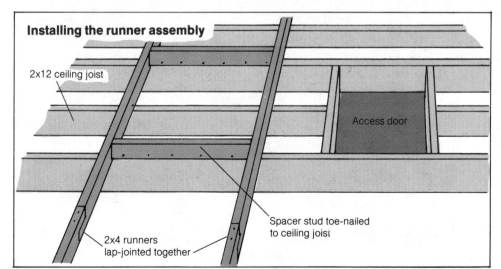

2x12 ceiling joist

Access door

Spacer stud toe-nailed to ceiling joist

2x4 runners lap-jointed together

This endview shows the alignment of track and casters on one side of the storage platform. When measuring the track fitting, be sure to allow ⅛'' clearance on both sides between runners and side casters.

4. Using the straightest 2x4 lumber you can find, make two continuous runners by joining shorter lengths with a lap joint (above). Line the runners up and join them together with 2x4 *spacers,* as shown. Position the spacers about six feet apart, directly over the ceiling joists, then toe-nail them in place to secure the runner assembly. Put the platforms in place, and connect them with heavy-duty hooks and screw-eyes.

Covering the cans

What it takes

Approximate time: Plan to spend a long afternoon on this one if you're building from scratch. (Two hours if you use a kit.)

Tools and materials: Tape measure, square, crosscut or circular saw, hammer, drill, screwdriver, four strap hinges with screws, two butt hinges with screws, one hook and eye fastener, four cement blocks, plus the following materials: 34' of 2x2 lumber, two 4x8 sheets of C/D exterior-grade plywood (¾" thick). **Note:** The grooved plywood used for the shed pictured here is a special exterior siding called *Texture III*.

A small shed like this one for concealing trash containers can be free-standing because it has a back and bottom. It's a great way to keep overflowing cans out of sight and to protect garbage from possible upset by animals or wind.

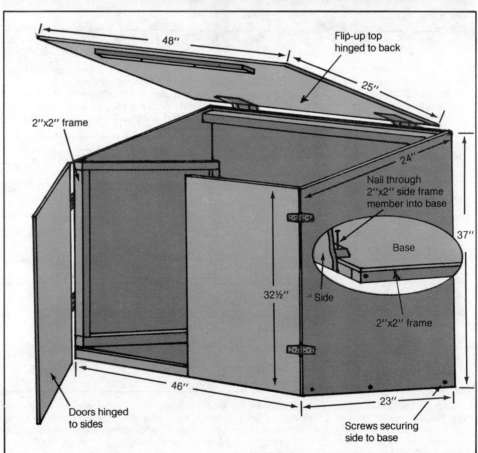

Some home centers and builders' supply outlets sell sheds pre-assembled or in kit form, but you can usually build one much cheaper from scratch in about half a day. This design is for a completely enclosed shed that holds two 32-gallon cans.

1. Shovel out a depression about 6 inches deep, two feet wide, and four feet long.

2. When your hole is uniformly deep and level to the eye, pack the bottom flat with a tamper or the back of your shovel.

3. Fill the flattened depression about half way up with pea gravel. You'll need about two wheelbarrow loads to do the job.

4. Spread gravel evenly over the bottom of the hole, using a rake to make the surface roughly level.

5. Position cement blocks to support corners of base, then seat blocks in gravel bed as shown. Use a level and straight length of 2x4 to make sure the blocks are level.

6. Place the base on the block foundation, then nail the sides to the base as shown. Here double-headed nails are used so that the shed can be disassembled easily.

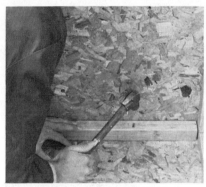

7. Attach the back to the base by nailing through the bottom 2″x2″ frame member and into the base.

8. Fasten sides to back with screws. Drive screws through plywood sides and into back frame member, as shown. Screw sides to base for additional strength and stability.

9. Attach the front doors to the sides. Have someone hold the doors in place while you attach the hinges.

10. Hold the top in place, then hinge it to the back as shown.

11. Keep the front doors closed with a simple hook and eye latch. Screw the hook in place first, then the eye.

12. Even though exterior grade materials have been used throughout, a coat of wood preservative will make it weather-proof.

Workshop storage

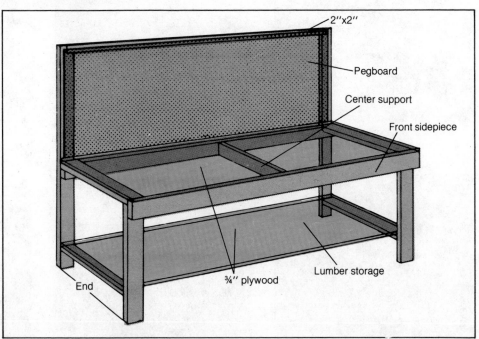

Here's a plan for a workbench with built-in storage space for tools and lumber. It's sturdy, as well as easy to build. The ends of the bench are assembled first, then joined with the front and back sidepieces. The rear corners are lap-jointed for strength. The center support is nailed in place, then

the workbench top is installed. The top is screwed rather than nailed in place because it may have to be replaced in the future. A 2x2-inch horizontal support is fastened to the rear uprights and the pegboard attached, then the bottom shelf is installed. Adjust workbench dimensions to needs.

Your workshop may be the best place to start building new storage space. It's a good first choice because a well-organized workshop makes subsequent projects go smoothly and pleasantly; you can concentrate on building instead of on locating tools or materials.

Whether your workshop is large or small, extensively or minimally equipped, there are several important items you should have on hand. Keep a fire extin-

guisher within easy reach. You should also have a first aid kit nearby. Your power tools should be out of reach if your workshop is accessible to children. You might even want to lock these tools up or, if that's not possible, construct a small box around the electrical outlet in your work area and put a lockable latch on it.

Once you've got these safety precautions out of the way, you can go ahead with the ideas on the next few pages.

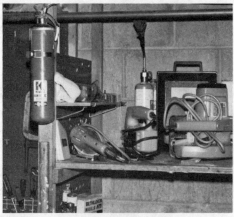

Safety first is the rule when it comes to workshop storage. Keep a fire extinguisher and a first aid kit within easy reach. Notice that safety goggles and a filter mask are stored right along with power tools.

Metal sawhorse brackets are inexpensive and surprisingly handy to have in your workshop. With a few 2x4s and a sheet of plywood, you can put up additional workbench or storage space in a matter of minutes to help you cope with a large project or a sudden case of storage overflow.

Putting pegboard to work

Because of its low cost, universal availability, and easy installation, pegboard is the perfect wall material for work areas of all kinds. It also helps you create an incredibly adjustable storage system. Making room for new tools or accommodating special tools and materials for a particular project is a quick and easy job.

When planning pegboard storage space in your workshop, remember that you can choose either ⅛" or ¼" thickness. Use the heavyweight perforated hardboard if you plan to store heavy items (axes, power tools, bar clamps) or install shelf supports.

Hand tools and pegboard were made for each other (see page 14 for pegboard installation instructions). If you or your fellow workers have trouble returning articles to their proper locations, trace the outline of the hanging tool, then paint in the silhouette, as shown above.

TIP: It's easy to go overboard with pegboard storage. Even ¼" pegboard is not suitable for long term storage of heavy items: after several weeks it starts to bow away from the wall; the shelves become slanted, and the clips start to pull out of their holes. To prevent this from happening, fasten your hardest-working shelf supports and hangers into the wall behind the pegboard.

You can really get the most from your pegboard by using both sides of it. Here one side faces the workbench, while the other faces a shelf storage area. There is one important limitation to getting double duty from pegboard: it's easy to overload, so use it only for lightweight items.

It's hard to beat this system of storing screws, nails, and other small items. The screw-on tops of these clear plastic containers are fitted with pegboard clips. Your hardware store or home decorating center should have them in stock.

Storing lumber

Having ample storage space for building materials means fewer trips to the lumber yard since you won't have to stop work in the middle of a project to go out and get more wood. Making more room for lumber will also enable you to take advantage of sales or special prices on building materials. Unfortunately, storage space for wood is often neglected in favor of tool and workbench space. To keep your wood supplies in top condition, all lumber should be stored away from moisture. This usually means you'll want to keep it off the floor.

Here's a good way to store plywood, paneling, and other sheet material. Suspend two five-foot lengths of 2x4 stock from the ceiling joists as shown. Using a chain enables you to adjust the height of your sheet storage area or remove it entirely.

With two pairs of large angle braces, you can convert unused ceiling space between the joists into storage space for boards.

Make a separate storage area for scrap wood. Longer stock that can still be used for building is stored on two horizontal supports which are nailed to studs and strengthened with a diagonal brace. Small kindling is kept in the box on the right.

Storing paints and finishes

It doesn't take long for the space you've allocated for stain, varnish, wood filler, paints, and enamels to become a disorganized array of cans and containers of all sizes (see photo). A secondary shelf for smaller cans will utilize your storage space more efficiently and prevent your quarts, pints, and half-pints from being hidden by the "big boys."

Separate your finish-related preparations into these groups: Thinners, solvents, brush cleaner solutions; wood stain and filler; sealers and clear finishes; paints and enamels; waxes and polishes; spray products. **TIP:** Keep a supply of empty cans near your thinner, solvent, and brush-cleaner section so you won't have an excuse for not cleaning your brushes right after you're through using them. You'll also need cans whenever you use finish, since it's bad policy (see margin) to apply straight from the original container.

Separate small cans from large ones by putting up a narrow secondary shelf. This is a quick, easy job with inexpensive shelf brackets like the one shown. Make sure your shelf is at least 8½ inches high so gallon cans can fit underneath.

Before

After

An open and shut case

I got on the wrong side of a paint expert friend of mine recently. He stepped into my workshop just as I was putting the lid on some enamel and really got an eyeful of my can-closing technique. To make a long story short, I ended up buying him a new shirt and he ended up giving me some important pointers:

1) Paint cans are made to be opened and shut gradually, not by prying or pounding in just one or two spots. Open the can by working all the way around the lip with a screwdriver or can opener. Close it in the same way, tapping the edge in place bit by bit. Once you've deformed the lip with a heavy blow, you can forget about getting a good fit.

2) Don't apply paint or finish straight from the container it comes in unless you'll be using the entire can. The original can is for mixing, storing, and pouring. Use a clean coffee can to hold the paint or finish while you're applying it.

3) Keep the lip clean. Before you start applying the paint or finish, use your brush to remove the excess from the groove around the top of the can. Keeping the groove free of dried finish makes reclosing the lid a simple and airtight job.

4) Sort through your paints and finishes at least twice a season. Give inactive paints a good mixing and throw away finishing preparations that have dried out or become too concentrated or contaminated to use.

Practical Pete

Other workshop storage ideas

A handy nail-file can be created in an empty drawer by building in small bins. Shallow drawers like this one are well suited for small item storage.

Screw-top jars and lids fastened to the underside of a shelf as shown make see-through storage space for nails, screws, bolts, and other small items.

A plastic dish tub functions as a drawer when slid on two pieces of U-shape wood molding nailed to the underside of a workbench or shelf.

Build a carry-all toolbox

If you and your tools have to do a lot of traveling, a simple tote/storage box like the one shown above will come in handy. You can make it in about an hour, using spare or scrap lumber, some 6d box nails, and a length of 1½" dowel rod. Toolboxes should be built to take a beating, so use ¾" exterior grade plywood if possible. Both sides of the interior should, for safety's sake, be slotted to hold and protect handsaw blades.

1. Cut the bottom and end pieces, drill out holes for the dowel rod, and cut an opening for your 2-foot level in one endpiece. Then join as shown above. A toolbox 19 to 21 inches in length will be long enough to hold most handsaws.

2. Cut the sides to size, then cut a slot for the saw blade near the top edge of each sidepiece. Locate and bevel the slot so it lines up with the top endpiece edge as shown, then join the sides to the ends and the bottom.

3. Divide one end of the box to hold nails, screws, tape measure, and other small items. When planning the divider, make sure you leave room for your level to lie flat. Also keep in mind the importance of evenly balanced weight in the toolbox, if you plan to be carrying it frequently.

4. Secure saws by driving a round-head screw in on one edge or endpiece. Sink the screw in just far enough to hold the blade. Tie down the handle at the other end with a length of leather cord secured to a screw-eye. Slide the dowel rod into place and lock it in position with a small nail. Finally, give your toolbox a coat of varnish for durability and easy cleanout.

Stowaway storage for toys

What it takes

Approximate time: About half a day.

Tools and materials: Carpenter's square, electric circular saw, electric or hand drill with ⅞-, ½-, and ¼-inch bits, hammer and a nail set, sandpaper, 6 dozen ½-inch finishing nails, 3 feet of ½-inch rope, two washers with holes at least ⅞-inch in diameter, acrylic enamel paint and/or stain; one sheet ¾-inch 4x8 plywood, 6 feet of 1x8 board, 40 inches of ¾-inch dowel.

Planning hints:
It is very important when constructing the two basic boxes involved in this project that your measurements allow for easy sliding of the engine box into the garage.
Measure all corners with a carpenter's square to ensure right angles.
Pieces should be glued as well as nailed for extra support.
For a more finished looking product, use dowels to cap the exposed nailing. Drill holes ¼ inch in diameter about ¼ inch deep where nails will go. Set the nails deep in their holes, and hammer glued pieces of ¼ inch dowel into the holes. Sand the tops flush.
When cutting the ends and sidepieces for the boxes, be sure to compensate for the various dimensional fractions lost to kerf (the width of the saw cuts, that is). Add the width of the saw cuts to your finishing strip measurements as you go, tailoring them to the large panels.
When cutting finishing strips as diagrammed, it's a good idea to make all lengthwise cuts before sawing crosswise measures.

Do all toys come complete with 50 losable parts, or does it just seem that way? And how do you keep open-shelf playroom storage from looking like the baseball toss in a penny arcade? Short of instituting martial law, why not try building an eye-catching closed storage box?

Here's a combination toy box/work table which kids will enjoy. The fire engine rolls in and out of its garage on wheels, holds all kinds of toys, and is sturdy enough for a small child to ride in.

To begin

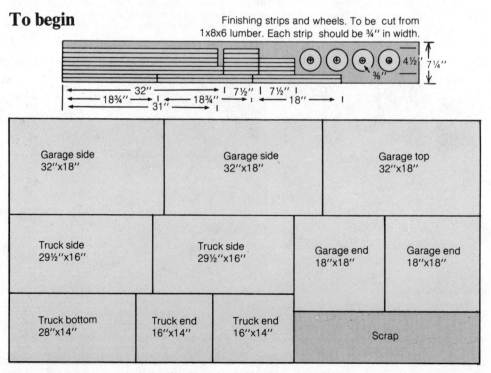

Finishing strips and wheels. To be cut from 1x8x6 lumber. Each strip should be ¾" in width.

1. Cut the measured pieces of plywood as shown. Use a circular power saw.

2. Cut out wheels and finishing strips. Remeasure. Use the larger panels as a guide.

Assembling the garage

1. Glue and nail the two 32-inch finishing strips to the top edge of each of the side pieces. Then glue and nail horizontally through each of the strips into either side of the ¾-inch edge of the top piece to hide the exposed laminations.

2. To make the back of the garage, glue and nail an 18¾-inch strip on each vertical side edge of the 18x18 plywood back end. The strips will stick up ¾-inch above the top. Fit and fasten one 18-inch strip along the top edge of the back. Then glue and nail through the strips into the exposed ends of the top and sides of the garage.

3. Attach the two remaining 18¾-inch strips to the top of the 18x18-inch plywood front. Lay this assembly aside. It will be painted and nailed to the front of the fire truck later when the body has been assembled.

Assembling the truck

1. Drill ⅞-inch holes through the bottom corners of both side pieces, 2 inches from the bottom and 4 inches in from the ends.

2. Glue and nail the truck pieces together as shown. Be sure to set the floor piece at least 3½ inches up from the bottom so that it will clear the axles.

3. Cut the two 17½-inch axle dowels and insert through the holes. Slip on the washers and hammer the wheels on flush with the ends of the dowels. If they are too loose smear glue on the end of the dowel.

4. Paint the truck as you desire. Carefully nail the front panel onto the truck so it will fit exactly into the open end of the garage when the truck is backed in all the way. We painted the truck red inside and outside, with gold grille and bumpers, white headlights, and black coats and hats on pink-cheeked firemen.

5. Round off the sharp rear corners of each 31-inch strip for the sides of the two ladders. Glue and nail them to the rungs as diagrammed here. Nail each ladder to a side of the truck, square ends facing forward.

6. Drill holes ½-inch or ⅝-inch in diameter through the front of the box, centered. (Here each is the center of a headlight.) Run the ends of a tow-rope through the holes and knot them inside.

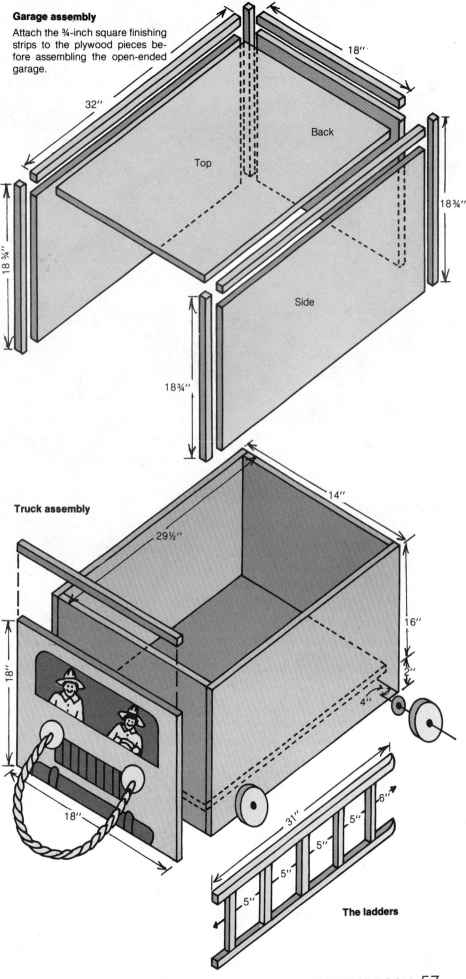

Garage assembly
Attach the ¾-inch square finishing strips to the plywood pieces before assembling the open-ended garage.

Top

Back

Side

32″

18″

18¾″

18¾″

18¾″

18¾″

Truck assembly

29½″

14″

16″

2″

4″

18″

18″

31″

6″

5″

5″

5″

5″

5″

The ladders

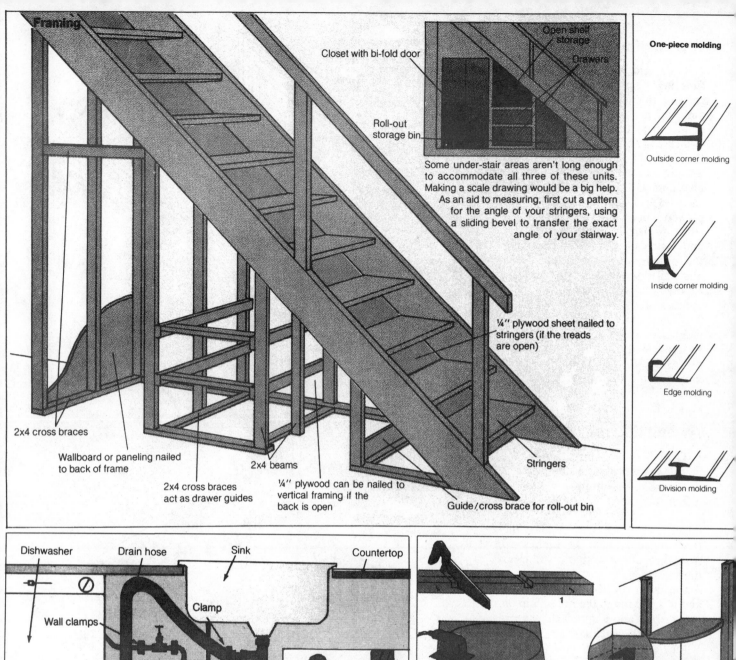

Framing

2x4 cross braces

Wallboard or paneling nailed to back of frame

2x4 cross braces act as drawer guides

2x4 beams

¼″ plywood can be nailed to vertical framing if the back is open

Guide/cross brace for roll-out bin

Stringers

¼″ plywood sheet nailed to stringers (if the treads are open)

Closet with bi-fold door

Roll-out storage bin

Open shelf storage

Drawers

Some under-stair areas aren't long enough to accommodate all three of these units. Making a scale drawing would be a big help. As an aid to measuring, first cut a pattern for the angle of your stringers, using a sliding bevel to transfer the exact angle of your stairway.

One-piece molding

Outside corner molding

Inside corner molding

Edge molding

Division molding

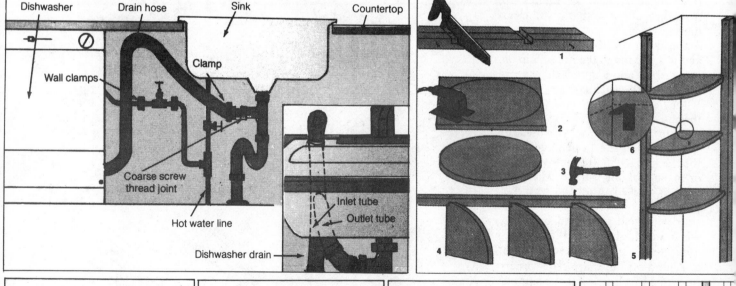

Dishwasher

Drain hose

Sink

Countertop

Clamp

Wall clamps

Coarse screw thread joint

Hot water line

Inlet tube

Outlet tube

Dishwasher drain

1

2

3

4

5

6

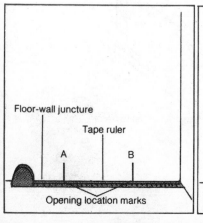

Floor-wall juncture

Tape ruler

A

B

Opening location marks

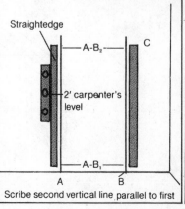

Straightedge

A-B₂

C

2′ carpenter's level

A-B₁

A

B

Scribe second vertical line parallel to first

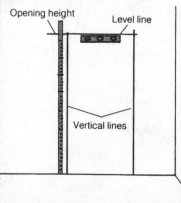

Opening height

Level line

Vertical lines

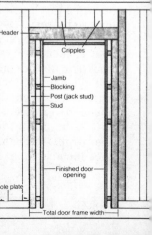

Header

Cripples

Jamb

Blocking

Post (jack stud)

Stud

Finished door opening

Sole plate

Total door frame width

Two-piece molding

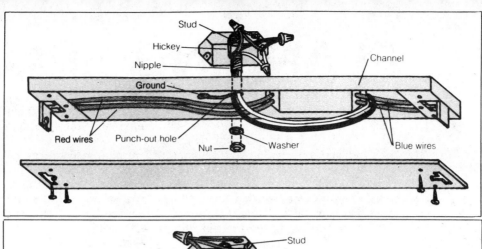

Two-piece corner
molding (inside)

Two-piece corner
molding (outside)

Decorative strip

Stud
Hickey
Nipple
Ground
Channel
Red wires
Punch-out hole
Nut
Washer
Blue wires

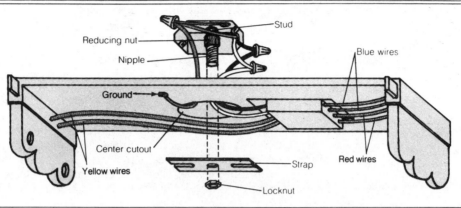

Stud
Reducing nut
Nipple
Blue wires
Ground
Center cutout
Yellow wires
Strap
Red wires
Locknut

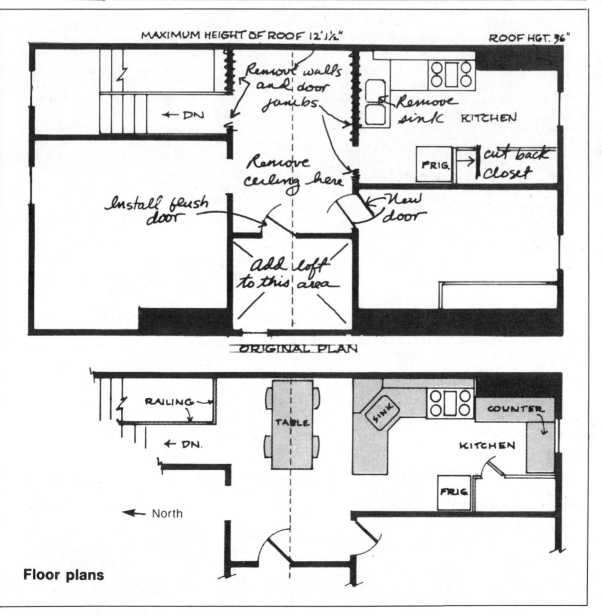

MAXIMUM HEIGHT OF ROOF 12'1½"   ROOF HGT. 36"

← DN

*Remove walls
and door
jambs*

*Remove
sink* KITCHEN

*Remove
ceiling here*

FRIG. *cut back
closet*

*Install flush
door*

*New
door*

*Add loft
to this area*

ORIGINAL PLAN

RAILING

TABLE   SINK

COUNTER

← DN.

KITCHEN

FRIG.

← North

Floor plans

PLANNING SPACE-

This section tells you what to think about before you spend a nickel, and how to schedule the work, just as a professional contractor does, to help you keep material costs and labor time within your estimate. Then it shows, step by step, how to do each of the jobs you are likely to have to tackle—and presents them in the general order that you will be doing them—from planning to hooking up your new lighting fixtures and final decoration.

Since no two remodeling projects are exactly the same, you may be able to skip some jobs that are outlined; you may change the sequence of work; and perhaps you may wish to seek help elsewhere for elaborate effects or special situations that require professional expertise. The latter part of the book contains descriptions of how specific renovation projects were actually executed, including step-by-step instructions for creating some unusual effects.

Remodeling living and utility rooms

Changing walls, cabinets and fixtures requires a kind of planning that isolated carpentry projects and maintenance jobs don't. Even if you have experience with the necessary trade skills—carpentry, electrical, plumbing—you can waste a lot of time and money if you do not plan the *sequence* of steps correctly.

Here, for example, are some real-life situations that demonstrate the kind of disasters that can happen if space remodeling jobs are not thought through carefully from the beginning.

• Imagine that you've installed the kitchen cabinets, with the sink snugly in place ready to be connected. Then you realize that the waste and water lines are covered by the cabinets so you can't get to them.

• The new acoustical tile ceiling is up and looks great, but the old ceiling fixture is not centered over the new dinette table where you wanted it so you could simply replace the fixture. Now you have to tear down enough tiles to run new cable from the old box to the spot where you want the new fixture to be—then put them all back up again.

• You have put up a partition wall to close off the tub and toilet and hung the new door. The new tub has been delivered and you are ready to take out the old cast iron one—but it won't fit through the door. What do you do? Tear out the door jamb? Break up the old tub with a sledgehammer? Careful planning averts such crises.

A contractor plans the sequence of jobs by working *back* from the way the finished renovation will look to the way it is now. He must line up specialists in each trade to come onto the job at the right time. Unless you are doing *all* the work yourself—rough and finish plumbing, electrical wiring, carpentry and cabinet-making, painting and decorating—you will have to tell a specialist ahead of time exactly when you will reach the stage

where he will be needed to do his thing.

Once you have decided what the end result should look like, work back to see what kinds of jobs you are letting yourself in for. For example, if your plan requires that you change the dimensions of the room by moving a load-bearing wall (one that helps hold the house up rather than a partition added only to divide space), you should be prepared to relocate in-the-wall basic plumbing and electrical wiring, and expect some pretty heavy construction work, along with disrupted family activities; plus the problem of obtaining building permits.

If you don't feel your experience matches some of the steps your remodeling plan requires, talk to a contractor or to individual artisans about doing those portions of the work. Get bids from them before you abandon your plan. They may also be able to tell you whether you will need permits from the municipal building authority in your town. If you are running new wiring inside the walls, have the electrical insurance underwriters inspect it. If they don't, and a fire starts because of faulty wiring, the amount of your home-owners' insurance coverage may be affected.

A professional contractor would want to pin down when as well as how much he will be paid. If you are doing your own work, total the costs of the materials, fixtures, appliances, and new tools required (see page 7 of this book); then add a contingency of about 20% to allow for minor changes of mind or surprises along the way.

Once you have your plan, have evaluated the skills you will need, and have arranged for permits and financing, set dates to start and complete the work. Even the professionals dislike being held to a completion date. The way they get around it is to ask for more time than they believe is necessary. So should you. For

CHANGING JOBS

example, if you estimate that you can finish the job in two weekends, you'd better not make plans for the third weekend in case something goes wrong. The less pressure you are under, the fewer mistakes you are likely to make.

Another aspect of job coordination is ordering tools, material and equipment. They will have to be delivered well in advance, so arrange for a place to store them safely. As soon as possible after delivery, unpack and inspect materials and fixtures for damage, and to be sure you have received the right model, color, size, etc. Plug in or temporarily hook up appliances and fixtures to be sure they work. Since some may have to be sent back to the supplier to be replaced, have them delivered to your home as far in advance as it would take to obtain replacements.

A contractor relies heavily on his own, or a supervisor's talents in certain specific areas. The professionals call it trade coordination. As your own contractor you will be doing that job yourself. Briefly, here are the requirements: knowing when a job is to be started and finished; seeing to it that enough time is allotted for the job; knowing when to order tools, material and equipment; checking on deliveries, as well as on quality of tools and materials; knowing how to blend the efforts of the different trades so as to expedite the work; being able and ready to devise alternative work methods when job conditions are not as expected.

Is the dream do-able?

Work back from your picture of the finished work to see if you want to tackle the kinds of jobs it will require. Here are some typical considerations.
• Replacing old appliances or plumbing fixtures is not difficult but changing their location in the room will probably mean opening a wall to extend pipes, or running new wiring, or both.
• Tearing out an existing wall and putting up a new one, or cutting openings in walls is easier, and lighter work if the walls are not load-bearing. Load-bearing walls support the structure of the house, rather than merely partition off space supported elsewhere.
• Relocating overhead electrical fixtures in a solid (not suspended) ceiling will mean cutting channels through plaster or tearing down tile or wallboard.
• Changing the location of hung cabinets

requires careful measuring, locating studs, patching walls, and installing new stringers to attach them to.
• Removing a ceiling is a strenuous, very dust-producing job, especially if it is plaster. Covering it with tile or hanging a suspended ceiling is relatively easy.
• Laying new tile directly on an uneven floor will usually look worse than what was there. The old flooring usually has to be removed and the sub-flooring leveled or replaced.
• Check the voltage requirements of new electrical appliances to be sure your existing wiring is adequate. An appliance that needs 220-volt wiring or more won't work in a standard (110 or 120-volt) circuit. Also be sure the total combined wattage of all new appliances does not exceed the capacity of the circuit or circuits they must be plugged into.

Job-sequence for remodeling

Most remodeling projects will require at least some of the following steps in the order given. Use this as a reminder when you plan the scope of your project. The chapters that follow provide specific detailed techniques for executing each of these steps, in this same order. See the how-to text for resequencing options in addition to those noted here. Because of the hazards and difficulty of roughing in new or relocated plumbing waste and water lines except by a professional, those techniques are not covered.

☐ Plan the extent of the job, in detail.
☐ Order and store materials, appliances, tools; after thoroughly checking.
☐ Protect the house from debris.
☐ Remove the plumbing fixtures.
☐ Remove the hanging cabinets (Note: The previous two steps can be reversed).
☐ Remove the countertops.
☐ Remove the base cabinets.
☐ Remove the old floor.
☐ Clean up the debris.
☐ Install the bathtub.
☐ Frame the walls for doorways,

windows, and trimmed openings.
☐ Frame in soffits.
☐ Route the electrical wiring.
☐ Secure the electrical outlet boxes.
☐ Patch or refinish the walls (gypsum board, plastic coated fiber board, tile, etc.).
☐ Refinish the floors
☐ Install cabinets and counter tops.
☐ Install plumbing fixtures (sinks, water closet, etc.).
☐ Connect the electrical wiring to the electrical fixtures.

Job survey checklist

General
- ☐ Plans
- ☐ Estimates
- ☐ Building Permits
- ☐ Insurance
- ☐ Financing
- ☐ _____

Appliances
- ☐ Refrigerators
- ☐ Ranges
- ☐ Ovens
- ☐ Dishwashers
- ☐ Disposal
- ☐ Freezer
- ☐ Washer
- ☐ Dryer
- ☐ Vacuum System
- ☐ Range Hood
- ☐ Exhaust Fans
- ☐ _____

Plumbing Fixtures
- ☐ Kitchen Sink
- ☐ Hot Water Heater
- ☐ Laundry Tubs
- ☐ Bathtubs
- ☐ Lavatories
- ☐ Water Closets
- ☐ Shower Cabinets
- ☐ Air Conditioner
- ☐ Disposal
- ☐ Dishwasher
- ☐ _____

Finishing
- ☐ Hardwood Flooring
- ☐ Underlayment
- ☐ Linoleum
- ☐ Floor Tile
- ☐ Ceramic Tile
- ☐ Millwork
- ☐ Doors
- ☐ Screens
- ☐ Storm Sash
- ☐ Floor Sanding
- ☐ Floor Finishing
- ☐ Blinds
- ☐ Shades
- ☐ Interior Painting
- ☐ Wallpaper
- ☐ Weatherstrip Doors
- ☐ Weatherstrip Windows
- ☐ General Clean-up
- ☐ Finish Hardware
- ☐ Medicine Cabinets
- ☐ Planters
- ☐ Stall Showers
- ☐ Tile Wainscot
- ☐ Carpets
- ☐ Drapes
- ☐ Paneling
- ☐ Shower Doors
- ☐ Patio Doors
- ☐ Bathroom Accessories
- ☐ Mirrors
- ☐ Closet Accessories
- ☐ _____

Cabinet work
- ☐ Kitchen
- ☐ Bathroom
- ☐ Laundry
- ☐ Basement
- ☐ Cabinet tops
- ☐ Counters
- ☐ _____

Framing
- ☐ Lumber
- ☐ Veneer
- ☐ Windows
- ☐ Air Conditioning
- ☐ Plastering
- ☐ Drywall
- ☐ Areawalls
- ☐ Nails
- ☐ Hardware
- ☐ Louvers
- ☐ Vents
- ☐ _____

Electrical service
- ☐ Range Circuit
- ☐ Dryer Outlet
- ☐ Convenience Outlets
- ☐ Switches
- ☐ Intercom
- ☐ Telephone
- ☐ Ceiling Lights
- ☐ Wall Lights
- ☐ Fixtures
- ☐ _____

COST ESTIMATE WORKSHEET

Quan.	Item	Rate	Outside labor		Materials		Actual results	
		Totals						

An island kitchen can be as big or as little (almost) as you like. It can include a stove, a sink, even a refrigerator; or it can be just a mix center. Here, you can also breakfast with the entire family.

Design and placement of kitchen cabinets

The first thing in planning your new kitchen is to see what the old one lacks. Very likely it is not as convenient as you would wish it to be; otherwise you wouldn't be planning a renovation.

Be specific. Do you have enough counter space? What about storage area? Can you reach things easily? Do your appliances work as they should? Does the refrigerator open in such a way that you have to walk around the door to take out the milk? How is the lighting, ventilation? Is the room attractive, a pleasant place in which to work? Do you also see your kitchen as a family center, a place for breakfast, coffee breaks, possibly lunch or dinner? There are four basic kitchen layouts that you should bear in mind: the U-shape kitchen, the L-shape, the corridor kitchen, and the one-wall.

Every kitchen is also made up of three main activity centers: storage (refrigerator), cleanup (sink), and cooking (stove). It is essential to have these three centers in a convenient work triangle.

When you realize that in order to prepare just breakfast and dinner for an average family the cook will walk 120 miles in a year, it raises the question of wasted movement which the cook will suffer due to bad kitchen planning. If you arrange the sink, the refrigerator, the stove in a good triangular relationship, you can save, the experts tell us, about 40 miles a year in walking.

The actual design of the kitchen will be regulated by three factors: the available wall space, the floor area, and your budget. You must also consider ventilation and lighting.

First, make a sketch of your existing kitchen—a "plan view." The plan view sketch will show the kitchen as though you were looking down from the ceiling. Use ¼-inch graph paper. Each square or box (¼"x¼") will represent one square foot (12"x12") of the area.

Draw the outline of the kitchen, indicating any breaks in the walls, such as doors, windows, an arch, a radiator, or boxed pipes.

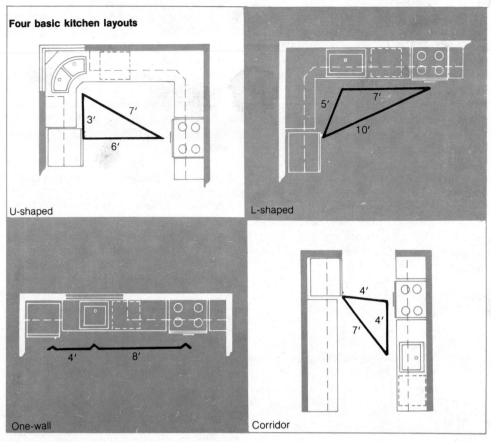

Four basic kitchen layouts

U-shaped

L-shaped

One-wall

Corridor

Recommended kitchen triangle distances:
- Sink to refrigerator 4-7'
- Sink to range 4-6'
- Range to refrigerator 4-9'
- Total triangle perimeter should be no more than 22', no less than about 12'. Plan at least 4' of counter or open space between major, installed appliances.

Base cabinets

Now sketch, still in plan view, the desired location of the new base cabinets. If you wish, use a color pencil to differentiate them from the existing kitchen.

Start with the kitchen sink. It is economically wise to put the new sink in the proximity of the existing sink. The piping may be altered to the right or left a little, but to put the new sink on the opposite wall or in an "island" in the middle of the room would involve major plumbing work. At the same time, don't eliminate a desired layout simply because of the additional work involved. Remember that you, as contractor, can sub-contract all or any part of the renovations. Moreover, a basic plan is still needed if you do wish to hire a local contractor.

The front of the base cabinets will be approximately 24 inches out from the finished wall. Count out 2 squares and draw a line parallel to the perimeter of the room where you desire the base cabinets.

You will have to decide whether to have your cabinets custom built by a cabinetmaker or buy them prefabricated. You may, of course, be able and willing to build them yourself. Of course, custom-built cabinets will offer the most flexibility, but they cost more.

Prefabricated cabinets may be constructed of wood, metal, plastic laminate, or even a combination of materials. Stock base cabinet widths start at 12 inches and increase in increments of 3 inches up to 36 inches. Beyond the 36-inch width, they increase by 6-inch increments to a maximum 60-inch width.

The best counter height

A happy cook makes for a happy meal, is an old saying. Remember this when you consider the height of your kitchen counters. A 36-inch height is said to be average. On prefabricated cabinets you can lessen this by reducing the kick space at the bottom. If, on the other hand, you wish to raise the counter a few inches, then consider raising the upper wall cabinets to keep the kitchen height in good proportion. As a rule, the work surface that is most agreeable will be about 3 inches below your elbow.

At this point give some thought to the size and design of the kitchen sink. The sink you choose will determine the size of the sink base cabinet; and this in

Locating the dishwasher

You can be flexible in placing your dishwasher. The discharge (waste pipe) from the dishwasher, and only one (hot) water supply pipe require tubing or hose of relatively small dimension. The dishwasher pump is capable of getting the drain water to the kitchen trap. The added expense of extra hose is negligible.

While a portable roll-around dishwasher has merit in an older kitchen, you would be wise to plan for an under-the-counter model. The portable type, when in use, will tie up the sink, and when not in use will present a storage problem.

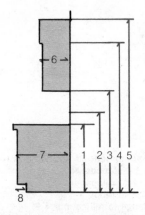

Some useful work heights and depths
1. Height of countertop—36"
2. Height of wall outlets and switches—44"
3. Bottom of wall cabinet—54"
4. Top of wall cabinet—84"
5. Ceiling—variable
6. Depth of wall cabinet—13"
7. Depth of base cabinet—24"
8. Depth of kick space—3"

A wall oven

If you plan a wall oven you will need a cabinet, unless you provide a "cabinet" of real or artificial brick, or fieldstone, to frame it. Be careful not to install the oven too high, and place it so that its door opens on about the same level as the countertops—36 inches from the floor.

turn will affect the sizes of the remaining base cabinets along the same wall.

Consider that for ease of installation, as well as for the sake of efficiency, the dishwasher should be adjacent to, or at least in the proximity of the sink base cabinet. And now, too, is a good time to locate the refrigerator and range; and also the oven, garbage disposal, and other appliances.

Sketch your appliances to scale and cut them out of paper. These figures can then be pinned to the floor plan layout and if necessary can be moved.

In your design you may have placed two base cabinets to form a right angle to each other. This makes a dead corner. A good way to deal with this is by installing a "Lazy Susan"—a cabinet with revolving shelves.

U- or L-shaped cabinets will require

U- or L-shaped counter tops. This could be a problem in maneuvering the countertop through the kitchen doorway. Consider the possibility of breaking up the length of counter with a strategically placed butcher block top over a built-in dishwasher, for instance. In that way you can retain the L- or U-shape and still have a functional piece of equipment.

Another means of breaking a long section of countertop is with a free-standing gas or electric range. Perhaps you desire a drop-in unit that will utilize the countertop. A cutout in the counter will of course be necessary.

Stock base and wall cabinets may not stretch from wall to wall because of an odd measurement. Filler pieces, of the same material as your cabinets, are available and are easy to install.

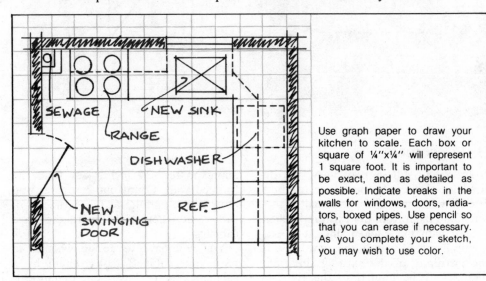

Use graph paper to draw your kitchen to scale. Each box or square of ¼"x¼" will represent 1 square foot. It is important to be exact, and as detailed as possible. Indicate breaks in the walls for windows, doors, radiators, boxed pipes. Use pencil so that you can erase if necessary. As you complete your sketch, you may wish to use color.

Wall cabinets

These should be placed above the base units, whenever possible, so that there will be a symmetrical appearance to the design. Because of the headroom space required above the kitchen sink, it is not desirable to place a wall cabinet in that location. If a window is above the sink, you have no choice anyway. Cabinets or shelves may of course go on either side of the window.

On your graph paper, indicate the distance from floor to ceiling. Sketch in the ceiling line, floor line, and adjacent wall lines. You now have a large box that will represent an entire wall. The height and width measurements of doors, windows, and other openings may now be located in their proper place on the wall. Be sure to identify the actual wall on the graph—left wall, front, right, or back.

The top of all wall-hung cabinets will be 84 inches above the floor. Count 7 squares from the floor line on your paper; draw a line from wall to wall to indicate the top of the cabinets.

A 30-inch wall cabinet will allow for 18-inch clearance between the bottom of the wall cabinet and the surface of the countertop over the base cabinets. If you place the tops of the wall cabinets higher than 84 inches it will be difficult to reach the top shelves.

Finally, your choice of cabinet finish, whether it be wood or plastic laminate, is a matter of preference. Go to the showroom or store and actually see the cabinets you are considering. Avoid choosing cabinets by photograph or brochure. While the idea may be there in a picture, the actual texture and feel of the cabinet cannot be truly appreciated.

Countertops

In any kitchen a major consideration has to be surface—walls, floors, countertops. These areas are the most visible, and the most vulnerable. Indeed, the countertop will receive almost as much punishment as the kitchen floor.

Nowadays there is an especially large variety of countertop materials to choose from. Ideally, the countertop would be attractive, stainproof, impervious to heat, moisture, scratches; it would be resilient to a certain degree, and inexpensive. Unfortunately, no one material combines all these qualities, though some do come close.

Of the many materials to choose from, about a half dozen appear to be the most popular.
- **Plastic laminate.** This is the most in demand. It's easy to maintain, comes in many colors, patterns and textures. It is resilient, non-porous, refuses grease and household chemicals. However, it should not be subjected to hot utensils, or used as a cutting surface.

- **Flexible vinyl.** It has a strong resistance to moisture, alcohol, stains, and abrasions. Don't use the surface for cutting or for placement of hot pans.
- **Laminated hardwood.** Butcher block is greatly in demand nowadays; good for cutting, but avoid prolonged moisture and hot pans.
- **Ceramic tile.** Tile wears well and comes in many patterns and colors. It resists moisture and heat, but dirt can collect in the crevices between the tiles.
- **Synthetic marble.** It is just about stainproof. However, it is less resistant to heat than tile, and it is also expensive.
- **Glass-ceramic.** This is a new heatproof material that is somewhat expensive. Yet, it is fine as a small chopping or cutting spot, or for holding hot utensils. It cleans easily and resists stains.

One-piece countertops are now available in various lengths, made from postformed plastic laminate with or without a drip-free front edge and a curved backsplash.

Countertop materials

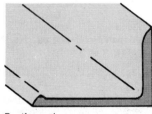

Postformed

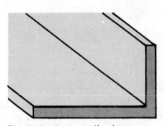

Plastic laminate, self edge

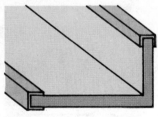

Plastic laminate with edge molding

Ventilation

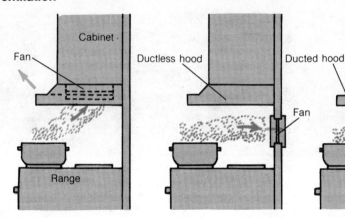

When you consider the fact that some 200 pounds of smoke, moisture, and grease in the form of vapors are released in a single year's cooking, you will realize the need for adequate ventilation in your kitchen.

To handle this problem you may either vent the vapors to the outdoors or remove them by filtering the air in the kitchen.

Venting is simply done with a kitchen fan cut into a wall close to the range. There are many sizes and shapes of exhaust fans, and all require cutting through the kitchen wall for installation.

Ventilating hoods come in two types: ducted and unducted. The ducted system vents directly to the outdoors. This type of vent is most easily installed when there is major renovation work in the kitchen—renewing walls, ceiling, and cabinets, for instance.

Ductless ventilators, on the other hand, fit in a hood right over the range and can be hung

on the wall, or suspended below a cabinet; and so will be part of your cabinet planning. This type of vent is not as efficient as the ducted ventilator. It draws cooking vapors through a charcoal filter, eliminating odors and grease, and then releases clean air back into the kitchen. It cannot, however, remove heat and moisture from the kitchen like a ducted system. The ductless system is favored where it is too difficult or too expensive to install a duct to the outside wall. But the filters, of aluminum mesh and fiberglass, activated carbon or granulated charcoal, should be cleaned or even replaced every few weeks. The ducted system, though, should be cleaned every six months.

It is important, in any ventilating system, that the correct fan capacity be taken into account. This must relate directly to the size of the space in which it is to operate. Check with your appliance dealer before you buy.

Suggested counter area around appliances:
- At least 15" on the latch side of the refrigerator.
- At least 30" of working counter on each side of the sink.
- 24" on each side of the range is a minimum working area.

Plumbing fixtures

The kitchen sink

Your best bet for selecting plumbing fixtures is to visit the showroom of a plumbing supply dealer or discount center specializing in building supplies.

Many of the newer sinks are self rim; this means that the unit is supported by the rim resting on the countertop. The weight of the sink and an adhesive/caulking prevent the sink from shifting. Self rim makes for an easy installation, but bear in mind that the top of the sink rim is ⅜ to ½ inch higher than the countertop. This means that if water is spilled onto the countertop it won't run into the sink.

The cast iron sink has proven its endurance over the years. The enamel is acid resistant, and the sink comes in white plus a multitude of colors, which cost about 10% more than the traditional white. The shapes and styles are also many—double compartment, triple, corner, waste disposal accommodations, and more.

The pressed steel sink (porcelain on steel) is light and not expensive. It has a coating of tar-like substance underneath the sink to deaden the sound caused by running water striking the thin body of the sink. Although pressed steel is also available in colors, the choice of shapes is limited. This is because of the manufacturer's effort to keep the price down.

The stainless steel sink offers durability, with little weight for handling problems, and it too comes in self rim. Various shapes are available, and you can get multi-compartment models. You also have a choice of gauge; that is, thickness of the steel.

Stainless steel sinks also have a soundproofing material adhered to the underside. While stainless steel will not chip, it does require more attention than cast iron. For instance, it should be wiped dry after each use to avoid water spotting.

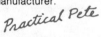
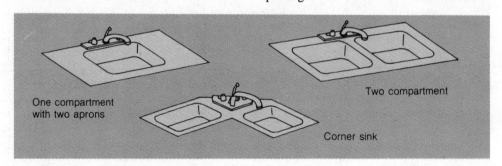

One compartment with two aprons

Two compartment

Corner sink

Types of vanities

Vanity or basin

Consider the bathroom as a whole. If you have the space, then by all means update the new bath with a vanity. You'll gain storage space, you'll have a countertop work area, and you'll have a brand new look in your bathroom.

On the other hand, if the bathroom is cramped for space, then a wall hung basin would be a sensible choice. While it is true that a small vanity will take up the same floor area as a basin, so to speak, all you actually gain with a vanity in this case is a little storage space; and the cabinet to accommodate the vanity basin will add to the cost. It could all end up looking like a small, crowded bathroom.

The wall hung lavatories are made of enameled cast iron, pressed steel, and vitreous china. Vitreous china lavatories are certainly attractive, but while serviceable under normal use, they are fragile. A jar falling from a medicine cabinet above a porcelain steel or an iron enamel basin might chip it, but it would crack a vitreous china one.

Vanity basins, besides coming in the above-mentioned materials, are also available in modern plastic and plastic variations. In many instances, the bowl is an integral part of the top. This is not only an attractive feature, but a sanitary one since the seams or joints formed when attaching a basin to a countertop are eliminated.

Another plus for the vanity is that the plumbing is inside the cabinet and out of view. Moreover, the vanity is probably easier to install for the home do-it-yourselfer because it does not rely on a bracket for support as does a wall hung basin. You can rely on it being firm.

Toilets

The water closet (toilet) is made of vitreous china, although some new tanks come in plastic. All modern water closets operate on the principle of siphonic action. It is the flushing and cleansing action that you pay for if you select an expensive fixture.

One-piece water closets (bowl and tank constructed as one piece) have a lower tank and are easier to clean than the conventional close-coupled bowl and tank. However, the one-piece is more than double the cost of the close-coupled combination water closet, which consists of a separate bowl and tank. The tank is bolted to the bowl by two and sometimes three bolts.

While the elongated toilet bowl is considered the most sanitary, and is required in public buildings according to strict plumbing codes, it is also the most expensive. However, a round front water closet with a reverse trap or siphon jet will be more than adequate for the average household. Most plumbing codes prohibit wash down bowls.

Before you order a water closet be sure that you know the rough-in dimen-sion of the bowl. You can find this by measuring, at floor level, the distance from the finished wall to the center of the bolts that secure the bowl to the closet flange. You won't be able to see the flange with the bowl in place but the bolts are easily located. They may be under two china or plastic caps. In the event that you find four bolts or caps, the ones you should measure will be the rear ones, those closest to the wall. This measurement will usually be between 10 and 14 inches. But if you get a measurement of 14½ inches, figure it as 14 for purposes of roughing-in.

If you remove a 14-inch bowl and replace it with a 12-inch bowl, you will find that when you connect the tank to the bowl it will be 2 inches away from the wall. On the other hand, if you remove a 12-inch bowl and attempt to replace it with a 14-inch one, the tank just won't fit. In either case, returning the wrong tank and bowl to the dealer will present a problem. For while it is indeed "brand new" from your point of view, remember that it will be considered "used" by the dealer.

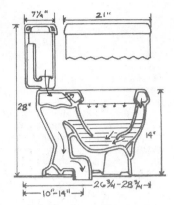

Close-coupled bowl and tank

The bathtub

The fixtures discussed so far are installed after the finished wall and floor material is secured. The bathtub, on the other hand, is built in; it is installed (set) first.

If you're planning a new tub or shower in the existing bathroom, you will have to cut the tile or plaster away from the perimeter of the present tub to free it from its recess. Of course, a very old bathroom may have a freestanding tub.

A new tub installation will almost always require alterations to the waste line and trap.

The easiest tub to install, because of its light weight, is the pressed steel tub.

Bathtubs are ordered by size; 4-foot, 4½-foot, 5-foot, 5½-foot, for example. The 5-foot tub is the most popular. In addition to the size, you must indicate whether or not the tub is to be recessed into a wall or set in a corner. The tubs that fit these requirements are called "recessed" and "corner," respectively.

You must also specify the location of the drain hole in the tub. It will be a left-hand or a right-hand waste outlet. To determine which it is, face the apron of the tub—the apron being that part of the tub that extends from the rim down to the floor. While facing the apron, if you find the tub drain is on your right, then the tub is a right-hand tub. If it is to your left, then it's a left-hand tub.

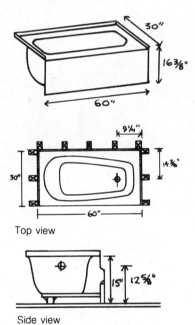

Top view

Side view

The shower

Why not plan to install a combination shower/bath fitting over the tub. The cost of the shower fitting is not high, and it will be there when you want it.

Prior to starting your bathroom remodeling, have the fixtures on hand. Ask your local dealer for rough-in sheets that give dimensions. Try to buy a lavatory or tub waste that is manufactured by the manufacturer of the fixture. Many dealers quote a price on a quality fixture, but supply competitive "trim" to keep the total cost down in order to make the sale to the customer.

You can gain space in the bathroom if you replace the tub with a shower receptor. There are many styles of shower in numerous materials, and installation is easy. Years ago the shower required a custom-made lead pad that was encased in mortar and tile. This was a little beyond the reach of the average do-it-yourselfer. Today, however, precast shower receptors and plastic shower enclosures allow the homeowners to do the job.

Only the rich can afford cheap plumbing

Remember that any money put into quality plumbing pays off. Stick to brand names, especially where you are buying small items that might need to be replaced—such as faucets. Besides long-life, quality parts are more likely to be available when needed years later.

Electrical needs

In remodeling a kitchen or bathroom you must expect some form of electrical work. The extent of the wiring will be determined very much by the age of the house. For instance, if you have an older house you may find that the house service (electric supply cables from the utility pole outside to the electric meter and panel box where the fuses or circuit breakers are located inside the house) may not be adequate to supply sufficient power to the electrical additions you contemplate. On the other hand, an older house may have been re-wired with an eye to updating the electric service. The important thing is to remember that any extensive remodeling with new cabinets, sink, floor, and appliances, warrants a modern, safe, and well planned electrical layout. Your local utility company can tell you how to determine the load that must be handled.

All kitchens should have what is called an appliance circuit. You might very well need more than one circuit. This means new runs of electric wiring from the main panel box location. The listing on this page will serve as a check sheet of outlets you may need. Look it over carefully, and you might even add some of your own. If you outline your needs before the walls are closed in or the cabinets hung, you won't have any problem. After that, though, you'll have to work a bit harder and improvise to install the wiring you want.

Lighting

Plan lighting so that you are sure that all small print on food packages is legible. You should not have to work in your own shadow, and you should be able to see clearly into all corners of cabinets. It is essential to plan in such a way that the kitchen wiring is adequate to handle all appliances and lights in use at any one time. Wiring for countertop appliances, such as toaster, coffee maker, blender should be on a different electrical circuit than your major appliances.

Nothing like a little light on the situation

I thought I had planned the best possible lighting in my kitchen. And, as a matter of fact I had . . . as far as the kitchen itself went. But I forgot about the kind of light needed in corners and closets. Remember that a good check is to place lighting so that you can always read the labels on jars, cans, and other items.

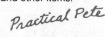

Electrical outlet checklist
A suggested list of kitchen and bathroom equipment requiring electricity.

Kitchen
- ☐ Refrigerator
- ☐ Freezer
- ☐ Electric range
- ☐ Electric oven
- ☐ Gas stove
- ☐ Wall oven
- ☐ Dishwasher
- ☐ Clothes washer
- ☐ Clothes dryer
- ☐ Trash compactor
- ☐ Waste disposal
- ☐ Air conditioning units
- ☐ Exhaust fan (through wall)
- ☐ Exhaust hood with light and fan (ductless)
- ☐ Ground Fault Interrupters
- ☐ Ceiling lights
- ☐ Recessed lighting (hung ceilings)
- ☐ Fluorescent lights; under hanging cabinets, or above cabinets for diffused lighting
- ☐ 3-way switches

Wall outlets (called convenience outlets) for operation of the following kitchen equipment:
- ☐ Toaster
- ☐ Mixer / blender
- ☐ Electric coffee pot
- ☐ Electric can opener

- ☐ Radio
- ☐ T.V. outlet
- ☐ Microwave oven
- ☐ Electric skillet
- ☐ Crock pot (slow cooker)
- ☐ Electric clock on wall or soffit (Plan to locate the outlet behind the clock)

Bathroom
- ☐ Ceiling and / or wall lights
- ☐ Medicine cabinet with lights and shaver / hair dryer outlets
- ☐ Ventilation exhaust fan (if no window)
- ☐ Exhaust fan / light combination (wall switch turns on both)
- ☐ Ceiling sun lamp
- ☐ GFI electric shaver outlet

Consider making provisions for the following items, which are not necessarily electrical in nature, but when concealed in the wall or ceiling will enhance the appearance of the new kitchen:

- ☐ Telephone outlets
- ☐ Smoke detector
- ☐ T.V. or FM antenna wiring
- ☐ Intercom wiring
- ☐ Speaker wiring

Ground fault interrupter

The 1975 National Electric Code (NEC) requires certain circuits to be protected by Ground Fault Interrupters (GFI) in new construction; in all 120 volt, single-phase, 15- and 20-ampere receptacles installed out of doors; in bathrooms of all dwelling units including single-family, multi-family, and mobile homes; in all 120 volt swimming pool equipment and receptacles. It is important to check this.

The code also recommends GFI protection for receptacles in workshops, laundries, and kitchen circuits.

Electricity travels in circuits. For example, it may flow from a wall receptacle through a turned on appliance, and continue in a path back to the receptacle. Normally, the same amount of electricity that flows from the receptacle returns to the receptacle. But if there is a leak, a loss of current which is escaping from the normal flow of electricity, then the same amount will not return to the receptacle. This particular leak may not be significant enough to blow a fuse or trip the circuit breaker; it is a hidden electric hazard called a ground fault. The leak flows into the housing of the appliance. Touching the housing causes the electricity to flow through your body to the ground.

A ground fault shock is potentially dangerous. The ground fault interrupter shuts off the electric power within 1/40th of a second when the leak is as little as 5 milliamps. A GFI is expensive, but a worthwhile investment.

Here is how a ground fault can travel. The GFI will shut off the current before it can cause injury, though that small a leak might not blow a fuse.

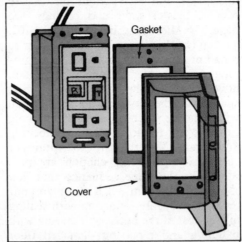

Gasket

Cover

GFI receptacle fits into an outdoor box. It looks like a regular duplex receptacle with two push buttons. The one labeled ''R'' resets the interrupter after it has tripped, while the one labeled ''T'' simulates a leak so the device can be tested.

The need to check your work

A voltage tester is a must if you are going to check your home's electricity. What you will be checking is whether or not there is voltage (power) in the circuit you are working on.

The voltage tester will light when its probes touch anything that is charged with electricity. The probes are made so that they will fit into the two slots of a receptacle, thus making it possible to know whether the power is on or off without having to remove the cover plate.

A continuity tester, unlike the voltage tester, has its own source of power; a small battery that will light a bulb when there is a continuous path for current between the alligator clip and the probe. The tester must only be used when the power to a circuit or an appliance is off. Attach the alligator clip to one point and the probe to another. If the bulb doesn't light, you will know that there is a break in the line of current between the two points.

Voltage tester at work. It works in many ways, but here it tests the grounding of a receptacle when one probe is inserted into the semicircular ground slot, and the other, successively into each of the elongated slots. The device should light when the probe is in the hot slot. If the tester does not light in either slot, it means that the receptacle is not grounded, and the wiring needs correction.

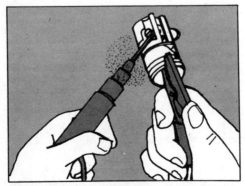

Continuity tester in action. You can check a suspected lamp socket, for example, by unplugging the lamp, removing the bulb, and taking the socket apart; then clamping the tester's alligator clip to the metal screw shell and touching the probe against the terminal. The tester should light. If it doesn't, then you will know that the socket has an open circuit, and should be fixed or replaced.

REMOVING THE OLD

Dust control

This chapter describes how to detach and remove the old cabinets, counters and fixtures that you want to relocate or to replace. For instructions on how to remove plaster walls and ceilings, see page 176. For patching, see page 101. The end of this chapter describes how to repair or replace an old floor. The beginning of this chapter shows, in great detail, how to protect the rest of your living space from the dust and debris that you will generate when you begin removing cabinets and fixtures and start knocking down walls. Note that the descriptions of each task within this chapter are presented in the same sequence that you should tackle them when you plan your own job in reality—starting with sealing off the rest of the house and ending with patching and repairing damaged floor areas.

The first, and absolutely essential, step before you start removing walls, fixtures and cabinets is to protect the rest of the house from dust and debris. Without this step, the irritation factor in your mind, and the lives of those who live with you, will be much higher than it needs to be. Most jobs take longer than one plans at the beginning. If the house is full of debris, that is a constant reminder that the work *still* isn't done. Tracking particles of plaster and dirt can scratch the finish on floors and mess up carpets. Cleaning up after a job is no fun, so the less of it you have to do the better you will feel about the work you accomplished.

Obviously, the inconvenience of keeping the room you are working in sealed. off must last until the job has been completed fully. This is another important reason to plan the job carefully before you start. If the materials and fixtures you will need are all there when you are ready to install them, and they all work, and they all fit correctly—then the job will move smoothly and life can return to normal in the time you predicted.

What you will be concerned with at this point is heavy dust generated by opened plaster or other types of wall structure. Although much of it may not be seen, the dust becomes airborne and can cover everything in the rooms adjoining the renovation. Rugs, upholstery, wall hangings and drapes—indeed, everything—will be affected. Unless protective measures are taken on the scene of renovation as well as in the adjoining areas, wood and plastic furniture can be scratched and dented, floors can be gouged, rugs may have to be shampooed, or inground debris may ruin the rug's fiber and shorten its life span. The odor of gypsum from broken plaster or gypsum wallboard may become so penetrating that it will be present in sofas and chairs weeks or months afterwards.

The first area to consider is, of course, the place of actual work. Resign yourself to the inevitable fact that the room you are renovating will certainly suffer from debris. The point is to minimize it. You can put down an overlay of plywood, or use drop cloths or tape down building paper. It will all help, but only to a degree. Nothing will really keep dust and particles from slipping underneath the covering and grinding into the floor. You'd better figure on refinishing the floor.

One of the best helps is to clean up your work area as you go along, rather than wait for the end of the day or the completion of the job. Remember, too, that there is always danger of tracking as you go into other rooms, especially if you've been painting, and haven't been careful about spills.

The adjoining rooms are the really important areas to protect. Paintings and all wallhangings are to be removed and stored as far from the renovation as possible. Immovable or heavy items needing protection—for instance, rugs and carpets, furniture—are to be completely covered.

Any openings such as doors or windows that connect the renovation area to the rest of the house should be sealed and not used, as should all doors that connect to the house beyond the adjoining rooms.

It is an asset if you have windows and exterior doors in the room that is being renovated. They can be left open providing the outside air is blowing by the house and can suck out the dust. On the other hand, if the outside air is blowing into an opened doorway or window, it will force dust into the adjoining rooms. In such an instance, it would be a good idea to shut the exterior door and place an exhaust fan in a window for a flow of air outward.

Protecting floors and rugs in adjoining rooms

The best way to protect a finished hardwood floor, carpet, or rugs from debris is with wide rolls of heavy gauge plastic, rectangular fabric, or plastic cloths.

The plastic material is better suited to protect against dust, but heavy fabric cloths are less likely to tear. Any breaks, however, must be immediately covered.

Material preparation

There are two systems that may be used to protect your floors. The first calls for removal of all furniture, the second bypasses it. Regardless of which system is used, the first three steps, in the box immediately below, should be completed before continuing with the operation. It is important not to rush this job.

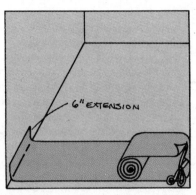

1. Allowing at least 12 extra inches, cut the floor covering to length. Use the first strip for a pattern, and cut enough strips, plus 2 extra, to cover the width of the room.

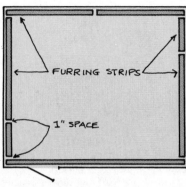

2. Cut enough furring strips to line the room's perimeter. Do not make tight fits, but leave 1 inch ends and edges of joining furring. Allow 1 inch clearance between furring and walls.

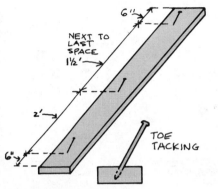

3. Starting and finishing 6 inches from each end, toe-tack an 8d finishing nail into furring strip every 2 feet. Spacing of next to last nail may be shortened. Spacing is approximate.

Covering the floors

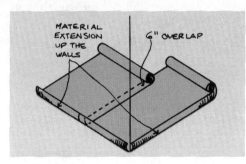

1. To thoroughly protect a floor, move all the furniture out of the room; or if that isn't feasible, move it to one end of the room. Then roll out the plastic with 6-inch overlaps, making sure that 6 inches of material extends up each wall. If using drop cloths, stretch them out with the same overlaps. 2. At the floor and wall juncture, fold the material twice to inhibit tearing. 3. Set the furring 1 inch away from the wall on top of the material.

Stationary or heavy objects: To protect the floor without moving the furniture, the same furring strip preparation must be made, as above, but with one exception. There will be no furring cut for any wall that has furniture against it. Start from an opposite wall that is bare, and stretch out the plastic rolls or drop cloths in the same way as previously indicated. Continue until the covering reaches the furniture. Cut the covering so that it will bypass sofa, chair, or table legs, or slip under them, and continue to opposite wall.

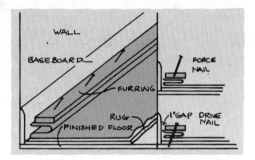

With one hand apply pressure toward the wall and downward at the same time. 4. When the material is squeezed tight to the wall and floor, drive the nails into the floor, but slanted toward the wall to insure a tight fit. After the protection has been stretched out far enough, relocate the furniture. Then, complete the rolling out of the floor protection. Be sure to clean the protection layer periodically.

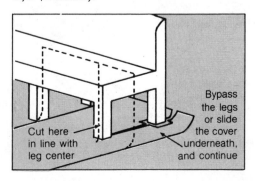

Covering the furniture

After the floor has been protected, the next step is the furniture. You will need the largest rectangular drop cloths that can be obtained. Use plastic sheets; woven cloth allows dust penetration.

You should take protective steps against heavy objects falling onto the furniture; tools for example. Use com-pressed fiber board as a cover.

Placement of the drop cloths over the furniture is probably the easiest part of the renovation; yet to their sorrow many people skimp when it comes to this particular task. Be generous with your drop cloths, and err, if you have to, on the side of over-abundance.

Fiber board is a good protection against heavy objects falling onto furniture. You can box a piece of furniture with it, or just cover vulnerable surfaces.

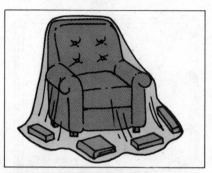

A drop cloth draped over small items and weighted at the ends with bricks or short pieces of lumber is good. Be careful about openings where dust could enter.

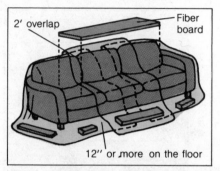

When covering large pieces, start at each end and work toward the center. Center cloth should overlap adjoining ends by 2 feet. Allow 12 inches extra at floor.

A barrier curtain

Whether it is a trimmed opening or doorway, any opening in the wall that leads to an adjoining living space has to be sealed. Again, the best material for a barrier curtain is heavy-gauge plastic sheets or rolls. With slight variations, it is hung in the opening in the same manner that you place a curtain in or over a window frame. You can support it with furring strips.

I thought I'd covered the situation—but it covered me!
I thought I had the dust and debris problem licked when I hung all that extra cloth in the doorway to my living room. But I forgot that cloth is woven, and so it's permeable. Next time I'll be smart enough to use plastic so that fine dust just can't get through.

Practical Pete

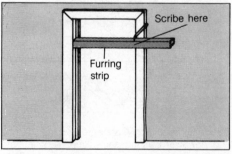

1. Place one end of the furring strip against a jamb face. Scribe a mark on the furring that is in line with the opposing jamb face. Using the mark as a guide, saw the furring to length, 1/32″ to 1/16″ short of the mark. Repeat the process at the bottom.

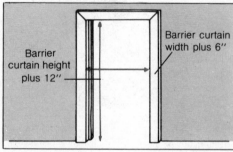

2. Cut the barrier curtain to length and width. Its length should be a minimum of 12 inches longer than the opening is high. The width of the barrier should be approximately 6 inches wider than the opening width. Staple the top and bottom ends of the plastic barrier to the furring strips.

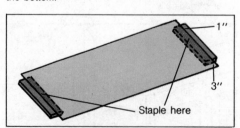

3. Expose one inch of the furring face and allow the plastic material extend to 3 inches past the furring ends. Staple the plastic to the furring every 6 inches.

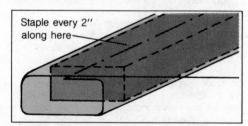

4. Rotate the stapled furring and plastic material under one revolution. Staple the two layers of plastic to the furring strip every 2 inches.

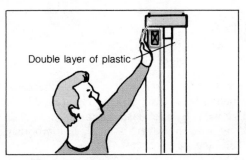

Double layer of plastic

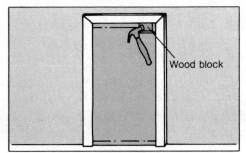

Wood block

5. A friction fit is used to place the barrier in the wall opening. Hold the top end of the barrier, keeping the double layer of plastic away from your body. Squeeze the second end of the plastic-wrapped furring into the opening. Repeat at the bottom.

6. Providing that 1/32″ to 1/16″ clearance was allowed when cutting the furring strip, it should squeeze in easily. If necessary, however, place a block of wood over the plastic covered furring to prevent tearing, and tap it lightly with a hammer to squeeze it in.

Sealing doors

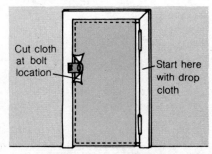

Cut cloth at bolt location

Start here with drop cloth

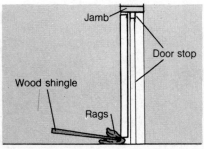

Jamb

Door stop

Wood shingle

Rags

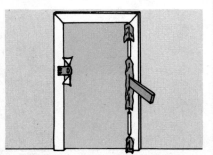

1. Place a drop cloth over the door, starting from the hinge edge and covering the lock edge. It should be a snug fit.

2. Stuff the bottom of the doorway with rags. A wood shingle will serve as a useful tool to press the rags into place.

3. Wedge a folded cloth between the length of the hinge edge of the door and the door jamb; use the wood shingle.

The daily cleanup

Just as providing a dust and debris barrier is essential to protect the rest of the house, so is the daily cleanup. It is also important for safety. Any rubbish lying in and around the work area can lead to an accident. Your best bet is to clean up as you go along, and not wait until the end of the day. As you finish working in one area, clean up, then go to the next part of the job. At the end of the day you can do a general cleanup, so everything will be ready for the next day.

Before removing rubbish, thought has to be given to where it is to be placed, and how it will be disposed of. You can stack it at the front of the house, along the sides, or in the back. When a truckload is ready, pay a commercial carter to haul it away.

Still, a load of debris at either the front or back of the house is unsightly. You may consider it necessary, but your neighbors could see otherwise. Check with them before you do anything. And check with the local authorities.

In any case, the debris will have to be placed in containers until it can be hauled off. Do not depend on the local sanitation department to handle debris.

Call sanitation headquarters to find out what the regulations are concerning construction debris.

For a fee, private sanitation companies will provide and haul away containers of varied capacities. Some of the smaller types—which hold up to 3 cubic yards—have wheels and can be located at any convenient place. The larger containers rest on steel skids, to be moved by a truck. This type is usually left in the street and this may require a special permit from the local authorities.

Remember that the trick in accomplishing a thorough and speedy cleaning is to do each part of it at its proper time. Take out the large debris first, then sweep what you can, and finally vacuum, being sure to catch any dust that has settled on top of the doors, window trim, or any other projections from the walls. After you have cleaned the work area, go into the adjoining rooms. After you have cleaned thoroughly, it will be safe to remove the seals placed around the doors, if you wish to do so at this point. Of course, if it isn't the final day of the job, you will have to seal the doors again on the following day.

What it takes

Tools and materials: Large rubbish container, between 1 and 20 cubic yard capacity, 20- and 30-gallon garbage pails, 6 cubic foot wheelbarrow, square-point shovels with 27″ and 48″ handles, 5- or 10-gallon drum vacuum cleaner, broom, gloves.

TIP: A good investment is the purchase of a drum (shop) type vacuum cleaner; 5-10 gallon capacity. It will save your expensive standard type from being damaged. Unlike a household vacuum, the drum type can suck up small bits of steel, such as nails and screws, and wood splinters with no harm to the machine.

Taking down wall cabinets

What it takes

Approximate time: To remove braces; 10-15 minutes per pair. To remove screws; depends on how quickly holes are located, and whether or not they are plugged.

Tools and materials: Saw, claw hammer, 6d nails, ruler; 1"x3" or 1"x4" wood stock; screwdriver (according to size of screwhead slot), scraper or knife, ¼" wood chisel.

As with everything else about construction and demolition (a renovation is both), a primary concern is safety. Therefore, when removing old cabinets, the hanging ones are handled first. The reason for this is that if one of the cabinets should fall, it can be stopped, or slowed, by the base cabinets. A further measure, however, is to place temporary bracing under them.

Temporary bracing

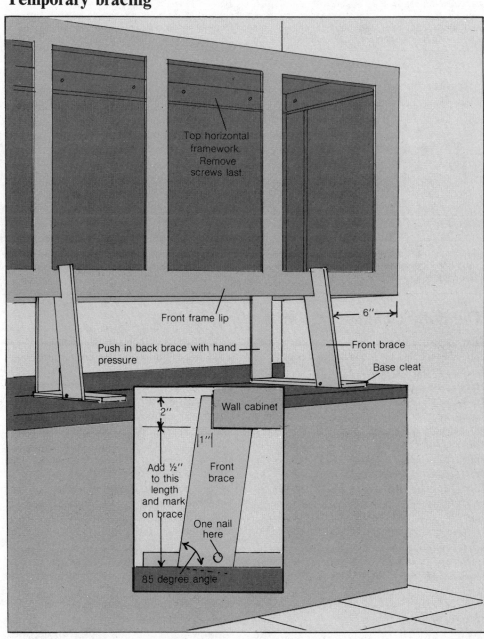

Top horizontal framework. Remove screws last.

Front frame lip

6"

Push in back brace with hand pressure

Front brace

Base cleat

Wall cabinet

2"

1"

Add ½" to this length and mark on brace

Front brace

One nail here

85 degree angle

TIP: Do not let yourself become distracted at any time you are balancing or supporting a cabinet during removal. When moving about, always look in the direction of travel. If the cabinet is over 3 feet long, get a helper.

1. Cut two 1x3 or 1x4 base cleats, 4 to 6 inches less than the depth of the base cabinet. Place each one on top of the base cabinet, 6 inches in from each end of the hanging cabinet.
2. To obtain the length of the back braces, measure from the top of the base cleat to the bottom of the bottom cabinet shelf, adding ¼ inch. Be sure to avoid the frame lip when measuring. The back and front braces will be 1x3 or 1x4 stock.
3. After you have cut the back braces, cut the bottom end of the front braces, at 85 degree

angle. This is in order that the braces will lean into the hanging cabinets when they are secured. From the top of the base cabinet, measure to the front frame lip of the hanging cabinet; add ½" and mark the length on the brace. Now add 2" to the brace length and cut it to the total length. Cut a notch 1" from the front edge and at the ½-inch mark so the brace fits over cabinet lip.
4. Secure with 6d nails. The bracing will look like this when the front and rear braces are in position. Now you can loosen the holding screws.

Locating/removing screws

One of the reasons for temporary bracing is the difficulty of locating the screws that hold the cabinet to the wall. Very often a missed screw thwarts the efforts to remove the cabinets. And without the bracing the cabinet will be apt to pivot around the remaining screw making it unsafe and difficult to remove. In addition, some screws hold the cabinets to each other. The bracing keeps the supported one from tearing a piece out of the adjoining one and supplying its extra weight for you to juggle.

Front frame holding screws

Hanging cabinets are usually secured by screws because they have greater holding power than nails. Wall studs were and still are used to anchor the screws. However, some contractors install large cleats or grounds in the walls for screws to anchor into. They claim that the time spent doing so is more than offset by the speed with which a carpenter could install cabinets when he doesn't have to look for studs.

Rear frame holding screws

The screws that really hold the cabinet weight go through the back framework into the studs, cleats, or grounds. Regardless of what they are anchored to, they always pass through the highest horizontal framing member. Frequently they will also be found in the lowest member. Rarely are any found in the center framing sections. Nevertheless, they too should be looked over for screws that will have to be removed.

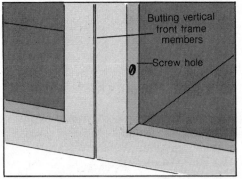

Check carefully along the inside edges of the front framework of any cabinet that abuts another. You will probably find some holes in the edges of the vertical members. These will most likely be screw holes. Using the largest screwdriver that will fit the slot, back the screws out.

On some of the old cabinet installations the screw holes have been plugged. The purpose was to provide a flush, more presentable surface when the cabinet doors were open. If the cabinet has a stained finish, the plugged holes can be located by a round discoloration that is slightly darker than the rest of the finish. Dig out the plug by first twisting a ¼-inch wood chisel part way into it; then use a screwdriver.

When the cabinet has a painted surface, it is more difficult to locate the screws. The paint must be scratched off between 2 and 6 inches from each end of the vertical framing member's edge. After the wood is bared, the round plug will be easier to locate.

You could have knocked me over with a (lead) feather!
It sure wasn't any feather that fell on me when I started removing that cabinet; but a good old tea pot that I never suspected was there.

Boy, I'll be sure to check next time for any loose items before I start taking a cabinet down.

Practical Pete

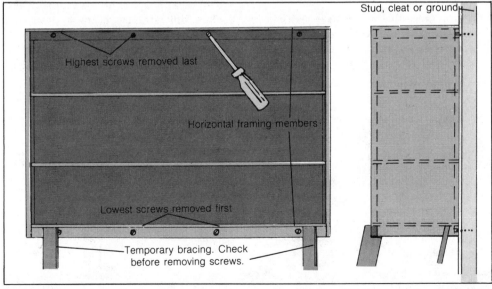
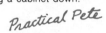

Always start screw removal in the lowest framing member, then go to the next highest. Continue until the screws are removed from the highest member. Be sure that the temporary bracing is securely in place while you work.

TIP: Stop cabinet doors from getting in the way by either removing the doors or taping them shut. On large cabinets, removal is better because it lightens the load and also provides more places to grip the cabinets while carrying them.

Removing sinks

Countertop method

Begin by cutting off the water supply to the sink. Depending on the original piping installation, the shutoff valves may be located in any of several places. First check under the sink or in the sink cabinet. There should be two valves coming either from the wall or the floor, with pipes going up to the sink faucets. These are the hot and cold water lines. Turn the handles on the valves in a clockwise direction. This should cut off the flow of water. But check by opening the sink faucets.

Remember, this is a preliminary check. If those valves don't turn off the water supply, you have a number of alternatives.

Go down to the basement and see if there are two valves in the ceiling area right under the kitchen. These may be in addition to the valves beneath the sink, or they may actually be the only valves that control the flow of water.

On the other hand, the valves controlling the flow to the kitchen sink may be under the bathroom, controlling both bathroom and kitchen. This presents a problem of inconvenience since when these are turned off, the bathroom will also be without water.

If you don't find the valves in the basement, then look for two valve handles protruding from the corner of a bathroom wall or in a closet adjacent to the bathroom.

You may have fixtures with old valves and so your only recourse then is to turn off the main valve. This will be just inside the foundation wall, near the water meter if you have one. This will cut the entire water supply for the house. In fact, in some old houses the fixtures have no valves and this is the only way to cut the water off.

Once the water is turned off you may disconnect the plumbing pipes from the sink. Of course, this must be done before the sink is removed from the wall or before the countertop can be removed from the existing base cabinets.

If the plumbing is enclosed in a cabinet, you will have to crawl partly inside, and lying on your back or side, reach up to the connection between the hot and cold supply pipes and the faucet. Place the "claw" of the basin wrench on the tailpiece nut. Since the faucet is probably embedded in putty, you may have dry, crumbling putty falling into your face and eyes. Better wear goggles.

Position the wrench claw so that the tailpiece nut will turn counterclockwise. Be sure that you have a good grip on the nut; if you have the wrench on the faucet shank, locknut, or riser pipe you won't loosen the supply pipe from the faucet.

If the faucet is tied in solid, it will be necessary to cut the supply pipes with a hacksaw or tubing cutter. With copper tubing for instance, it's usual to make a solid hookup.

The next step is to disconnect the kitchen sink strainer tailpiece from the sink. Although special wrenches are available for this, such as a trap/spud

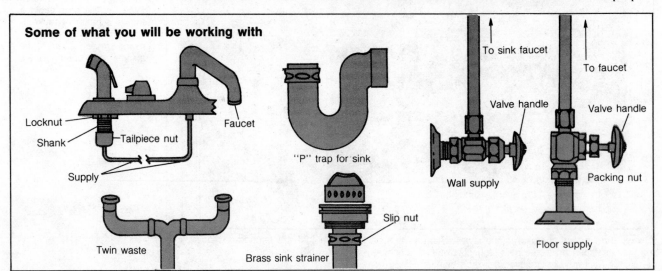

Some of what you will be working with

Locknut · Shank · Supply · Tailpiece nut · Faucet

Twin waste

"P" trap for sink

Brass sink strainer · Slip nut

To sink faucet · Valve handle · Wall supply

To faucet · Valve handle · Packing nut · Floor supply

wrench, the number of times you would use such a tool doesn't really warrant the purchase.

Actually, the slip nut(s) can be loosened with a pipe wrench, monkey wrench, or channel lock pliers. To avoid damaging the finish on the slip nut, place a piece of cardboard or cloth around the nut to protect it from the "teeth" of the wrench or pliers. A monkey wrench has smooth jaws and will not mar the finish.

Place the wrench on the nut, adjusted for a snug fit, and turn it counterclockwise. In the event that you have a twin waste (double sink) then you must loosen both slip nuts. This will free the sink strainer(s) from the waste tubing. It is not necessary to remove the strainer from the sink.

With the screws that extended up from the base cabinets into the bottom of the countertop removed, you can now take off the countertop. If the top is large and the sink heavy, you would be well advised to remove the sink from the countertop before lifting off the top.

It is difficult to lift the countertop and the sink as a unit straight up (10 to 12 inches) so that the bottom of the sink clears the base cabinet. Another difficulty that may arise is a window sill above the counter. The backsplash of the countertop will become wedged under the windowsill before the unit is raised high enough for the bottom of the sink to clear the top of the base cabinet. Realize that you may wish to use the countertop at some future time in garage or basement, and so take care to avoid damage in removing it.

Once having decided to remove the sink from the countertop you will be wise to remove the trap and any other drain pipes from under the sink. This will provide you with more room to work and will also lessen the chance of damage to the piping while the sink is being taken out. If you are able to get the top and the sink out as a unit then the waste piping can wait. Once the top is removed and the base cabinets are pulled away from the wall you will find it a whole lot easier to remove the remaining plumbing pipes.

The sink is secured to the countertop by clips in older installations, or by a sink flange and channel/lever type anchoring bolts. In either case the clips or retaining screws must be removed; and for this you will have to work under the countertop.

Again, work with goggles, but you should also secure the sink to the countertop while you are underneath it loosening the retaining clips.

Pete the Magnificent!
I figured the best way to get a tight connection was to really "sock-up-on-it," as the pros put it. So I gave it the muscle—and cracko! I was just too strong for that porcelain.

Next time for sure I'll hand-tighten first, then just snug the nut with a wrench.

Practical Pete

Securing the sink while you work

You can do this quite simply with the "sandwich" method. All you need is a short length of ⅜-inch or ½-inch threaded rod and a length of 2x4, plus nuts, washers, and a wrench.

The 2x4 should be at least 12 inches longer than the width of the sink cutout in the countertop. Center it over the sink opening, with an equal overlap on each end.

Drill a hole in the 2x4 slightly larger than the diameter of the threaded rod, and directly over the sink strainer.

Now take another piece of 2x4 and drill a hole about 3 inches from the end. Cut off a 6-inch length of the 2x4 so that you will have a 6-inch piece with a hole in the center. You must drill the hole first, before you saw, so the short piece of 2x4 will not spin on the drill bit.

Now cut the threaded rod so that it will be of sufficient length to pass through from the long 2x4 to the short piece, as shown in the drawing.

Place a washer and nut on the rod. Feed the rod through the hole and down through the sink strainer. Place

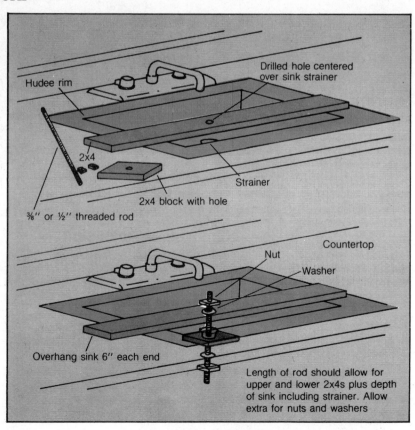

Hudee rim

2x4

⅜" or ½" threaded rod

Drilled hole centered over sink strainer

Strainer

2x4 block with hole

Nut

Countertop

Washer

Overhang sink 6" each end

Length of rod should allow for upper and lower 2x4s plus depth of sink including strainer. Allow extra for nuts and washers

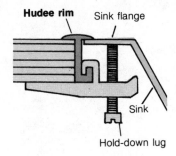

Hudee rim Sink flange

Sink

Hold-down lug

the 6-inch 2x4 with the hole, over the rod extending below the sink strainer. Now place the washer and nut over the rod protruding through the 2x4.

Tighten the nuts, holding back on the bottom nut with a second wrench to prevent it turning while you tighten the top nut.

The countertop and sink should now be sandwiched between the long 2x4 and the 6-inch block which acts as a big washer at the bottom. Now, when all the sink retaining clips are removed the sink will not fall through the countertop opening and down into the cabinet.

If the sink has a flange-type Hudee rim, then you can lift the sink and rim up and out from the countertop. Grasp the spout of the faucet near the faucet body with one hand and place the other hand on the threaded rod directly under the 2x4. You should be able to lift the sink out. On the other hand, if it feels too heavy, ask someone to help you.

The sandwich method is ideal for heavy cast iron sinks, but a stainless steel or pressed porcelain on steel sink is light enough for one person to hold while you are working underneath. Just make sure it's someone reliable. Remember, you, not your helper, are the one who is underneath.

An older method of anchoring the sink is with clips. The top of the sink is recessed the thickness of the countertop. A stainless steel or aluminum frame covers the edges of the sink cutout. In this case, the sink cannot be lifted up and out because its length and width exceed the cutout.

When you are ready to lower the sink down and away from the countertop, have a helper grasp the threaded rod firmly just above the sink strainer. Remove the top nut and washer so that the rod can slide free from the upper supporting 2x4. The countertop can now be lifted or slid off the base cabinets.

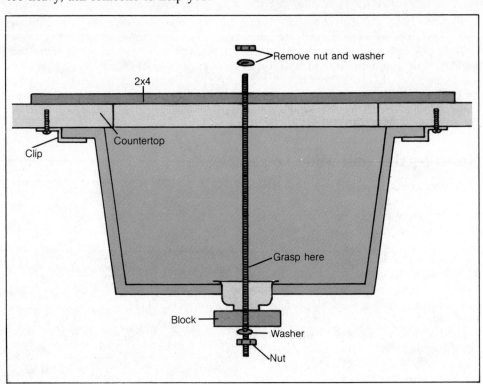

Remove nut and washer

2x4

Clip

Countertop

Grasp here

Block

Washer

Nut

Removing a small sink

Removing a small bathroom sink takes the same basic action as for a heavy kitchen fixture. Again, it's a matter of loosening nuts and bolts, and remembering where parts that have been removed will go when you reassemble.

It's always a good idea to take a hard look at old fixtures to see how they are mounted and connected to the piping. Old sinks and lavatories are mounted in a number of ways. They can be suspended from a countertop, or set on a pedestal, or they can hang from a wall. The faucet assemblies may pass through holes in the countertop or wall, or they may extend down through holes in the fixture itself.

Remember, too, that fixtures are fragile, and if dropped or knocked with some hard object they can be damaged. You can save the parts of a fixture by removing them carefully and listing, and even sketching them before storing them in a solid container.

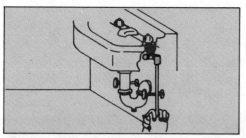

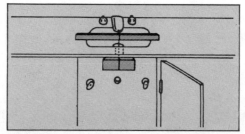

First step is to disconnect the water supply lines. Simply turn off the hot and cold valves. Unscrew the coupling nuts at the top. If the space is too tight for an adjustable wrench, use a basin wrench, as shown. If the supply lines have shutoff valves, unscrew the coupling nuts above the valves. This will free the supply lines.

To dismount this smaller countertop, lay a 2x4 across the top of the basin and tie a wire to it. Pass the wire through the drain hole to a wood block. This is essentially the same method as shown for the kitchen sink on page 23. Twist the block until it is right up against the tailpiece. Unscrew the lug bolts and lower the basin by untwisting the block.

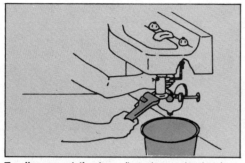

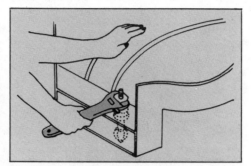

To disconnect the trap, first place a bucket beneath it and unscrew the cleanout plug so that it will drain. Unscrew the slip nut to free the trap from the tailpiece.

To remove the faucets, place the basin on its face on the floor. Put some padding under it. Unscrew the lock nuts from the faucet shanks and lift out the washers. Now turn the basin face up and tap the faucets to break the putty seal. Lift out the faucet assembly.

Capping pipes

It is necessary to seal pipes when a fixture is removed. For a supply line with a shutoff valve, just tape over the valve outlet hole. Supply lines without shutoff valves, as well as drain outlets, should be capped securely. For a threaded pipe, use a cap of the same material. Use plugs for elbows, and short pipe extenders, which have female threads. You can cement on a plastic cap if the pipe is unthreaded plastic. If the pipe is unthreaded copper, solder on a copper cap.

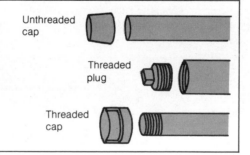

Unthreaded cap

Threaded plug

Threaded cap

Wall hung sink and laundry tub

Removing this type of sink will require a helper. If the faucets are deck type, the removal of the water supply pipes is the same as the countertop method. However, older styles of sinks used swing-spout faucets with the water supplying the faucet coming out of the wall or the supply piping exposed on the surface of the wall. The faucets would then be connected at a right angle to the piping.

To remove faucets of this type, place the monkey wrench jaws on the flat surface of the faucet union. Loosen the union until the faucet is free. Be careful it doesn't drop into the sink.

With the body of the faucets off, you now must remove the faucet couplings.

They are held against the sink by nipples (short pieces of pipe) that pass through the sink and connect to a fitting behind the sink. You can use the monkey wrench to remove the faucet couplings. In some cases it will be necessary to insert a seat wrench or old screwdriver into the internal opening of the faucet couplings. The opening is "square," and the tool or device that you insert into the opening can be turned with a pipe wrench and the sink couplings removed. Disconnect the waste tubing as described earlier.

Be careful, though, if the sink has a supporting leg. Remove it, for the chances are it will fall free when the sink is lifted.

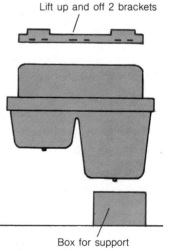

Lift up and off 2 brackets

Box for support

Removing toilets and tubs

In a bathroom renovation, the toilet bowl should usually be the last fixture removed.

The first step is to turn off the water supply line.

Yours is very likely one of the two standard bowl and tank setups. Either the tank is bolted to the bowl, or it is secured to the wall with several screws with a flush elbow connecting it to the bowl.

Remove the tank cover and get it out of the bathroom. The temptation is to put it on the basin or in the tub, but that might be hazardous. Eventually it will have to be moved out anyway, so you might as well do it right away.

Trip the flush tank handle, holding it down until the tank is clear of water. The small amount of water remaining in the tank can be sopped up with a rag or sponge.

The water supply line to the tank must now be disconnected. Follow the water supply pipe as it leaves the valve and enters the shank of the ballcock which extends below the bottom of the tank. There is a nut or collar below the shank which makes the connection watertight. The nut must be loosened entirely from the threaded shank. As you back off counterclockwise on the collar, using a small pipe wrench or water pump pliers, it is advisable to reach into the tank and grasp the ballcock to prevent it from turning. Failure to do so may result in damage to the float rod and float ball, as well as other working parts.

With the tank supply free from the ballcock, you can proceed to remove the tank from the bowl.

The tank is secured to the bowl by two, and in some instances, three bolts. The heads of the bolts are inside the tank. Each has a screwdriver slot. The bolts pass through the tank, and the nuts (sometimes wing nuts) are located under the upper rear portion of the bowl. A small adjustable wrench will perform nicely in this spot. An open end or box wrench will also do the trick.

Remove the nuts and washers from the tank bolts. The tank should be free to lift clear of the bowl. The easiest way to separate a wall hung tank from the bowl is to cut through the flush elbow with a hacksaw.

Locate the two or three bolts that are visible near the top-rear part of the tank. You can use a stubby screwdriver that will fit inside the tank or a long screwdriver that will allow the handle to remain outside the tank when the blade is in the screw slot. At this point, just loosen the bolts slightly. When you are sure that all the mounting bolts will turn freely, you must prepare to support the tank while the bolts are being backed out all the way.

This is best done by sitting on the toilet seat cover as you face the wall and tank. In this position the weight of the tank can be supported by your knees and legs. The bolts can now be removed completely. With the tank free from the wall and supported across your legs, you can grasp it firmly and remove it.

To remove the bowl, first take a look at the area around the base of the bowl. You will see nuts and washers protruding from the top of the base. They may be concealed by china or plastic caps. If, as is frequently the case, the caps are embedded in plaster of paris, you may have to break them off.

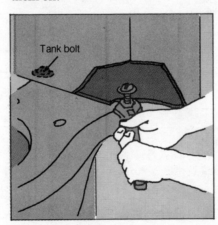

1. Disconnect the tank and bowl by first turning off the supply valve, flushing the toilet, and removing all the water remaining in the tank and bowl. The supply line should be disconnected. Should the tank be mounted on the bowl, unscrew the nuts under the rear rim of the bowl. On the other hand, if the tank is wall-mounted, take off the L-shaped spud pipe that connects it to the bowl. Loosen the slip nuts at each end and remove the bolts or screws that hold the tank to the wall. Pry off the caps over the flange bolts. Unscrew the nuts. Move the bowl, rocking it, in order to break the seal of putty with the flange. Finally, lift the bowl.

There are usually four caps on a toilet base. The rear pair hold the bowl to the soil pipe. The front two attach the bowl to the floor. But you may discover that the front two caps do not in fact cover bolts. It is not always necessary to bolt the bowl to the floor, and the front two caps may be there simply to cover the front holes in the bowl base.

Remove the two rear nuts and washers. If you have a problem with the entire bolt turning before the nut is removed, you can probably wedge the bolt with a screwdriver to prevent it from turning. If that doesn't work, the bolt will have to be hacksawed, directly under the nut. If the hacksaw frame will not fit, you can tape the ends of the blade and use the blade alone. Sawing these bolts is not a major effort, as they are made of soft brass. Once sawed half way through, the bolt can probably be wiggled back and forth until it snaps off.

The bowl is probably grouted to the floor with a layer of plaster of paris. There will also be a seal underneath, made of putty, wax or a felt gasket. This won't be visible until the bowl is removed, so don't be alarmed if the bowl does not move freely when all the nuts and washers have been removed. To break the seal, give the rim of the bowl a sharp blow with the heel of your hand. Repeat from the other side, and the bowl should be free to lift from the bolt.

Be certain to thoroughly scrape off the old sealer and gasket from the soil pipe to ensure a perfect join

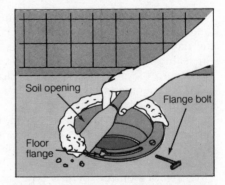

2. Take out the flange bolts and scrape the gasket with a putty knife. Check the flange closely for any cracks or other signs of wear, and if necessary, replace it. Be sure to stuff the hole with rags or paper so that sewer gas will not escape, and nothing can fall into the hole.

when the new sealer is applied.

When this is done, insert a wad of newspaper or an old burlap bag into the soil opening in the floor. This will keep odors from backing up into the room and prevent debris from getting into the system. Remove the bolts from the floor flange that is secured to the soil pipe inlet. The bolts can be tapped around or slid until the elongated heads line up with the corresponding elongated slots in the flange. These bolts should probably be replaced when you install your new toilet.

Taking out a bathtub

Of all the plumbing fixtures you may want to remove and replace, the bathtub is by far the biggest job. For this project you must be prepared to remove and alter sections of wall and floor. Your best tool will be patience.

The standard bathtub is built in and rests on the subflooring and against the rough wall. The finished floor and wall material are installed after the tub is in place. To remove the tub, you will have to reverse this procedure, first cutting away the tile or plaster around the tub and the floor area that abuts the tub apron.

There are two major safety considerations in this project. The first is to protect your eyes. Wear goggles while working, and keep onlookers clear of flying chips. The second safety concern is to keep wall and floor material from entering the tub waste pipe and clogging the trap below. Before the drain is removed, use masking tape to seal it.

If you intend to use the tub elsewhere or give it to a friend, you will have to take more care in cutting the wall and floor. An old blanket placed inside the tub will absorb the shock of falling objects and catch debris. You should stand in the tub as little as possible, to avoid grinding wall debris into the tub surface.

The wall area adjacent to the tub must be removed down to the bare studs and adjacent flooring removed to a depth of 2 or 3 inches. When this is done, the tub is free. But the big job is to get it clear.

First remove the strainer on the drain and the face plate from the overflow. Removing the face plate will reveal screws or a threaded ring with ears. Unscrew the ring. The tub is now free of waste and overflow drains. The remaining waste parts can now be unscrewed from the trap.

Remove the tub fill spout. To do this, place a chisel or small pipe inside the pipe and apply pressure until the spout turns. After one or two turns with a tool, the spout should

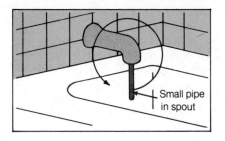
Small pipe in spout

turn easily by hand.

Now comes the tough part—getting the hefty tub out of the bathroom. In a small bathroom you may have to remove the sink and/or toilet to be able to maneuver the tub. If the tub is enclosed on three sides, you will probably have to cut through one of the end walls to get it out. Two men can carry a standard metal and fiberglass tub, but the tub must first be maneuvered far enough out from the back wall that you can safely get a hold on it.

Lift the apron of the tub at floor level by levering with a pinch bar. Place metal bars or scrap pipe under the front edge of the tub, at a right angle to it. Be sure to keep your fingers clear. The object is to form a metal surface on which the tub can roll or slide. Use the pinch bar again to pry the tub out and away from the wall. The back edge of the tub is probably supported on a horizontal 2x4 running the length of the tub. When the tub is pushed away from the wall a distance equal to the thickness of the horizontal support, it will drop slightly.

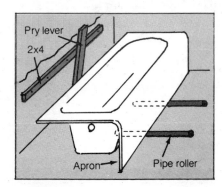
Pry lever
2x4
Apron
Pipe roller

Continue to pry the tub away from the wall. You may have to use a long 2x4 to pry as the distance between the tub and the wall increases. Position this long lever so that it is not in front of your face. And be sure to have the lower end of the prying lever butted against a wall stud. Placed in the space between the studs, the end of the pry could poke through the wall on the other side of the partition.

When the tub is about two feet away from the wall, it can be tilted forward so that the apron rests on the floor. In this position the tub can be manipulated from the bathroom, using pipe rollers or a strong assistant. The tub should be at least two feet from the wall during this operation to ensure that it clears valve stems and shower handles.

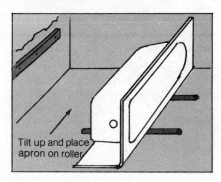
Tilt up and place apron on roller

With the tub out, you can remove the waste pipe that is exposed and connects to the trap. Put a wad of paper or a rag in the trap to prevent any accidental obstruction during construction. Removal of additional wall and floor material can be made at this time if necessary. Refer to a rough-in sheet (get it at a plumbing supply store) to check the trap location for the new tub. With a little luck and planning, no alteration will be required. If alteration is necessary, it might be minimized with a swivel trap; the lower part of a swivel trap can rotate to vary location. Make further alterations with pipe nipples and drainage fittings.

If you are considering a shower stall to replace the tub, it is especially important that you check first with the plumbing supply house for a rough-in sheet with the exact dimensions.

Removing electrical fixtures

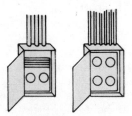

Plug light bulb sockets with bulbs into every wall receptacle that will have to be moved or removed.

Fuse boxes

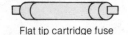

Screw type fuse

Flat tip cartridge fuse

Round type cartridge fuse

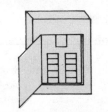

Circuit breaker entrance panel

Circuit breakers

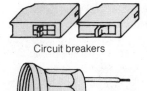

Plastic weatherproof socket

The first and most important step in removing (or in repairing) any electrical fixture is to turn off the current. Should you need light in the work area, it's easy enough to rig up auxiliary lighting, either with an extension cord that is plugged into an outlet in another room, or by using plastic weather-proof sockets connected to the house wiring.

Turn on all lights that are to be removed; then plug light bulb sockets with bulbs into every wall receptacle that will have to be moved or taken away.

Locate the main power source box, which is usually in the basement. If it is a screw-in type fuse box, unscrew the fuses one at a time until you find which are the work area lights. Keep that fuse or fuses out of the box so that someone else will not inadvertently put them back in while you are still working.

If your house has a cartridge-type fusebox, use a fuse puller to pull the cartridge until the work area lights go out. Store cartridge away from the fuse box.

A fuseless box is another type. This is a box with circuit breakers. Move the breaker switches on and off until you locate which breaker switch is the one for the work area. Close the breaker and put tape over it. Then shut the box and tape it, so nobody else will turn the power on.

Disconnecting the fixtures

Several types of assembly methods and hardware are used to secure lighting fixtures to the ceiling or walls. There are certain general rules to follow, however, that pertain to any type of fixture being disconnected. After turning off the power source, loosen the fixture from its mounting. Next, identify the house wiring, and separate it from the fixture wires. Lastly, connect temporary lighting if needed.

Before disconnecting any wires, make sure that they are color coded. The insulation on the wires should be either white, black, red, green, or blue. This makes the work easier when connecting new fixtures or reconnecting the old. Sometimes when the wires in the walls or ceiling are old, especially those with the fiber type insulation, the color fades, or the fiber disintegrates leaving no coding. In such a case paint the old wires the same color as the fixture wires to which they are attached.

Quite often one of the fixture wires will be attached to two house wires that separate as soon as they are disconnected. Be sure to reconnect those two wires before going on to some other work. You can identify which fixture wire they were attached to by color coding. An alternative method of identification is to tape them together with colored electrical tape.

Connecting a temporary light

With the fixtures disconnected, provisions for temporary light will have to be made in the work area. A common method is to simply plug an electrical extension cord into a live receptacle in another room. The problem here is that you will have an obstacle in your path as you work.

A more practical way to provide this sort of lighting is to connect plastic weatherproof sockets to the house wiring. They will accept standard, large size incandescent bulbs; and you can hook up as many as you will need.

Connecting a socket requires only that the color coding be followed. Use solderless wire connectors. Connect the socket's black wire to a red or black house wire. Connect the socket's white wire to a white house wire.

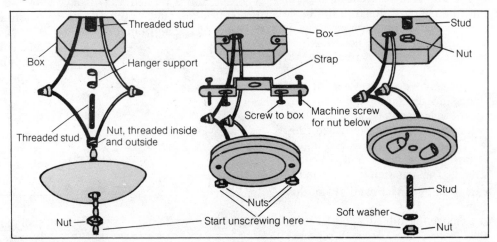

The principles involved in removing any type of fixture are the same. Start from the outermost part of the fixture. Unscrew any nut, screw, or stud that is visible. It is important to feel the loosening of the fixture with one hand if it is heavy, so that it won't fall on you. At the same time, you may wish to reuse the fixture, and so you have another reason for exercising care.

Countertop and floor cabinets

Large, solid countertops are heavy, yet they will still slip around on top of a base cabinet if not secured. The usual method of holding down a countertop is to screw into it from the base cabinet frame below. The hold-down screw locations vary according to a cabinet's construction. The sketches on this page show probable screw locations. Bear in mind that the framework shown is a composite of various types of construction.

The ease with which the hold-down screws can be removed depends upon how well they were put in to begin with. Another factor is the quality of wood used. Screws are more difficult to remove from plywood that is solid throughout than the less expensive type that has some honeycombing (hollow spots) within it. Another condition which will affect screw withdrawal is water damage. If the countertop wood base has been periodically soaked with water, it may have rotted to the point where the removal of the hold-down screws is unnecessary. In such a case the countertop can just be pulled up.

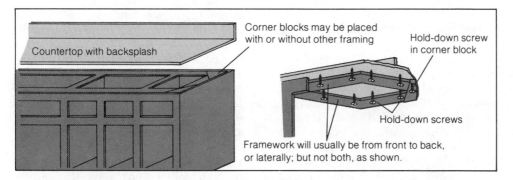

Countertop with backsplash

Corner blocks may be placed with or without other framing

Hold-down screw in corner block

Hold-down screws

Framework will usually be from front to back, or laterally; but not both, as shown.

Base cabinets

Because base cabinets rest on the floor, they are much easier to detach from the wall than the hanging kind. On the other hand, since they are bulkier and heavier, they may be more difficult to remove.

First, remove the cabinet doors, drawers, and all loose shelves. Next, locate and remove the hold-down screws, plus any screws that may hold the vertical framework of one base cabinet to another.

Locate the screws in the top rear horizontal framework or special cleat. Turn the screws counterclockwise to back them out. Should they spin and not back out, grasp the front framework and pull the cabinet away from the wall. The screws will then either come loose or tighten up enough for you to back them out.

Base cabinets can be removed by one of three basic methods. The first method would be to roll the cabinets out on pipes or rollers. When done properly this requires only average strength. It does require a bit of space to maneuver cabinets.

As a second choice of method, you can carry out the cabinets on a hand truck. This takes less time and space than the roller system. Still, you must be sure that there is adequate space to safely maneuver the hand truck, plus the cabinets and yourself without being trapped into a corner halfway through the operation. In addition, caution must be exercised when placing the cabinet on the hand truck. Both must be kept in balance, otherwise the load may pull out of your hands and fall away from, or toward you, striking items not intended to be removed and damaging them. If possible, tie the cabinet to the truck.

Finally, you can cut the base cabinet into smaller sections to ease handling.

This kickback really kicked . . .
Take a tip from a practical man! Any power saw can easily kick back when its cutting blade is pinched by the wood it is cutting.

To avoid a kickback, be sure to leave one end of any wood you are cutting free to fall or roll away from the blade. OR—use a hand saw.

Practical Pete

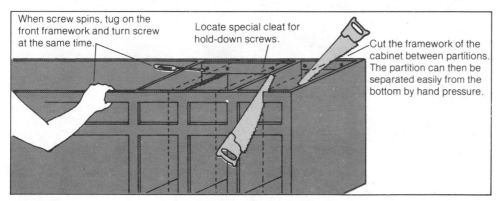

When screw spins, tug on the front framework and turn screw at the same time.

Locate special cleat for hold-down screws.

Cut the framework of the cabinet between partitions. The partition can then be separated easily from the bottom by hand pressure.

Older flooring

Linoleum, vinyl, or ceramic tile
Construction paper
Top floor; tongue and groove
Subfloor; wide planking

Joists

Newer flooring

Finish vinyl or tile floor
Underlayment; particle board, hardboard, or plywood
Subfloor; wide planking or ⅝″ exterior plywood

Joists

A sound floor is the beginning of a sound bathroom or kitchen renovation. This means a clean, solid, and level surface that is also attractive.

A floor is usually in three layers. The subfloor lies directly on the floor joists. This can be tongue and groove lumber or exterior-grade plywood sheets. Over this comes the underlayment, which may be hardboard, particle board, or more plywood. Exterior plywood in ⅝-inch thickness is often used because it resists moisture well. The finish flooring is on top of the underlayment.

If the finish flooring is in pretty good shape you might simply lay the new one right over it. But flooring that has deteriorated should either be removed or covered with new underlayment. Of course, adding new underlayment and new flooring on top of the old will add height, and you will have to trim the bottoms of any doors. All the same, it is quicker than tearing up the existing floor and putting down a new surface.

It is important to make sure that there is no decay under the finish flooring. Check for broken tiles, loose bits of flooring, curling seams, buckling, or any signs of moisture such as dampness, discoloration, or odors underneath sinks and lavatories, and around bathtubs, dishwashers, or toilets.

Check especially at any place where the floor feels soft or gives when pushed. Remove a section and probe for rot. You may need to patch or replace the underlayment, the subfloor, or possibly both, depending on the damage.

Don't forget that susceptible area for leakage around the toilet; that is, at the ring that seals the toilet to its flange.

If your floor is in such poor shape that you need to replace it completely, start by removing the floor molding and the finish flooring. In the event that the bathtub is resting directly on the floor joists, you can leave it where it is, for the old flooring can be pulled from around it. On the other hand, if the tub is resting on the subfloor, inspect the floor underneath. If it is in good condition, leave this part intact and take up the old flooring around it. In any other situation, take the tub out of the room.

Figure out the combined thickness of the subfloor plus the underlayment, and set your circular power saw to that exact depth. You must turn off the power to any circuits that enter or pass through the room to avoid the chance of accidentally cutting a live wire.

Cut through the flooring as close to the walls as possible, and go around the entire room. Start at the side of the room which is opposite the door, prying up and taking out the underlayment and subflooring. Take out all nails from the floor joists.

With all the joists exposed, lay down two or three sheets of subflooring as a temporary work surface while you inspect each joist carefully. If you see any signs of rot, you can just cut away the area; but only if it is no more than an inch or so deep. Treat the surrounding wood with preservative. Extensive rot means you should call a professional.

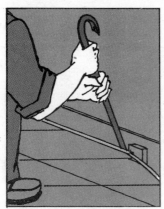

Removing the floor molding.
Your first step before you add or take away a layer of flooring is to remove the *base shoe,* the rounded strip that is attached to the floor. Start close to the center of the wall, pry with a thin blade to get it started, then insert the end of a pry bar. Work along the wall in both directions, placing small wedges as you go, so that the shoe comes off evenly and without breaking. Remove the baseboard in the same way.

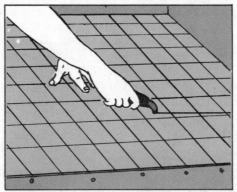

Removing continuous flooring such as cushioned vinyl or linoleum. Cut it into pieces that are a handy size, then roll or peel. If it doesn't come up easily, use a scraper with a stiff blade.

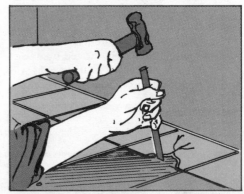

Taking out ceramic tile. You must wear safety goggles whenever you remove ceramic tile from a floor or a wall. Start at a place where you can work the edge of a cold chisel under the edge of a tile. You may have to break one of the tiles with a hammer to get a start. Chisel out the fragments, then work on the adjoining tile's edges, tapping gently with a hammer on a cold chisel.

Patching

You can take care of any minor damage in underlayment and subfloor by replacing damaged areas with solid patches. Remember to plan your patches so that the joints of an underlayment patch correspond with the joints of the subflooring. When patching the subfloor, make certain that you cut out an area of underlayment that is larger than your proposed patch of subfloor. If it is just the underlayment that you are patching, remove enough old underlayment so that the patch will span all the subfloor underneath it.

Most patching is simple work and such obstacles as a toilet flange which go through the floor are easy enough to work around.

Removing underlayment. Set your circular saw to the depth corresponding to the thickness of the underlayment, then make your cut.

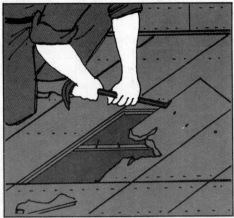

Removing tongue and groove subflooring. Take out the finish flooring and underlayment from the area you wish to replace. If you're taking up the whole floor, then just proceed as shown, making your start as close to the wall as you can.

Removing and repairing damaged resilient flooring

When floor tile is cut, scratched, or damaged in any way, and you feel the need to replace it, hope that you had the foresight to save some extra tiles when it was originally installed. If you haven't done that, you'll have to buy extras. If they're unavailable or do not match, take a tile up from inside a closet or underneath an appliance where it won't be noticeable.

When removing any tile, the point is to heat the tile until the adhesive melts underneath. The quickest way to remove a damaged tile is with a blowtorch (this is not recommended for use on undamaged tiles). A slower but safer method is heating the tiles with an iron to soften the adhesive and make them more pliable. Set the iron at medium and place aluminum foil between it and the tile. When the tile has loosened, pry it out with a putty knife or similar tool.

It is also possible to remove a tile without using heat. If the tile surface is soft you can cut an X through it with a utility knife and pull the pieces out. Cold also breaks the bond. Put a block of dry ice on a tile for just a few seconds, then pry.
Caution: Don't touch dry ice with bare hands, and keep the room well ventilated.

Resilient sheet flooring. This is not as easy to repair as tile, and again hope that you have saved a scrap of it. Place the scrap over the damaged area so that the pattern matches. Cut a square piece, using a utility knife and straightedge. Tape the piece down firmly, and cut a smaller square through the top piece deeply enough so that you score the flooring underneath. It is important to hold your knife vertically. Take away the top piece and finish cutting through the score lines into the subfloor. Remove and replace the damaged section just as you would a tile. In this way you should have a perfect fit and pattern match—only the barely visible outline of the patch may remain.

TIP: When putting down new tile, make sure that the area is completely clean before spreading fresh adhesive on the subfloor with a notched trowel. Set (don't slide) the new tile in place, and go over it with a rolling pin. Weight it until the adhesive is dry.

REFRAMING & WIRING

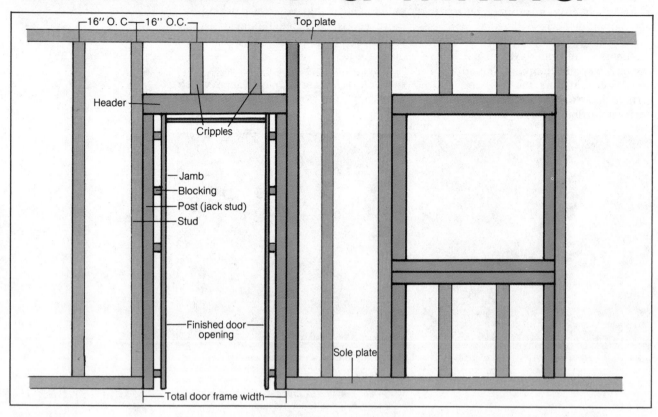

16" O. C.—16" O.C.

Top plate

Header

Cripples

Jamb

Blocking

Post (jack stud)

Stud

Finished door opening

Sole plate

Total door frame width

What it takes

Approximate time: 15 minutes for measuring and marking; another 30 to 45 minutes for cutting.

Tools and materials: Ruler and pencil, straightedge, carpenter's level, claw hammer, broad cold chisel, crosscut saw (or reciprocating saw).

You may or may not be willing to engage in major renovation on your own, but whether you hire a contractor or do your own work, you will still need to know the procedures for cutting through walls, and

for framing a doorway, a window, or any wall opening. The important thing is to plan well. Allot your time carefully in order to minimize inconvenience to the members of the household.

Cutting an opening in an existing wall

There is a general procedure when cutting an opening in a wall. Whether cutting for a doorway, sash frame, or trimmed open-

ing, the steps are the same. Only the measurements and frame assembly may change, depending on the situation.

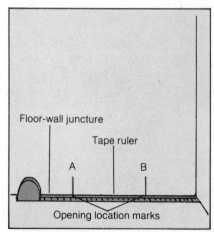

Floor-wall juncture

Tape ruler

A   B

Opening location marks

1. Mark the location of the opening on the wall at its juncture with the floor.

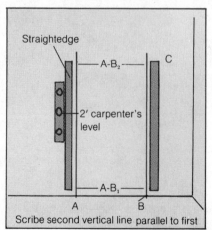

Straightedge

A-B₂   C

2' carpenter's level

A-B₁

A   B

Scribe second vertical line parallel to first

2. From Point A plumb a line upwards to obtain the first vertical line. Measure distance A-B₁ at the floor-wall juncture. Duplicate the measurement at location A-B₂, approximately one foot from the ceiling. Scribe the second vertical line with the assistance of a straightedge placed on B and C.

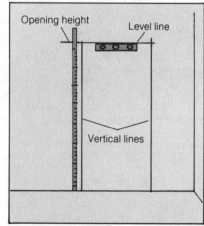

Opening height

Level line

Vertical lines

3. Measure and mark the opening height on one of the vertical lines. From the opening's height mark, scribe a level line between the two vertical lines.

Locating electrical wiring and plumbing lines

Any planned wall opening alteration must take into account the possibility of existing plumbing or electrical lines. A nearby plumbing fixture (sink, bowl, tank, etc.) definitely points to the existence of water supply and waste lines. Unless you are prepared to go through the expense of relocating plumbing lines, it is suggested that no wall opening be planned where plumbing lines may exist.

It must be remembered, however, that most plumbing lines (this includes steam or hot water heating) occur in exterior walls, or the walls between kitchen and bathroom. Electrical lines, on the other hand, may pass through any wall in the house. Consequently, they present a problem. If cut while the wall is being opened, the circuit will be useless. The chief problem is the cutting edge of the tool that goes into the wire. At the least it will be burned at the point of electrical contact. In the case of an electrical saw that cuts swiftly through a wire, that is all that may happen. On the other hand, should the tool not be properly grounded, the user may receive a severe shock. You can safely figure on any planned wall opening having an electrical wire passing through it; and so it will be necessary to open the wall with caution, and at the same time to make provision for the wire's relocation.

I really blew it!
When I opened my kitchen wall I checked all the electrical lines leading to outlets so I wouldn't cut into any of them. But I forgot about the room on the other side of the wall, which had its own outlets and wiring. I really blew a fuse!

Practical Pete

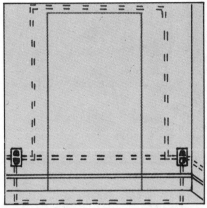

1. When electrical outlets are located as shown (in relation to the projected cutting lines), it can be assumed that there will be electrical wires running between them. Make your opening cut carefully at this point. To keep this electrical circuit intact, you will have to rerun the wiring connecting these outlets either under the floor or around and over the opening, as shown by the colored lines.

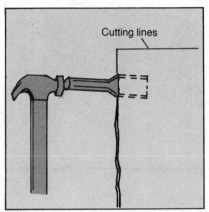

2. Score the cutting layout with a broad cold chisel and hammer—just enough to break the surface. Now go over the scored line again. This time hammer the chisel through the gypsum board or plaster. Repeat the process on the opposite side of the wall. With the hammer, break an opening large enough to put your hand in, and pull the section out. If there is much resistance, break the wall into smaller pieces.

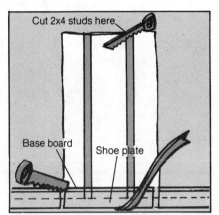

3. Cut the shoe plate and baseboard which are at the bottom of the opening. Use a hand saw. Now cut each stud at the top of the opening. Pull on the stud until it is loosened from the shoe plate. Pry the shoe plate and baseboard loose with a crow bar.

Framing a new doorway in an existing wall

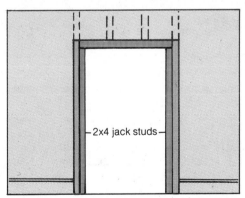

The jack stud length is determined by the door height. To figure the proper jack dimension, add 1⅝″ to the height of the door. Then cut two 2x4s to that dimension. The header length is determined by the door width. Add 4½″ to 5″ to the width of the door and you've got it. Either measurement allows clearance for squaring the door jambs. This allowance has not been codified, and diverse practices exist in different parts of the country.

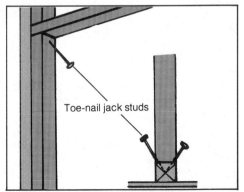

After the wall opening has been cut, it is time to assemble the framing members. 1. Slip a full-length stud into place and nail through the wall and the stud edges into the plate faces. 2. Place the header in position. Toe nail it to the cripple studs and full-length trimmer studs. 3. Toe nail the lower ends of the jack studs to the shoe plate and the upper ends to the header. When secured top and bottom, face nail to the trimmer.

What it takes

Approximate time: Allow 2 hours.

Tools and materials: Claw hammer, 8d and 10d nails; 2x4 framing stock.

Framing a window

To frame a window, follow the same method as for a door. As a rule, most windows, with the exception of kitchen pass-through openings, are in exterior walls, and so involve structural support.

Walls that run parallel to the ridge of the roof are generally supporting walls, while those running across the gable ends are not. If the window is wider than average, you will need a larger header, even if the wall is not load-bearing. Otherwise, there will be the tendency for cracks to appear in plaster or wallboard.

Base the dimensions of the window (and door opening) on the actual size of the window/door to be installed.

Framing a bathroom

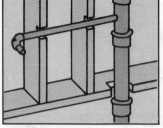

Framing details

Studs notched for pipe

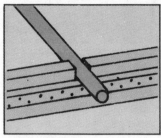

Reinforced joints

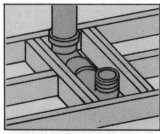

Brace for a closet bend

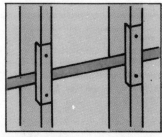

Studs reinforced with steel strips

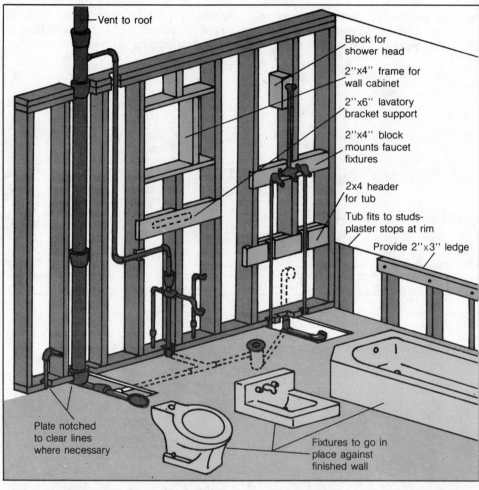

Vent to roof

Block for shower head

2''x4'' frame for wall cabinet

2''x6'' lavatory bracket support

2''x4'' block mounts faucet fixtures

2x4 header for tub

Tub fits to studs- plaster stops at rim

Provide 2''x3'' ledge

Plate notched to clear lines where necessary

Fixtures to go in place against finished wall

In any bathroom or kitchen renovation that involves plumbing, it will be necessary to support pipes and fixtures. In the kitchen, this will generally mean the sink, and as a rule this item will be supported by the countertop. In the bathroom, there are three basic fixtures requiring special supports—the toilet, lavatory, and bathtub.

The lavatory. It could be said that the lavatory is the simplest of the three. Because many lavatories are set in a countertop, special supports are not needed. Some models, however, hang from a crosspiece set into the wall.

To install a crosspiece and brackets for a lavatory, cut a 2x4 crosspiece 3 inches longer than the distance between the studs. Hold the 2x4 across the two studs at the height of the lavatory; each end of the crosspiece should overlap a stud by 1½ inches. Check with a level, and mark the top and bottom of the crosspiece on the studs. Now notch the studs within the marks, and wedge the crosspiece into the stud notches so that the front of the piece is flush with the fronts of both studs. Nail it in place, making sure you maintain your alignment. Finally, close the wall, and screw the bracket to the wallpiece, right through the surface of the wall.

The toilet. As a rule the toilet stands closest to the DWV (drain-waste-vent stack). Its waste pipe curves beneath the toilet at a part called the closet bend. This needs strong support because of the pressure of the water and wastes rushing through. If the toilet waste pipe crosses a joist, you should cut out a short piece of the joist and frame the cut section so that it is supported.

The bathtub. This is the largest of the bathroom fixtures, and strangely, in certain ways it is the easiest to support. Still, it is necessary to cut an access hole in the floor for the tub drain and the overflow pipe, and also to install crosspieces in the wall to support the faucets and shower trim. Should the assembly for the overflow and drain rest on a joist, and you can't move the tub to a new position, then cut the joist and frame that section for support.

Now, with all the supports in place, you can run supply pipes and drainpipes to the fixtures. In running pipe through holes or notches, joists, or top plates, you must be sure to reinforce the cutouts. At the same time, the pitch of a long section of drain-waste pipe running along joists may require running the pipe underneath. Pipes running below joists are not very attractive, but you can hide them with an easily installed dropped ceiling.

It is important to remember that a bathtub will need an easy access to the trap in the event of emergency repairs. When you are finished connecting the fixtures and the wall surfaces are completed, go into the room that adjoins the wall next to the tub, and cut a square between two studs, directly behind the tub and at the level of the floor. Close the opening by screwing in a piece of plywood. This panel can be easily removed when necessary.

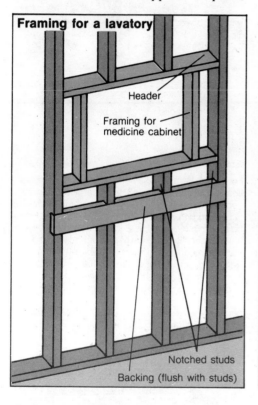

Framing for a lavatory

Header

Framing for medicine cabinet

Notched studs

Backing (flush with studs)

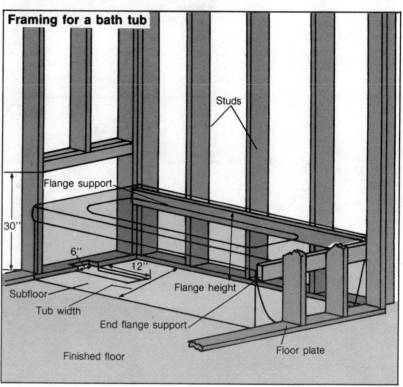

Framing for a bath tub

Studs

Flange support

30"

6"

12"

Subfloor

Tub width

Flange height

End flange support

Finished floor

Floor plate

Rules for notching

- Joists should be notched only in their end quarters; not in the center half. Notch no more than ¼ of depth of the joist.
- Drill the joists to a maximum diameter of ¼ of the joist depth. Then locate along the span, centered if possible, but not any closer than 2 inches to an edge.
- Notches on the studs should be no larger than 2½ inches square. After installing the pipe, nail a steel strap reinforcement over each notch. If the notch is 1¼ inches square it doesn't need to be reinforced.
- For larger cutouts in framing members, it will be necessary to add a 2x4 or heavier bracing nailed on both sides of that particular member.

Wiring

Potential electrical problems—overloaded circuits from too many kitchen appliances working at the same time, or water-soaked surfaces in the bathroom causing shock—are easily solved by improving the existing wiring or installing new lines.

To obtain power for a single use—say, a kitchen fan or a special light fixture over a work area—you can tap from an existing box. Large appliance additions, a garbage disposal or broiler oven for instance, will require their own circuits.

While you may need a professional to connect the circuit at the house service panel, you can do a good deal of the electrical work yourself.

Wiring along foundation sills

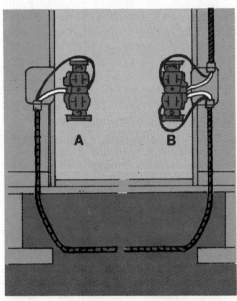

Wiring new wall outlet A from existing outlet B on ground floor is simple. Drill through the floor and then run your wire (armored or sheathed cable) across the basement ceiling. The drilling methods shown here apply to outer wall, but if either outlet is on an interior wall, you can drill straight upward between the walls. Use cable strap every three feet to secure the cable to the basement ceiling or side of joist. Connect the black wire to the brass terminals of the outlet, the white wire to the light color terminals.

For wiring from a basement ceiling light to a first-floor outlet, use armored or sheathed cable in a continuous length. 1. Select the location for the outlet and prepare the opening. 2. If the outlet is to be on an outer wall, use a long-shank bit to bore a hole diagonally (as shown) through the floor from the basement. If the outlet is to be on an interior wall, then bore straight up between the walls. 3. Push a length of fish wire up the hole from the basement; then, with wires attached to it, you can simply pull the wires through to the outlet. 4. Connect the black wire to the brass-color terminals; the white wire to the light-color terminals.

Wiring from the attic

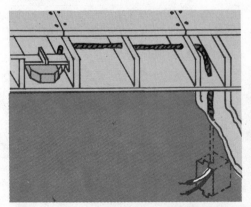

Where the attic is accessible, the attic floor boards can be raised, the joists notched and a hole bored to accept the cable. When you replace the floor boards, be careful not to nail through the cable.

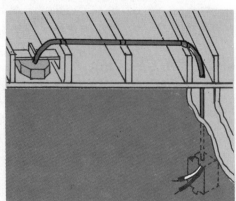

If there is no flooring, then the simple thing is to run cable across the joists and secure it with cable straps. The cable is non-metallic.

Wiring around doors

Running wire around a door frame. First remove the base board and door trim, as shown. Notch the wall and the spacers between the door frame and the jamb. Replace the door trim and baseboard.

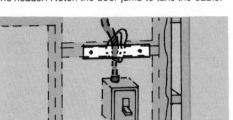

Going around a header. If the switch or outlet is to be next to a door, remove the door stop, drill a hole through the door jamb and frame above and below the header. Notch the door jamb to take the cable.

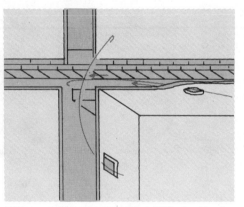

Going past a header. An alternate method is to notch out a piece of plaster, lath and header from top to bottom, as shown. Of course, this means that you will have to patch the plaster.

How to mount a ceiling box from below

1. Cut away plaster to size of a shallow box, and cut away the center lath.

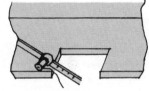

2. After removing locknut, insert hanger and put wire through threaded stud. Hold the stud above the ceiling with one hand; pull the wire with your other hand and the hanger will center.

3. Connect the cable to the box. Pull the wire, from the hanger, through the center knockout and install locknut on the threaded stud.

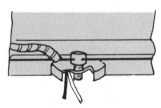

4. And this is how the completed installation will look.

How to fish wires

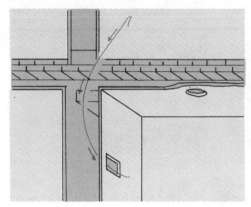

1. After drilling hole, use a fish wire (about 12 feet) with hooks on both ends. Push it through the hole on the second floor, then pull the end out at the switch outlet on the first floor.

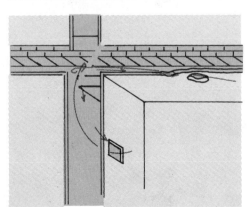

3. When the two fish wires have touched, withdraw either wire (see the arrows) until it is hooked on the other one. Then withdraw the other wire until the hooks are securely together.

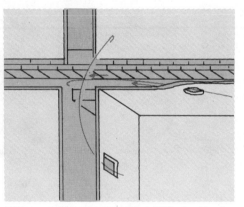

2. Push a second fish wire (20 to 25 feet) with wire hooks on both ends through the ceiling outlet as indicated by the arrows. Continue to fish until you contact the other fish wire.

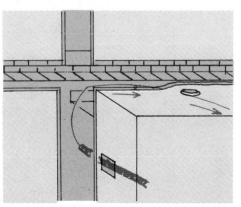

4. Finally, pull the shorter fish wire through the switch outlet until the hook from the other wire appears. To the end of this wire attach a continuous length of cable. Pull it through the wall and the ceiling.

Installing outlet boxes in an existing structure

All switch and outlet boxes should be located between studs at a spot 4 to 5 inches from the stud on either side. Make certain that you place the switches at convenient heights: roughly 48 to 50 inches from the floor. Convenience outlets can be 12 to 18 inches above the floor, or at table height in a kitchen. You should place wall light fixture outlets at about 65 to 70 inches above the floor. Never place a switch on the hinge side of a door, but rather on the opening side.

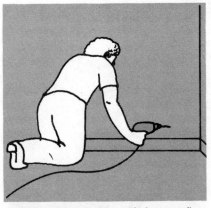

1. If you cannot locate studs by sounding the wall, then drill every 2 inches until you strike solid wood. Drill just above the baseboard so that the holes will not be noticed.

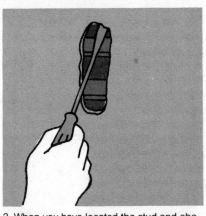

2. When you have located the stud and chosen the right place for the box, notch out plaster. Expose one full lath, but only sections of top and bottom laths.

3. Outline the position for the box with a template and soft pencil.

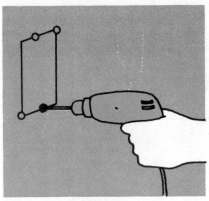

4. After the template has been outlined, drill four holes in the wall (as shown on the template) using a ½-inch bit.

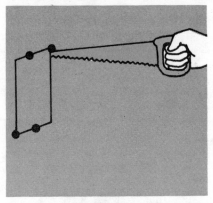

5. The holes provide space for your hacksaw. Draw the blade toward you to avoid loosening plaster. Hold your hand or a board against the plaster to prevent cracking.

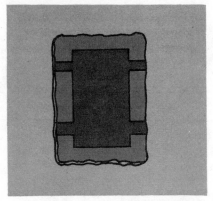

6. When you cut the opening, do not cut away two full laths. You will have a stronger mounting if you cut the center lath completely and half sections from the others.

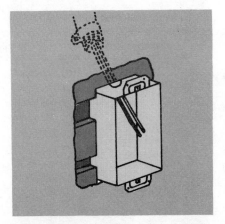

7. Draw the cable out of the hole in the wall, attach the connector less the locknut and pull lead wires through the knockout and into the box. Leave an 8-inch length on the lead wires.

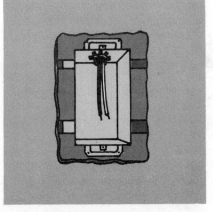

8. Now pull on the lead wires to bring the connector into place. Bear in mind that armored and sheathed cable boxes are available with built-in clamp for easier hook-up.

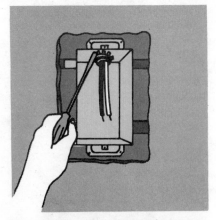

9. Finally, screw the locknut to the connector and tighten. Then anchor the box securely to laths using No. 5 wood screws.

Installing outlet boxes in a new structure

Installation in new work, directly over the bare studs, is certainly a lot easier than cutting electrical openings in old walls. In new work, your goal is to find the most practical route along which to run the wiring which connects various switch boxes and outlets.

Local regulations frequently require that new wiring be done with conduit, rather than armored or sheathed cable. The reason for this is that conduit is sturdy and makes future rewiring easier—wires can simply be pulled out of the conduit and larger load-bearing wires installed.

A conduit run is put in place before the new house or addition is finished. After the walls have been plastered, wires are run through and connected.

Handling conduit. It is important that you bend conduit gradually. Sharp bends will make it difficult, if not impossible, to insert wiring, and may potentially damage wire insulation. Be careful when running wiring from one outlet to the next

that you don't have more than four quarter bends in the conduit.

Conduit running vertically should be clamped or strapped every 6-8 feet. Horizontal conduit should be laid into notched studs or run across the subflooring.

When running wires through the conduit, make sure the wires used conform to the color code: in a two-wire circuit, one black, one white; in a three-wire circuit, one black, one white, and one red. Use the same wire from outlet to outlet; don't splice. Junction boxes must be placed where they are accessible at all times.

In a short run with few bends, you can probably push wire through a conduit. In a longer run, you will have to use fish tape, available in 50 and 100 foot lengths. If you are having trouble getting the tape past a bend, use soapstone or talcum powder as a lubricant.

Tip: Be sure to check your local electrical code before installing any wiring in your home. Regulations vary from region to region.

TIP: Take care that you punch only the knockouts you intend to run wire through so that the box will not have an unused hole at any time. Open holes in boxes are a fire hazard and should always be plugged with knockout filler.

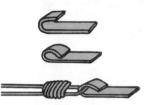

Fish tape hooks are made by heating the end of the tape over a flame and bending it with pliers.

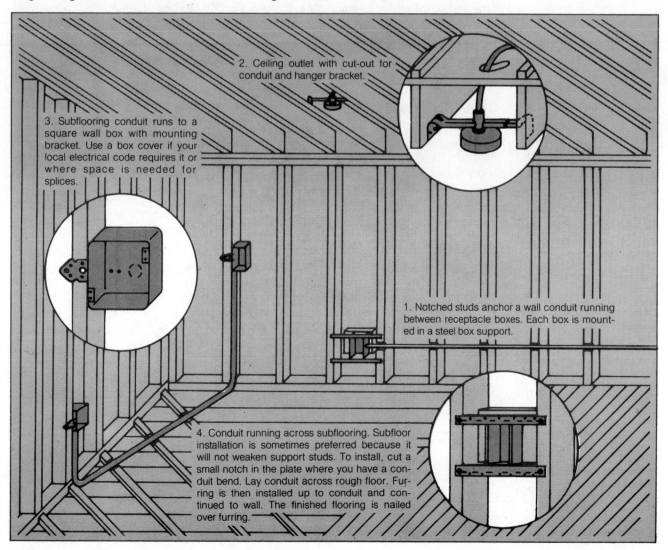

2. Ceiling outlet with cut-out for conduit and hanger bracket.

3. Subflooring conduit runs to a square wall box with mounting bracket. Use a box cover if your local electrical code requires it or where space is needed for splices.

1. Notched studs anchor a wall conduit running between receptacle boxes. Each box is mounted in a steel box support.

4. Conduit running across subflooring. Subfloor installation is sometimes preferred because it will not weaken support studs. To install, cut a small notch in the plate where you have a conduit bend. Lay conduit across rough floor. Furring is then installed up to conduit and continued to wall. The finished flooring is nailed over furring.

WALLS & FLOORS

You might decide that part of your kitchen or bath renovation will be to replace one or more of the walls. If the existing wall is solid, it can be used as the base support for new gypsum board, plastic laminate, plywood, or a combination hardboard of some type.

If the old wall is not sturdy enough to build on, it will have to be removed (see "Removing Ceilings and Walls," page 176). Furring over the bared wall studs provides an excellent base for new walls.

Durability, water and fire resistance, and easy maintenance are important considerations when choosing wall material for these high traffic areas.

Sturdy wall paneling, suitable for use in a kitchen or bath, is available in a wide range of materials, surfaces and prices.

A few of the more popular choices:

Gypsum wallboard, also known as plaster board or Sheetrock (a brand name), is flame-proof and highly resistant to cracking and shrinkage by humidity or extreme temperatures. The board is made of a gypsum core covered with a smooth glazed surface paper suitable for any decorative treatment. It is also available with a prefinished vinyl surface, or can be papered with a vinyl wall covering. Gypsum board can also be used as the backing for plastic laminate. For a kitchen or bath select waterproof gypsum board.

Plastic laminate. Probably the most rugged of wall surfaces, plastic laminate is available in a wide range of textures and patterns. Because sheets of laminate are quite heavy, the 1/32″ thickness is preferred for use on walls, when backed with gypsum, plywood, or hardboard. Plastic laminate prebonded to plywood might be a practical alternative.

Prefinished hardboard. Plasticized or vinyl coated hardboard is tough, moisture proof, and available in many colors. Hardboard, like gypsum board, comes in standard 4x8-foot sheets, though longer lengths can be ordered.

Installing wallboard

Preparing old walls

If you are willing to screw or nail your new wall material to the old wall or to build wall framing first, you need not knock out the old wall even if it needs some repair. When using adhesive alone to put up new paneling, be sure that the subwall is sound. In either case, the existing wall will need some preparation.

Remove all trim and loose or poorly bonded plaster. Repair any holes (see pg. 101). Extend electrical outlet boxes to make them flush with the new wall. In general, make sure that the subwall is clean, smooth and solid.

Planning for the new

Careful planning will save you time, money, and probably give you a better looking result. Figure out how much wallboard you will need, where you want the joints to be, and for economy try to use the longest practical lengths obtainable.

Cutting wallboard

It was like living under London Bridge
I thought I'd give my battered plaster walls a face lift, so I used the best wall adhesive money could buy to put up new gypsum wallboard. What I didn't realize was that adhesive is only as good as the wall to which it's applied. If the plaster works loose, so will the adhesive and mounted wallboard. Next time I'll remember that screws or nails are the only sure way to keep a board mounted on an old wall. Nail or screw along a panel edge at intervals of 6 or 7 inches for the best result.

Practical Pete

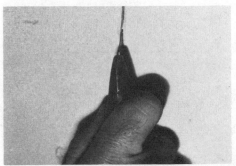

1. Using a utility knife, first score the face paper along your measured line.

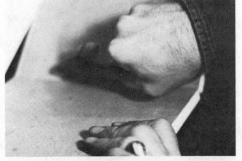

2. Snap through the gypsum core, but do not tear the face paper on the reverse side. Cut the reverse face paper with a sharp knife.

3. Use a power saw with guide for a mitered cut or one where perfect fit is essential.

4. Use a rasp to smooth rough edges, being careful not to tear the face paper.

Curved walls and archways

Gypsum can be shaped around a gentle curve with a little special handling. You may wish to use a slightly thinner board for curved surfaces than you would use on a flat wall.

First, measure the area to be covered, and cut the wallboard to size. Then score or cut through the back paper at intervals to increase its flexibility. Moistening the board will also ease the curving process. Secure one end of the board to the wall and gently bend it into the curve. Nail at closer intervals than you would on a flat wall. When completed, spread a little joint compound around the curve to guard against cracking.

When taping the edges of archway wallboard, cut notches in both sides of the tape at intervals where it will have to ease around the curve. You will probably need two or three coats of joint compound to cover this area.

Finishing wallboard seams

When wallboard installation is completed, you must finish off the seams. For joints you will want to use joint compound and drywall patching tape.

Patching tape for wallboard is available in paper, perforated paper and mesh. Paper tape is standard. It has a ridge that's easy to fold for taping inside corners. Perforated tape has holes in it to permit the compound to seep through, which is good for spreading, but it can form ridges where the holes are as it dries. Mesh tape is used where wallboard joints are particularly prone to expansion and contraction, or when joining old wallboard to new. It is also the best material for bonding a crack that keeps coming back after repair.

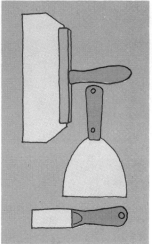

Taping knives are used to smooth the plaster compounds. They are flexible metal knives available in ½-inch to 12-inch widths. For cracks and small holes, a 2-inch putty knife is suitable. Larger areas require wider blades so the compounds can be blended with the surface of the wall.

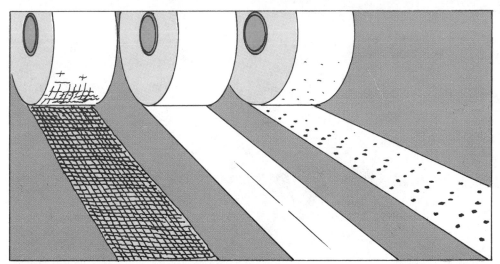

Drywall patching tape will form a permanent bond to seal patches or the seams between wallboard sections. It is 2 inches wide and is available in plastic mesh, paper, or perforated paper. The mesh is best for joining old and new wallboard or where a wallboard joint may expand or contract; for instance, where the edge of a sloping ceiling meets a dormer. Paper patching tape has a ridge in the middle that makes it easy to fold for joining inside corners. Perforated patching tape has holes in it that allow the wallboard compound to seep through.

Taping wallboard seams

1. To fill gaps between adjoining sheets of gypsum wallboard, force joint compound into the seam with a 5-inch taping knife. If the seam is very narrow, you can use spackle

2. Press mesh tape into the wet compound and run the blade of the taping knife along the mesh to squeeze the compound through. Feather the edges to blend with the wallboard. Let it dry overnight, then apply another thin layer of compound. Sand it smooth when it has dried about 24 hours.

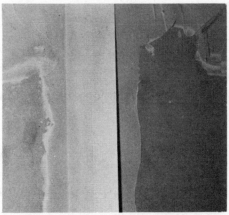

3. Apply paper tape in the same manner. Press it into the wet compound and run the blade over it in one long continuous stroke. When you put on the final coat of compound, use just enough to cover the tape. Feather smoothly outward using a 10-inch taping knife.

4. For inside corners, fold paper patching tape at the ridge that runs down the center of it to seal the gap where two sheets of wallboard make an inside corner. Apply the joint compound and feather it out from the corner as previously described. Sand when it dries.

Metal corner bead

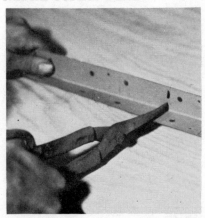

1. Use metal shears to cut a length of metal corner bead. It's easier to smooth the edge if it's cut at an angle. If the bead will turn a corner, as in a door jamb, cut out a small triangular piece from both sides, leaving the middle ridge intact.

2. Bend the corner bead to fit tightly around the corner. Attach it to the wall with screw-type, plasterboard ring nails driven into the wood of a door jamb or into the studs beneath the wallboard where two walls join.

3. Use a 5-inch tape knife to spread a generous coat of joint compound on the bead, smoothing it as even as you can to make sanding easier later. But don't fuss with it. Let it dry for 24 hours. Apply a second coat, feather the edges, and let it dry completely (about 24 hours) before sanding.

Wallboard computation chart. Computation for square footage of wallboard required in a room with an 8′ ceiling. (For net footage, deduct wall openings.)

	2′	3′	4′	5′	6′	7′	8′	9′	10′	11′	12′	13′	14′	15′
2′	68	86	104	122	140	158	176	194	212	230	248	266	284	302
3′	86	105	124	143	162	181	200	219	238	257	276	295	314	333
4′	104	124	144	164	184	204	224	244	264	284	304	324	344	364
5′	122	143	164	185	206	227	248	269	290	311	332	353	374	395
6′	140	162	184	206	228	250	272	294	316	338	360	382	404	426
7′	158	181	204	227	250	273	296	319	342	365	388	411	434	457
8′	176	200	224	248	272	296	320	344	368	392	416	440	464	488
9′	194	219	244	269	294	319	344	369	394	419	444	469	494	519
10′	212	238	264	290	316	342	368	394	420	446	472	498	524	550
11′	230	257	284	311	338	365	392	419	446	473	500	527	554	581
12′	248	276	304	332	360	388	416	444	472	500	528	556	584	612
13′	266	295	324	353	382	411	440	469	498	527	556	585	614	643
14′	284	314	344	374	404	434	464	494	524	554	584	614	644	674
15′	302	333	364	395	426	457	488	519	550	581	612	643	674	705

Applying plastic laminate

Plastic laminate is applied directly to gypsum or other unfinished wallboard material with wall adhesive.

Bonded laminate hardboard does not require a wallboard base, but should not be applied directly to a plaster wall. Furring strips nailed to the wall studs will support hardboard glued to it with wall adhesive. Obviously you want as few nail holes as possible in a plastic laminate finish, but it is best to lightly nail the top of each sheet to the framing at ceiling level. Most manufacturers sell color coordinated finishing nails for this use.

The tough part of plastic laminate installation is not putting it up but cutting it out. Great care must be taken when measuring, and cuts should be carefully executed with a saber saw. Edges should then be smoothed with a router, laminate cutter or file, depending on the length and accessibility of the cut.

Plastic laminate molding

Plastic laminate is mounted in metal molding strips. On a plaster or wallboard surface, they are nailed to the wall. For use over tile, they are glued with a wall adhesive.

There are two basic types of panel molding: one-piece and two-piece. One-piece molding is installed as the paneling progresses, a strip at a time. Two-piece molding has a base strip which can be installed before any of the paneling goes up. The paneling is fitted into the base strip and glued to the wall. A decorative molding strip, which snaps into the base molding, is then laid on the outside. As with one-piece molding, there are several styles of two-piece molding. **Division molding** goes between panels and has a double flange. **Edge molding** is used to define the outside edge of a partially paneled wall and can also be used as cap molding for a wainscot installation (where the paneling only extends part way up the wall). **Inside** and **outside corner molding** join two paneled walls.

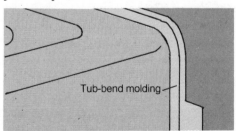
Tub-bend molding

When cutting paneling for installation in molding, remember to cut each dimension about ⅛-inch short, to allow for expansion due to climate changes. Never force paneling into a molding. It should extend into the molding flange only about half way. If the fit is a bit tight, you can bevel the back of the panel to ease it, but never nail panel edges.

Where edge and ceiling molding meet, both pieces should be mitered for a per-

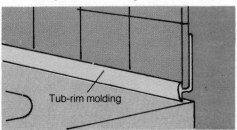
Tub-rim molding

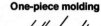
One-piece molding

Outside corner molding

Inside corner molding

Edge molding

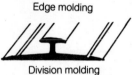
Division molding

Two-piece molding

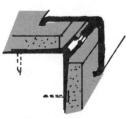
Two-piece corner molding (inside)

Two-piece corner molding (outside)

Decorative strip

fect fit. To mount plastic laminate panels, use some cardboard shims about 1/16 inch thick along the floor. If you are using two-piece molding, your base molding is already installed. Using panel adhesive on the wall, the panel, and in the flange of the molding, attach paneling as soon as the adhesive has reached the tackiness recommended by the manufacturer. Go

over the entire surface with a hammer and wood block to make sure that the bonding is complete. When the installation is finished, remove the shims and attach a vinyl edge or cove molding along the base of the wall.

Start at a corner when installing panels with a one-piece molding. Cut and fit panels and molding strips as you go.

Cutouts and special fittings

In a bathroom or kitchen area particularly, there are a number of fixtures, appliances and outlets to work around. All panel fittings should be cut before the panel is installed. Make a template on a piece of heavy paper taped over that part of the wall where a cutout is needed. Then transfer the cutout lines to the face of the panel and cut them with a saber saw.

Electrical and plumbing control open-

ings won't need further finishing. A face plate will do the trick. But tub and counter openings will need an edge molding. Molding strips specially fitted for curving tub edges are available, and their installation is the same as for wall molding. Before attaching molding around a tub or sink area, be sure to caulk all around the rim for a watertight seal. Do the same before attaching faucet and spout fittings.

About panel adhesives

Panel adhesive comes in bulk form or in cartridges to be used with a caulking gun. Many laminate manufacturers carry their own brand of panel adhesive, though it is certainly not necessary to restrict yourself to one adhesive.

There are two types of adhesive generally used with laminate paneling. The first is contact cement, particularly suited for bonding laminates to plywood. Contact cement bonds instantly, so care must be taken in positioning the panels before the glued surfaces touch.

The preferred panel adhesive is epoxy. Epoxy is a two-part adhesive, one a resin and one a hardener, which must be mixed

in equal parts—so measure carefully.

Since both of these adhesives are petroleum based, they are extremely water resistant, but for complete moisture protection a sealer should be used around all panel edges.

Their petroleum base also makes contact and epoxy adhesives highly flammable. Be sure that the room in which you are working is well ventilated and sustains a temperature of about 75°. Take a break every couple of hours when working and don't smoke in the area. Also avoid alcoholic beverages while working, as the combination of alcohol and adhesive fumes is toxic.

Patching plaster

Cracks, gouges, and holes in solid plaster or plaster-filled wallboard are easy to fill and smooth with one of the following compounds. These are applied with a putty knife or broad-bladed taping knife. Inside joints are reinforced with tape made of paper, plastic mesh, or metal; outside corners with metal corner bead.

Mixing tips. If you plan to be taping seams, attaching corner bead, or smoothing large areas with joint compound, you can make a terrific holder with scrap lumber.

Make a handle about 8 inches long that you can grip firmly. Nail one end into the middle of a piece of scrap lumber about 18 inches square. Carry a supply of compound on it and use the edge of the board to scrape excess compound off the taping knife.

Compounds for patching plaster

Spackling Compound

Form: Premixed in cans: easy to work with, lasts indefinitely. Powder: less expensive. Mix it with water.
Use: Filling small cracks (⅛" max.), shallow holes, and bulges in solid plaster.
Application: Putty knife. Thin layer.
Handling: Scoop small amount out of can and mix only what you can use in 5 minutes. Doesn't shrink when applied thinly. Be sure to reseal can.

Patching Plaster

Form: Dry powder to mix with water.
Use: Filling large holes or cracks. Contains fibers for strong bond.
Application: Broad-bladed putty knife or taping knife. Difficult to apply smoothly. Let dry overnight before sanding.
Handling: Mix small quantities. Starts setting immediately. Doesn't shrink even in wide cracks or holes.

Filling a crack

The most common problem with plaster walls is the inevitable crack that forms from age or climate, or from the house settling. Small cracks can be filled with spackling compound; cracks that run the length of a wall should be filled with joint compound. If you have a crack that will not fill or that keeps coming back, apply a length of mesh patching tape with the joint compound.

What it takes

Approximate time: Half an hour or more, depending on how much patching you have, plus drying time. Sanding is a few minutes.

Tools and materials: Putty knife for small cracks or 10″ taping knife for long ones, joint compound, sandpaper or, for large areas, an electric sander, goggles, and dust mask.

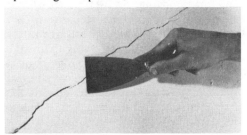

1. Scrape loose plaster from the surface of the wall with a putty knife. Don't dig into the crack—it only makes it worse.

2. A 10-inch taping knife is the best tool to use to spread a thin layer of joint compound over the crack. Run the knife straight along the line in a continuous sweep.

3. To "feather" the edge of the compound so it blends with the wall surface, place the blade parallel to the line of compound and gently pull the knife towards the edge. Let compound dry 24 hours.

4. You can sand small areas with a piece of medium sandpaper wrapped around a small block of wood. For large areas or particularly rough walls, use an electric sander and wear goggles and a dust mask.

Patching a hole

What it takes

Approximate time: A few minutes.

Tools and materials: Brush or sponge, putty knife or tape knife, patching plaster, scrap piece of wallboard or plywood.

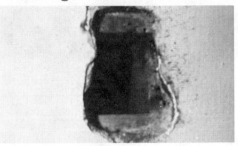

1. Holes in wallboard that are too large to fill easily with patching plaster must first be patched. The hole left after removing an electrical switch or outlet is a common example. Scrape away loose plaster and dampen the surrounding area with a brush or sponge.

2. When wood studs are visible, break off a piece of scrap wallboard small enough to fit in the hole but large enough to bridge the studs. Cement it to the studs with patching plaster.

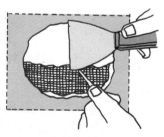

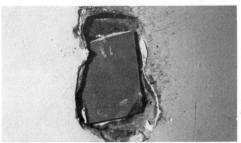

3. The patch fills the hole and gives support to the patching plaster. Starting from the bottom, use a putty knife to fill the remaining space with patching plaster.

4. Fill the rest of the hole with plaster. Let it dry for 24 hours before sanding it smooth.

Alternative method
When there are no studs behind a large hole, cut a piece of stiff wire mesh an inch or so bigger than the hole. Thread a string through the center. Smear a thin layer of plaster around the edge. Bend it just slightly to fit it through the hole and pull it tight. It should be larger than the hole. Hold the string tight while you fill the hole with plaster. Then cut the string off flush after the plaster has dried.

Replacing ceramic tiles

What it takes

Approximate time: A couple of hours to remove tiles in a fairly small area; a full day plus drying time to lay new tile.

Tools and materials: Hammer, chisel, straight bar or crowbar, notched trowel, tile cutter, tile nippers, rubber-surfaced trowel, sponge; tiles, wall-tile mastic, grout.

Ceramic tile is a popular surface in bathrooms—it's durable, water resistant, and attractive. See page 104 on laying a tile floor; the same techniques will apply to tiling walls.

Tiles surrounding a bathtub and shower get a lot of abuse from water. When the grout gets old and begins to chip away, water can seep behind the tiles. If the tiles are not re-grouted, they loosen from the adhesive beneath. Where grout is beyond repair, it's best to replace the tiles.

Choosing new ceramic tiles can be fun. And don't forget that a variety of accessories are available to set in with the tiles.

Before you begin, protect the bathtub with a sheet of plastic so tile chips don't scratch the surface.

After removing the tiles, the first—and perhaps most important—step is to square off the area to be tiled. Walls are rarely perfectly rectilinear, and trying to line the tiles up by eye is a mistake. To mark off a squared area, start at the lowest point of the bathtub line. On the wall, measure the height of one full tile and mark. Use a level to make a horizontal mark with a straightedge or chalk line. Mark perpendicular lines on either side of the wall to site the placements of the first and last full tiles. To tile, start the work from either vertical line.

1. When ceramic tiles surrounding the tub are beyond repair, loose tiles bulge from the wall, chunks of grout have fallen out, and some tiles may be cracked.

2. Use a straight bar or chisel to loosen the top tile. Strike it gently with a hammer—the tile should come free readily.

3. Continue working down, loosening the tiles with a bar or chisel. Around fixtures, work extra carefully to avoid damage.

4. Beneath the tiles you'll find an uneven surface of old adhesive. Thoroughly remove the old adhesive, and sand the surface with a belt sander. Make sure the whole wall is clean.

5. Spread wall-tile mastic adhesive with a notched trowel, as evenly as possible. Press the tiles in place—do not slide them or you will push adhesive up into the joints. Allow 24 hours for mastic to dry before grouting.

6. A rubber-surface trowel is the best tool to use to apply grout, but you can apply the mixture with a putty knife and sponge.

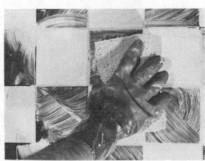

7. Once all the gaps between tiles are filled, wipe the surface clean with a dampened sponge. Let it dry for at least 24 hours.

8. Ceramic tiles in a checkerboard pattern cover two walls of this bathroom. What an improvement!

Those necessary accessories

A bathroom without certain accessories—soap dish, towel bars, toilet-tissue holder—is not complete. These accessories are available in three types: flush-set, surface-mounted, and recessed.

Flush-set accessories are mounted on the wall rather like tile or paneling. They are put on at the time the wall covering is applied.

Surface-mounted accessories can be installed at any time over the wall covering. Some are glued on, but screws and mounting clips give better results. The way you fasten the accessory to the wall will depend upon whether the accessory is ceramic or metal.

Recessed accessories, which are installed either when the wall covering is applied or at the time of framing, are fitted into holes in the wall or directly into wood blocking in the framing. They are usually made to fit snugly between studs.

In addition to the essentials mentioned above, there are optional accessories available for the bath. For instance, grab bars (vertical or L-shaped) are handy. They are affixed on top of the wall covering and must be solidly mounted. Do not use plastic anchors to hold the mounting screws. Screw a grab bar directly into wood blocking which is placed behind the wall when the framing is done.

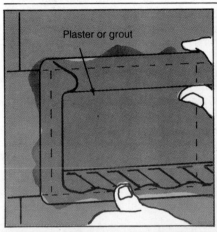

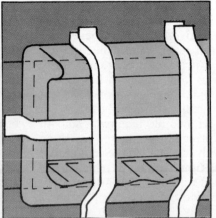

Flush-set. Mix water and plaster of paris in a bowl slowly, stirring well and continuously. The material must hold its shape but not be hard. Trowel about ¼ inch of the mixture on the back of the accessory, keeping it thinner at the edges. Set the accessory against the wall, moving it slightly to work the plaster of paris into any irregularities. Wipe off any excess. Hold in place a few minutes until the plaster of paris grips. An alternate method is to use a coating of grout consisting of white Portland cement and water. Secure the accessory with masking tape until it sets firmly.

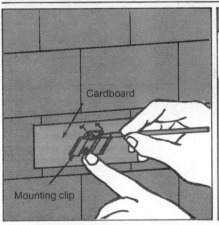

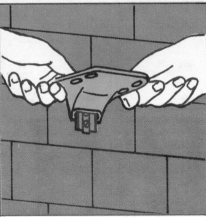

Surface-mount. First position the accessory so that its screw holes are as close as possible to the center of the tile. Using rubber cement, place a piece of thin cardboard on that tile. Hold the mounting clip against the card, and mark the screw holes. With a carbide-tip bit, drill at low speed using light pressure so as not to break the tile. Remove the cardboard. For a ceramic accessory, screw the metal mounting clip into the plastic wall anchors. Slip the accessory down over the clip until it is snug against the wall. Grout the joint between the wall and the accessory. A metal accessory is similarly installed, except that it is not grouted. A set-screw on the bottom is tightened to hold it to the clip.

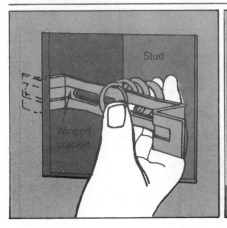

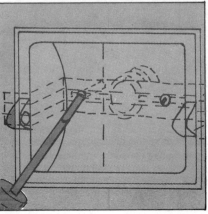

Recessed. If you planned to install a recessed accessory before the wall was surfaced, screw it right into the wood blocking at the time of framing. If you are installing it after the wall has been surfaced, cut an opening, and use a winged bracket to secure the bracket behind the wall. Mount the accessory by running a bead of caulking compound around the back of its front flange. Carefully insert it into the opening, then place and tighten the screws.

New floors

There is no question that the kitchen and bathroom floors receive the major punishment in a home. And so your choice of floor covering is an important decision when you renovate. There is a number of flooring materials to choose from: resilient sheet or tile, ceramic tile, and carpeting are the most popular. Other possibilities include wood, marble, poured, and painted floors.

Bear in mind that rarely will one floor finish have every quality that you desire. For instance, wood floors, though beautiful, need to be refinished, comfortable carpeting needs to be cleaned, and practical vinyl tile can loosen or get scratched.

Ceramic tile

Cutting tiles

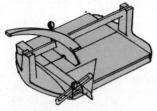

A tile cutter can be rented.

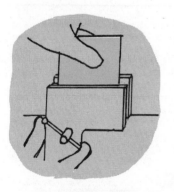

To do it without the cutter, score the tile with a glass cutter. Clamp the tile in a vise along the score line, and snap off. Another way is to lay the scored tile over a nail or piece of metal and press down on both sides.

For the bathroom, one of the most popular as well as durable floors is ceramic tile. It is not difficult to install, and it is certainly attractive. When properly put down, it will resist water. The tiles are generally square or hexagonal. They come in sizes from 1 to 12 inches square, and in a wide range of colors. A great variety of trim tile is also available.

Laying ceramic tile requires a smooth surface, a planned pattern, and attaching the tiles with adhesive. Make certain that the floor is firm, flat, and level. Remember that you will have to adjust the door to accommodate the thickness of the tiles.

Tile adhesives include epoxies, latex-mortar and epoxy-mortar combinations, organic adhesives, and cement-based mortars. The organic adhesives are relatively inexpensive and are easier to apply than the epoxies because no mixing is required.

When you buy adhesives make sure the product meets your needs—setting time, bonding ability, and water resistance.

As a rule, floor adhesives harden more quickly than wall adhesives. While you can spread adhesive over a fairly large area of wall before you set tile, it is better on a floor to work in small areas.

The floor plan

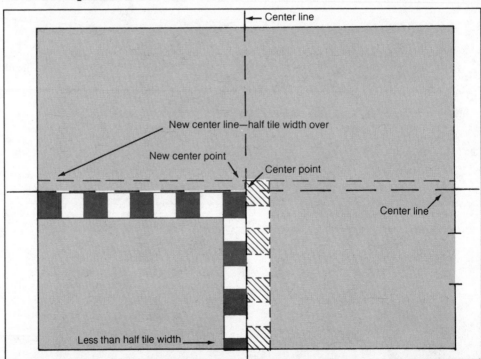

Center line

New center line—half tile width over

New center point

Center point

Center line

Less than half tile width

Plan the pattern well. First, lay a row of dry tile from the middle of a doorway to the opposite wall. The row will be guided by a string nailed from the doorway to the wall. Should there be a gap of less than half a tile width at the end of the run, take away the first tile and center those that are left. The spaces left for the two border tiles will equal more than half the width of a tile, which makes for a better-looking floor, and also avoids difficult cuts on very small pieces.

How to set separate tiles

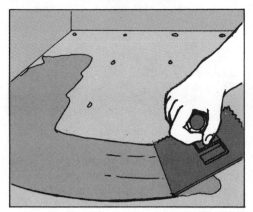

1. Spread the adhesive, using the kind that is right for your particular surface. Spread this as thinly as you can with the side of the trowel that does not have the notches. Allow the coat to dry thoroughly.

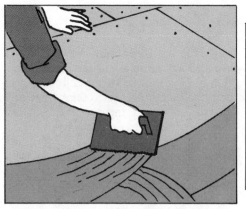

2. Spread adhesive with the notched edge of the trowel, over about 10 square feet. Hold the edge of the trowel against the surface at a 45° angle. In order that the adhesive will flow freely from the notches, use only about a cup of adhesive each time. Do not cover any lines that you have drawn on the floor for alignment or reference.

3. Set tiles by starting at reference lines near the middle of the room, and work toward the walls. Press each tile into place, carefully yet firmly, twisting it slightly with your fingertips to set it well into the adhesive. Be careful not to slide the tiles into place or the adhesive will fill up the joints, and you won't be able to grout. In the event that you are setting thick tiles that have indentations on the backs, also put adhesive on the back of each tile.

4. To "beat in" the tile, take a scrap of 2x4 about the length of three tiles, and pad it with several layers of cloth. With the padded side down, place it on the tiles that are set and tap gently with a hammer, going up and down its length several times. This beating will set the tiles more firmly into the adhesive and will help to achieve a level floor. When the adhesive has hardened for 24 hours, the floor can be grouted. If you must walk on the newly-laid tile, cover it with plywood sheets.

If you add, then you've got to subtract
I forgot that adding tile to my bathroom floor would mean I'd have to adjust the door so it could close. Remember that even a hair's thickness can make all the difference between an open-or-shut door!

Practical Pete

Grouting

The next step is to fill the spaces between the tiles with grout. This is a mortar, available in many colors, that seals out water and dirt. Since ceramic tiles have many different uses, it is best to consult your dealer to make sure you get the grout best suited to your project. For instance, the tiles used in the sunken bathtub on page 166 require a silicone grout. In other cases, such as the mosaic tiles (page 106), you can mix your own.

Mix mortar-type grout to the consistency that has been recommended by the manufacturer. This type of grout needs to dry slowly so that it can cure properly. At the same time, some floor tiles absorb water from the grout to the point where they hinder proper curing. And so, before grouting, put a drop of water on the back of a tile. If the tile absorbs it right away, then use more water in the grout.

In order to make floor grout joints flush with tile surfaces fill the joints with grout that has in it a water-retaining aggregate. Sprinkle dry grout of the same kind over the grout joints and rub the joints with a piece of burlap. Rub in a circular motion for the best effect.

After you have tiled the floor, cover it with polyethylene sheeting. If there is no sign of condensation under the sheeting the following day, remove it, sprinkle water on the floor and put back the sheeting. Allow the grout to cure for three days. In 10 days seal the grout joints. This sealer will protect the grout from dirt or mildew.

Mosaic floor tiles

What it takes

Approximate time: About half a day for a standard 5'x8' bathroom, plus underlayment and drying.

Tools and materials: ½-inch exterior grade plywood, saw, hammer, and nails if underlayment is required. Tape measure, 1-foot square sheets of mosaic tiles, mastic, spreader, grout, mixing bowl, squeegee, rolling pin, sponge.

Mosaic floor tiles are popular and easy to install. They come in 1x1-foot, or 1x2-foot sheets. Some have a paper backing to hold the sheets together; others have protective paper covering the top, and this must be peeled off after installation.

As with any new covering, the floor underneath must be leveled, all cracks must be filled, and if it's a rough hardwood floor, it should be sanded. If your floor is badly warped, you can put down a plywood or hardboard underlayment.

Mark off the floor area as you would for standard tiles. Apply adhesive with a notched trowel. Cover a 3-foot square area at a time. Place the sheets of mosaic tile lightly on the adhesive. Then slide each into its correct position, and press firmly in place.

Make certain that the spaces between the sheets are the same as the spaces between single tiles.

When the main part of the floor is done, you'll have to fit narrow pieces of tile around the edges. Cut carefully, following the pattern. Use tile nippers for cutting and shaping.

For this tile you may mix grout yourself. Mix 3 parts Portland cement with 1 part water. Continue to add water until you have a creamy consistency. Spread the grout over the tile with a rubber-surfaced trowel. Force it into the cracks. The grout should be allowed to dry for at least 12 hours before you walk on the floor.

Wipe excess grout from the floor immediately, using a damp sponge. When the floor has dried thoroughly, the cement will leave a film. This should be removed with a mixture of 1 part muriatic acid to 10 parts water. Apply with a rag, wipe thoroughly, and finally, dry with a clean rag. When working with this solution you should wear rubber gloves.

1. If the floor is at all uneven, cover it with an "underlayment" of ½-inch exterior grade plywood or heavy hardboard. Leave a ⅛-inch crack where the edges butt so the underlayment will not buckle if the wood becomes moist and swells. Offset the panels so the four corners don't meet.

2. The adhesive for ceramic tiles, called mastic, is highly flammable. Leave the windows open until it hardens. Spread it evenly with a trowel that has a serrated edge with teeth about ⅛ inch apart. Cover an area large enough to lay three 1-foot square sheets of tiles.

3. Small (½ to 1-inch square) mosaic tiles are usually sold in 1-foot square sheets. The tiles are perfectly aligned and held in place either with their bottoms glued onto a square of paper mesh or with a sheet of paper glued to their tops. Lay the squares the same distance apart as the divisions between the individual tiles on them.

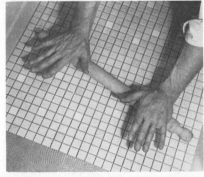

4. Imbed the tiles in the mastic, pressing them down evenly with a length of 2x4 or a kitchen rolling pin. If the tops of the tiles are attached to a sheet of paper, soak it in warm water after the mastic has dried (about 24 hours) and peel the paper off.

5. Fill the spaces between the tiles with a waterproof plaster-like material called grout. Grey is better than white for floor tiles because it won't show the dirt as much. Spread it with a squeegee, completely filling all the cracks.

6. Wipe the grout off the face of the tiles with a damp sponge before the grout dries. Wet the sponge slightly and wipe again to smooth and remove any excess grout between the tiles. Polish the faces of the tiles with a dry cloth.

Carpet in the bathroom

It's warmer in the winter, it's softer if you drop something, and it is quieter than ceramic tile. Use washable carpeting with a non-slip back, loose-laid so it can be taken up easily for cleaning. Kitchen carpeting can be used in the bathroom, too. Indoor-outdoor carpeting is durable, although it tends to hold water. You can often pick up inexpensive carpeting at overrun outlets and remnant sales stores.

What it takes

Approximate time: One hour

Tools and materials: Washable, non-skid carpeting, heavy kraft wrapping paper to make a full-size pattern, tape measure or ruler, scissors, single-edge razor blade, masking tape, marking pen.

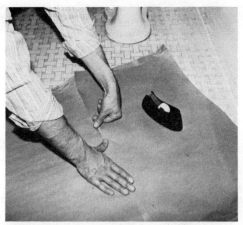

1. Make a full-size pattern of the floor with heavy wrapping paper. Overlap the seams about ½ inch and tape them together.

2. To cut around a protruding fixture such as a toilet bowl, measure and cut a slit in the pattern from the wall to the front edge of the bowl and another slit the width of the bowl.

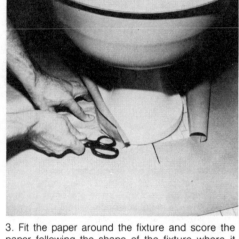

3. Fit the paper around the fixture and score the paper following the shape of the fixture where it meets the floor.

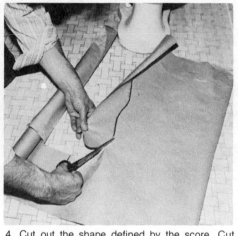

4. Cut out the shape defined by the score. Cut score and trim if necessary after refitting the paper pattern.

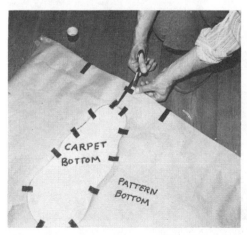

5. Place the *bottom* of the pattern on top of the *bottom* of the carpet, tape them together, and cut around the pattern with scissors.

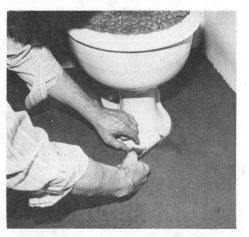

6. Trim the carpet for exact fit. Long-pile carpeting is more forgiving because the pile will hide small cutting errors.

Covering an old floor

To make sure you will have a solid tile floor, install a hardboard underlayment.
- Never butt sheets of underlayment flush together. Leave roughly ⅛" between them for expansion.
- Stagger seams to avoid having four corners meeting together at one point.
- Use annular-ring nails or cement-coated nails to fasten.

INSTALLING PLUMBING & ELECTRICAL FIXTURES

Toilets

What it takes

Approximate time: A half hour but it is wise to allow yourself a little extra time.

Tools and materials: Wrench, screwdriver, hacksaw, putty knife/trowel, folding ruler; Teflon tape, plumber's putty, plaster of paris; fixtures.

Installing most bathroom fixtures—tubs, toilets, and sinks—is a simple reversal of the procedures used when removing old fixtures. Any pipe connections will require only the tightening of slip nuts. But be careful not to over-tighten nuts or you can damage the parts. Hand tighten first, then snug the nut with a wrench. The main thing to keep in mind is that even the sturdiest porcelain fixture will break under undue pressure or if it's dropped. Notice particularly the careful handling of the toilet bowl in the installation photographs here.

When you want a watertight seal, use plumber's putty; apply joint tape or pipe-joint compound to threaded connections, plastic as well as metal. You can check your work by turning on the water to see if there are any leaks.

Connecting a toilet

1. If there isn't a shutoff valve at the location, you'll have to install one. Cut the supply pipe 2 inches away from the wall. Wrap the end of the pipe with Teflon tape or use a little pipe compound.

2. Slide an escutcheon over the pipe and press it against the wall opening. Then slide the coupling nut and compression ring over the pipe. Slip on the valve, with its outlet hole up, and tighten the nut.

3. Remove the burlap or paper (which prevented dirt entering the pipe) from the soil opening and slip flange bolts into their slots (see page 26). (In most cases these will be replacement bolts, since the originals may have been cut when removing the old bowl.) If using a felt gasket, slip it on over the bolts.

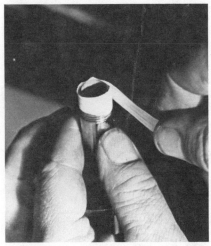

4. If using a wax floor gasket, turn the bowl upside down and press the gasket down over the horn around the waste horn.

5. Lower the bowl onto the flange so that the two flange bolts protrude through the rim holes. If using a wax gasket, press down and twist firmly on the bowl to seal it.

6. Make sure the bowl is level. Use copper or brass washers to shim, if necessary. But don't raise the bowl enough to break the gasket seal.

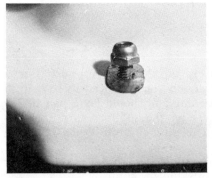

7. Snug a washer and nut over each flange bolt just enough to hold the bowl in place. Don't overtighten. Cover the bolt ends with plastic or porcelain caps.

8. To install a bowl-mounted tank, first check to make sure that the spud lock nut is secure. Again, don't overtighten. If it seems secure, leave it alone.

9. Place the tank cushion over the spud lock nut and drop the tank bolts through either side.

10. Lower the tank onto the bowl, guiding it so the tank bolts slide into the two holes on the back of the bowl.

11. Snug a washer and nut up onto each bolt.

12. To install a flexible supply pipe, first measure for the bend needed. (1 inch here.)

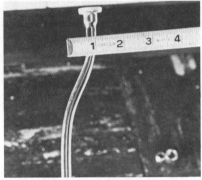

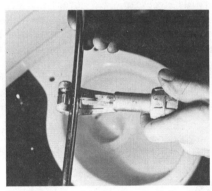

13. The copper tubing can be bent by hand. Then measure again. Mark the bent pipe for required length.

14. Cut the measured pipe carefully with a tube cutter.

15. Daub the upper end of the pipe with pipe compound.

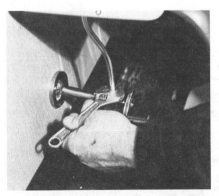

16. Slide a coupling nut up the pipe and hand fasten it to the inlet stem.

17. Slide the valve coupling nut and compression ring onto the lower end of the pipe. Insert the pipe into the valve and tighten both nuts with a wrench.

Finishing up:

Grout around the base of the bowl with plaster of paris. Smooth the plaster with a putty knife or trowel. A coat of clear lacquer applied after the plaster has dried will ensure that it's moisture-proof. The plastic or china caps over the closet bolts can also be anchored down with plaster at this point. Connect the water and test for leaks. Finally, install the lid and seat.

Bathtub/shower combination

The bathtub is the first fixture to be installed in a new or renovated bathroom. It goes in before the floor and walls are finished, since flooring and wall material will extend to the edges of the tub fixture.

Tub positioning is a heavy chore. Even the most maneuverable fiberglass and pressed steel tub needs two men to lift it. Moving a cast iron tub is a four-man job. The three-sided tub enclosure, which is standard, affords extremely limited work space for installation. Good planning is essential.

Tub support. For a three-sided tub enclosure, nail 1x4 tub supports horizontally to each of the three walls. The height of these supports should be carefully measured and the 1x4s leveled exactly. The tub flange must rest evenly on the supports with the tub base sitting on the sub-flooring.

Pipes. Consult manufacturers' rough-in plans for the exact height of overflow pipe, faucet assembly, and shower head, as well as the prescribed location of the floor drain opening. Extend all piping horizontally as necessary. Be sure that the shower pipe is braced on a vertical 1x4 nailed between studs.

Setting in the tub. Two men can position a steel and fiberglass tub in front of its wall enclosure and slide it straight back to the rear wall, being sure to lodge the underside of the rear flange securely on the wall support. For a heavier tub you will need more help in positioning and should lay a pair of 2x4 runners on the subfloor as a track on which to push the tub. When removing the 2x4s, do so as gradually as possible, again settling the tub flange on all three supports and the subfloor.

Once the tub is in position, level it again and shim under the flange, if necessary, with wood shims. Make sure the tub does not wobble. Nail or screw the tub flange to its wall supports. A cast iron tub needs no fastening.

The walls and floor around the tub can be finished at this point.

Plumbing provisions. An access panel in the head wall behind the tub will give access to hidden plumbing. If you do not plan to install an access panel, use permanent drain connections and large enough faucet face plates to facilitate faucet repair from the tub wall. The trap installed in a no-access tub fitting should accommodate an auger through the tub drain for cleaning.

Attaching drainpipes. Remove the overflow plate, lift linkage, and strainer cap. Join the waste and overflow pipes with a slip nut and washer, and set the assembly on the waste T. Position the large beveled washer between the back of the tub and the overflow pipe. Place the large flat washer between the drainpipe and the tub bottom. Position the

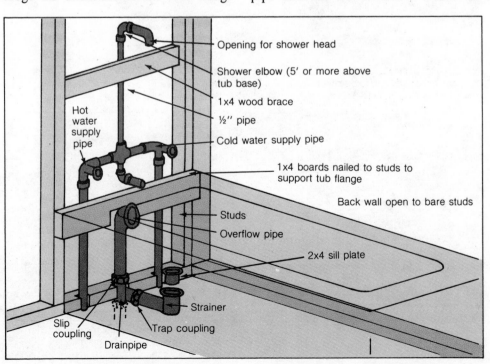

Opening for shower head

Shower elbow (5' or more above tub base)

1x4 wood brace

½'' pipe

Cold water supply pipe

Hot water supply pipe

1x4 boards nailed to studs to support tub flange

Back wall open to bare studs

Studs

Overflow pipe

2x4 sill plate

Strainer

Slip coupling

Trap coupling

Drainpipe

whole assembly and tighten the slip nuts. Use a strand of plumber's putty around the underside of the strainer, then handscrew it into the drain hole.

Hardware. Slip the lift linkage into the overflow hole and attach the overflow plate. For faucet handles, slide escutcheons and sleeves onto spindles, then screw on handles. If your faucet handle requires another kind of installation, consult the manufacturer's instructions.

To install the tub spout, remove the rough-in nipple, and replace it with a nipple measured to extend from the face of the pipe behind the wall to the threads of the spout *plus* ¾-inch allow-ance (for threaded fitting). Daub the nipple threads with joint compound and then hand screw the spout as tightly as possible.

To install the shower arm, remove the nipple from that supply pipe. Use joint compound on the threads of the arm, fit the escutcheon over the arm and hand screw the arm to the pipe.

When installing faucet handles, spout, and shower arm, be sure to use some form of caulking or sealant around the pipe fittings before the escutcheons go on. Also be sure to caulk around all the tub edges and check for leaks before installing floor and wall materials.

Prefab possibilities

Many manufacturers offer prefabricated fiberglass shower stalls and shower/tub combinations. These lightweight units are available in one-piece packages or four-piece snap-together assemblies. A one-piece tub/shower unit is usually positioned in a new bathroom before the framing is roughed-in. Four-piece units are easier to bring in through the door frame of a pre-existing bathroom. You may want to install support framing and sound-proofing insulation. Check all specifications before purchase, to ensure getting the right unit for your needs.

Custom showers

Custom showers as a rule are more expensive than the standard ones. However, in certain cases they are the only ones that will fit into the area available.

Tiled showers are fairly expensive, and it can be a job keeping the joints clean. The use of a silicone grout will discourage the growth of mildew. The tile can be put on with mastic over gypsum wallboard or plaster, or it can be set into wet mortar. Pregrouted tile shower *surrounds* are available in sizes that will fit the most popular receptors: that is, the floor of a custom shower, be it a pre-fab waterproof unit or one constructed on the site from ceramic tile or some other suitable material. To install the shower receptor:

1. Select the appropriate size, unless it is to be custom made.
2. Measure the receptor to locate the center of the drain outlet.
3. The center of the trap inlet must be directly under the drain outlet.
4. Place a short pipe nipple in the trap.
5. Lower the receptor over the trap. If it is a concrete type receptor, it will be heavy.

6. Mark the pipe so that the mark will be even (flush) with the socket of the cast in the strainer.
7. Remove the pipe; and cut the pipe on the mark.
8. Remove the receptor.
9. Replace the pipe and tighten.
10. Apply packing, and pack firmly between the outside wall of the pipe and strainer body.
11. Run a heavy bead of caulking onto the packing; smooth for a watertight joint.
12. Place the strainer grille in place.

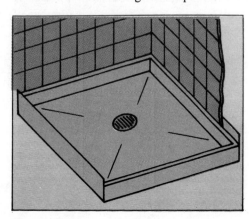

Installing shower doors

Plastic panels or metal-framed glass are the usual tub-shower doors. They come in a number of patterns and fit showers and tubs of varying dimensions.

Nowadays in new houses that have shower doors, safety glass is used. This is written into the building codes as a requirement. But older houses are liable to have shower doors made of ordinary ¼-inch glass. This type of door might resist a glancing blow, but will shatter if hit with great force.

Dangerous glass can be replaced by putting approved safety glass or acrylic plastic in the existing frame; or you can install a whole new door.

Tub enclosures come in three styles. **Horizontal sliding panels** containing either plastic or tempered glass. They're simple to install, replace, and repair. The disadvantage to this type of door is that cleaning is harder because there's no smooth tub edge, and the panels block off half the tub, even when opened.

Plastic vertical panels that raise and lower like double-hung windows give you clear access to the tub. However, installation is more complicated—the panels must be exactly aligned so they don't stick. Moreover, the panels may not be as watertight as other types of doors. Since they are not as widely available as the horizontal type, there might be some difficulty in finding replacement parts.

Accordion-fold doors have a strong advantage in one respect; when folded, the panels store at one end, thus taking up very little space, which makes cleaning easier. But they often are not as watertight as sliding panels, and they have been known to wear around the hinges. They are made of plastic and consequently are not as rugged nor as long-lived as glass doors.

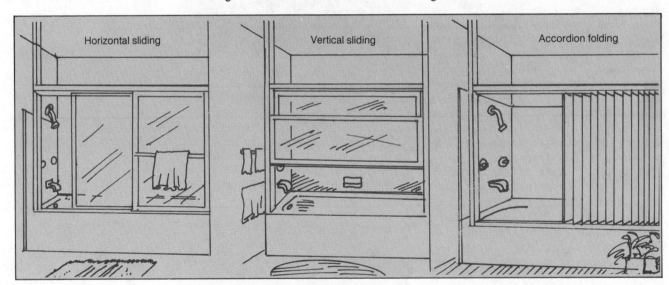

Horizontal sliding   Vertical sliding   Accordion folding

Soundproofing the bathroom

When renovating, measures to minimize bathroom noise are best done before the walls are put up. There are a number of ways to accomplish this. Gypsum wallboard folded in accordion fashion between the studs is quite effective, as is installing blanket insulation. Bathroom wallboard should be thick, and adding sound-deadening fiberboard to the back of it increases its ability to muffle sound.

The plumbing system when well planned, eliminates another source of unwanted noise. When pipes are located close to fixtures and drainpipes slanted to slow the flow of water, it is easier to achieve quiet. You can wrap noisy pipes with layers of asphalt building paper and fiberglass insulation. Remember that a steel bathtub or shower stall will make a lot of noise when water hits its surface, and you may prefer to install either fiberglass or porcelain fixtures.

The bathroom door should be solid rather than hollow core, and it should fit snugly to the threshold. Thicker glass—or even the sound control kind—will reduce noise through windows to the outside, as will weatherstripping around any doors.

There is ceiling material available that is not only moisture-resistant but also sound-absorbing. Carpeting the floor also softens the sounds.

Caulking

A tub-to-wall crack looks ugly and lets water leak against the wall, damaging it. The remedy is to rake out all the old caulk and reseal the joint with silicone tub caulk, which lasts more than 20 years outdoors and even longer indoors.

For the patch to work, the gap between the tub and wall must be wide enough for a decent-sized bead of caulk, and its depth should be roughly the same as its width. If your tub-wall joint is deeper, fill it in with rope oakum (jute fibers coated with preservative) or closed-cell plastic foam to a depth of about ¼ inch before you caulk.

If the wall has been damaged by water, you may have to replace it with one of the waterproof materials made for bathroom walls. If you do, leave a ¼-inch gap between the tub and wall material, even if it's tile.

Silicone tub caulk tends to bulge in spots and dip in others as you apply it. Apply masking tape above and below the tub/wall gap and have dampened cloths handy to wipe off hands and spills. Hold spout at a 45-degree angle and parallel to the joint and move it forward as you squeeze the bead in the joint.

A bathtub has two ends and two long edges, including the one at the floor. Do the end away from the faucet first, because it is looked at least. Apply caulk to the entire end joint. Try for neatness but not perfection. Fill the joint with caulk, then immediately tool it down—before any skin-over, or surface-hardening, can occur. Use a finger, the curved handle of a spoon, an ice-cream stick, or a tongue depressor to put a concave surface on the bead of caulk. Wetting the tool will keep fresh caulk from sticking to it.

When you have the first tub/wall section tooled into shape, go on to the next section. If the bead gets worse instead of better as you tool, stop. The more you try to smooth skinning-over silicone caulk, the rougher it is likely to get.

The use of toxic silicone caulk solvents is not recommended, especially in an unventilated bathroom or bathtub enclosure. If the smell of caulk seems strong, open a bathroom window for ventilation. Also, if you have a skin allergy, better not touch the caulk. Use rubber gloves.

A day later, you can repair any serious roughness by slicing excess caulk with a single-edged razor blade. At the same time, you can scrape off any unwiped caulk spills. Since the silicone bead cures clear through, this is like cutting soft rubber, which is what the bead is. Do not try to paint silicone tube caulking, however. It comes in colors so you won't need to.

Don't mess around
Have trouble caulking without getting all messed up? I did too until I tried using masking tape. Lines of tape laid along both sides of the tub-wall crack lets the bead of caulk go only where you want it. The bead can be tooled after applying, still without messing you up. Finally, when the caulk has gotten a little "tack" to it, you can pull off both strips of tape, leaving a nice, neat bead. Hey, and no mess.

Practical Pete

1. Apply masking tape above and below gap between tub and wall. Lay a bead of caulk in the gap, pushing tube forward as you go so that spout forces caulk into the gap.

2. If the caulk won't hold or you think it is unsightly, you can cover the gap with a quarter-round ceramic tile, which is available in kits from plumbing supply houses.

What tub caulk to use in the bathroom

Caulk type	How sold	Advantages/disadvantages	Solvent	Colors	Relative cost
PVA tub-and-tile	Tubes, cartridges	Easy to use. Excellent adhesion, but shrinks. Should be painted. Short-lived.	Water	White	Lowest
Acrylic latex tub-and-tile	Tubes, cartridges	Low cost, easy to use. Excellent adhesion. Cheapest type recommended. Should be painted.	Water	White	Low
Silicone rubber tub-and-tile	Tubes	The best. Lasts and lasts. Accepts great joint movement. Never becomes brittle. Needs no painting, but hard to use neatly.	Paint thinner, naphtha, toluol, xylol	White, blue, pink, green yellow, beige, gold	Highest

Sinks

Whereas in former times the kitchen contained principally the range, icebox, and sink, many modern kitchens also have a garbage disposal and dishwasher. These, along with the sink, can almost be considered a single unit when it comes to installation, and in many new homes are treated as such. This is because the disposal is actually an extension of the sink drain, and all three appliances use the same waste pipe. Indeed, if there is proper preparation, the installations of all three consist chiefly of tightening screws and nuts.

The simplest method for mounting a sink is to attach as many fittings as possible before you place it into the countertop. Clearly, if you have the faucets, spray hose, tailpiece, and strainer already attached, it will reduce the problem of having to work in a tight space.

For the garbage disposal you will need a handy wall switch. It is a simple matter to connect the disposal with the sink, and to connect the wires, once you've installed and tested the wiring.

A dishwasher has three connections; a hot-water supply line, a waste line, and an electrical connection. These connections are made through an access panel at the lower front. This is done after the dishwasher is in position.

Sink and disposal installation

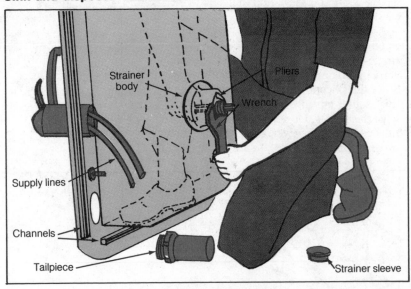

Strainer body

Pliers

Wrench

Supply lines

Channels

Tailpiece

Strainer sleeve

1. First attach the fittings. Stand the sink on its side for easier access. If the faucet body has a rubber gasket, slide it over the stems; if not, apply an ⅛-inch bead of plumber's putty around the body base and then slide the stems through the holes that are provided. If it is necessary to straighten the attached copper supply lines, bend them carefully. If there is a spray hose, follow the instructions of the manufacturer for attaching it to the faucet body and the sink opening. If the sink has no garbage disposal, apply an ⅛-inch bead of plumber's putty to the bottom of the lip of the strainer body before you place it in the drain hole. Place the metal and rubber washers plus a lock nut onto the threaded bottom of the strainer body. Tighten the locknut, carefully, by hand. Insert plier handles into the hole to keep the strainer body from turning before tightening. Assemble the strainer sleeve, tailpiece, and lock nut and attach the tailpiece to the strainer body.

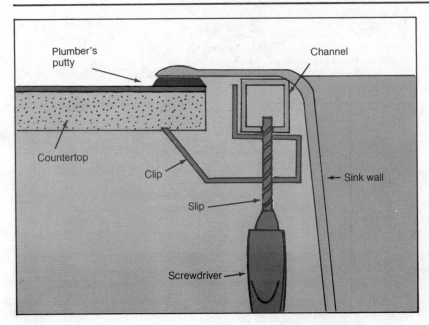

Plumber's putty

Channel

Countertop

Clip

Slip

Sink wall

Screwdriver

2. To attach the sink, apply a ¼-inch bead of plumber's putty along the top edge of the countertop opening. Place the sink into the opening. From beneath, slide 8 or 10 clips into the channels that rim the underside of the sink and position them to grip the bottom of the countertop. The clips should be evenly spaced. With a screwdriver tighten the slips, being careful not to crimp the rim of the sink by overtightening. Check the top to see that you have a good seal between the countertop and the sink rim. Adjust the level if necessary by drawing on the clips.

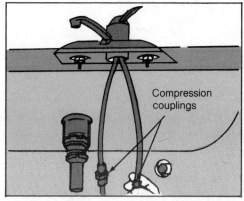

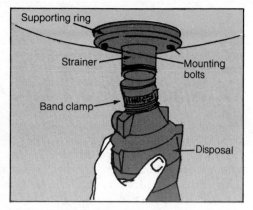

3. To connect the pipes you must first attach the shutoff valves to the stub-outs. If there are supply pipes attached to the taucet body, fasten them to the valves in the same way that you would to a toilet supply (page 48). If there are no pipes, or if they are not long enough, use compression fittings to attach copper tubing.

Add a coupling to the drainpipe, after first uncapping it. For a disposal, see the instructions in Step 4; otherwise, place a slip nut and washer on the tailpiece. Place the drainpipe so that the trap fits correctly, and cement the drain to the coupling. Place an escutcheon, slip nut and a washer over the drainpipe. Install the trap.

4. To attach the disposal, insert the disposal strainer in place of the strainer body (see Step 1). Place the rubber and metal gaskets and thread the mounting bolts loosely before you snap on the support ring. Tighten the bolts, but don't buckle the support ring. When the sink has been mounted (see Step 2), put the clamp around the disposal collar. Lift the disposal so that it locks into the sleeve of the strainer, as shown here. Install a P trap to connect the drain and the disposal waste pipe. Tighten the clamp, and connect the electricity.

Keep in mind that certain disposals require you poke in a knockout plug at the top if you plan to attach a dishwasher drain. You will have to retrieve the plug, so be sure to use long-nose pliers.

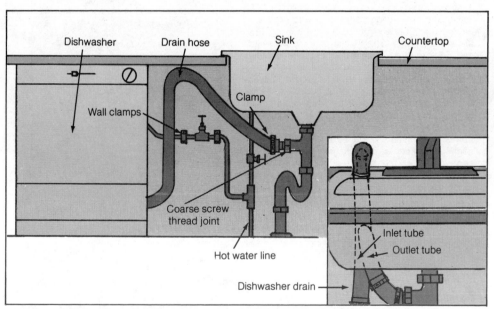

In order to connect the dishwasher, you will need to prepare the space. It will also be necessary to cut a hole about 6 inches wide in the lower rear section of the cabinet wall that lies between the dishwasher space and the sink. This will accommodate a line of flexible copper tubing along with the dishwasher drain hose, as well as the electrical cable if required. Take away the access panel and kick plate from the lower front of the dishwasher before you move the dishwasher into its opening. Level the unit so that it is flush with the countertop. You can then make the connections with the dishwasher in or out of its space. To connect the copper tubing to the inlet pipe, use a compression fitting. A hose clamp connects the drain hose to the outlet pipe.

With the dishwasher in place, secure it with screws to the countertop through the precut

holes in the front. Connect the wiring and put back the access panel and kick plate. Attach the other end of the tubing to the sink hot-water pipe with a separate shutoff valve, and the drain hose to the sink tailpiece or air gap.

To provide electricity, 120 volt, 60 Hz, AC only, 15 ampere fused supply is required. It is also advisable that a separate circuit serving only this appliance be provided. *Do not* use an extension cord; grounding is also a must.

If you require an air gap, pull the stem up through a hole in the countertop or sink, screw on the plastic top and press in the outer cap. Use a hose clamp to connect the dishwasher drain hose to the inlet tube of the air gap. Use a section of hose and clamps to connect the outlet tube to the sink drainpipe.

All you have to do is ask the right person!
My friend told me that our local code insists on an air gap for a dishwasher waste line. This prevents siphonage of waste water back into the cleaning chamber. So okay—only thing is *he* forgot to tell *me* to make sure my new sink had a precut hole, so I wouldn't have to cut through all that steel.

Practical Pete

Electrical connections

You are now ready to make the final wiring installations and connections. From the planning stage through the removal operation to re-wiring, it has been necessary to understand the nature of electrical power as well as the fundamentals of wiring and the functions of various devices. (see page 68).

It's a good idea to keep in mind that an electrical system is very much like a pressure water system in that electricity flows from the power lines through the meter and into the switch at the entrance to your home. From this point the electricity is distributed as needed to various circuits, and to lighting fixtures and appliances.

Here's a good place to be reminded of the importance of safety:
- Turn off power in the circuit you plan to work on.
- Test wires in a box with a voltage tester to be certain the power really is off.
- Never stand on a damp or wet floor when working with wiring.
- Do not touch parts of gas piping or plumbing system when working with electricity or while using an electrical appliance.
- Before working on a lamp or appliance, be sure to unplug it.
- Check your work after you are done.

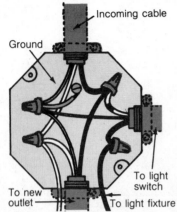

Taking power from a ceiling box.
First, take the light fixture out of a ceiling box and check the wiring. If there is only one cable, do not use the box as a source for power. If you see two or more cables coming into the box, as in the illustration here, connect the black wire of the new cable (dotted lines) with the black wire of the cable that is coming in; the white wire should be connected to the other neutral wires; and the bare wire is connected to the other ground wires.

Dishwasher and garbage disposal circuits. Run a single three-conductor cable, wired for 240 volts, from the service panel to a junction box in the kitchen. Connect the black wire coming from the service panel to the white wire of the switch cable. Either tape or paint both ends of the white wire black so that it is marked as a voltage-carrying conductor. Connect the black wire of the disposal cable to the black wire of the switch cable. Connect the black wire of the dishwasher cable to the red wire of the service-panel cable. Then fasten the three remaining white wires with a wire nut, and connect all the bare ground wires to each other and to the junction box. Finish the connections at the switch and the appliances, then cover the junction box with a cover plate which you can screw on.

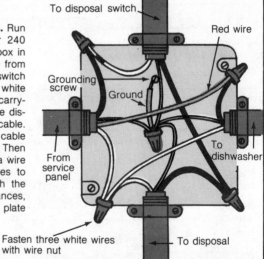

An electric range operates on 240 volts at high heat and 120 volts at low heat. It therefore requires a separate 3-wire No. 6 cable run from a 50-ampere circuit in the main entrance box to a heavy-duty wall receptacle. Check with your power company for the type of wire specified by the local code. In a good many cases, service entrance cable is used and the uninsulated wire is connected to the neutral terminal on the range receptacle.

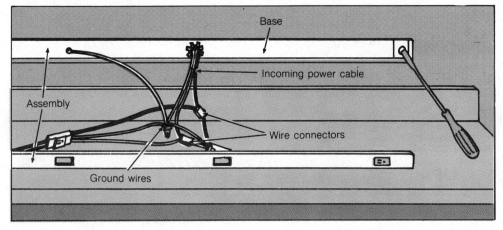

Base
Incoming power cable
Assembly
Wire connectors
Ground wires

To install a surface-mounted receptacle strip, run a two-conductor, No. 12 cable from the service panel to a spot about 8 inches above countertop. Clamp cable to knockout in base of multioutlet assembly; screw base to wall. Near incoming power cable, cut black, white, green wires of assembly; strip ½ inch of insulation from each. Join incoming black and white wires to matching assembly wires; use pressure-type wire connectors. The code forbids using these connectors for ground wires. Join the two green assembly wires, the bare cable wire, and a short grounding jumper wire; use crimp-type connector or wire nut. Fasten other end of jumper wire to assembly base with a grounding screw.

Hanging a new ceiling fixture

You may just want to exchange one simple incandescent fixture for another. Here's what to do. Turn off the power at the entry box, either by removing the fuse, or by throwing the circuit breaker. Then follow the steps as shown here.

What it takes

Approximate time: Depends upon the particular job; but allow sufficient time so you never have to hurry. From an hour to a day

Tools and materials: Hammer, ⅝-inch drill and bit, keyhole saw, hacksaw, test light, level, folding rule (6-foot), wire cutter, stripper, chisel, electrician tape, jack knife, screwdriver; fixtures and accompanying hardware.

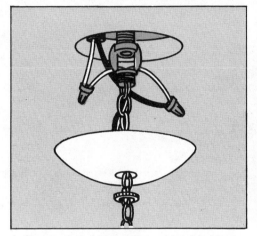

1. Remove the plate that is covering the hole in the ceiling.

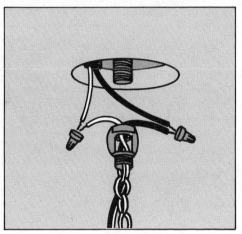

2. Disconnect the existing fixture. Note carefully how it is wired. Is there anything other than a white and a black wire coming out of the ceiling? If so, how is it hooked up?

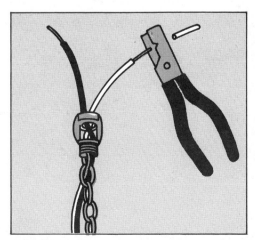

3. Peel back about an inch of insulation from the wires on the new fixture.

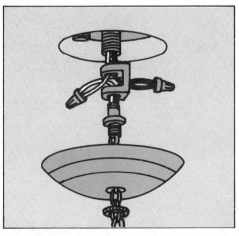

4. Connect the wires from the ceiling box to the wires from the new fixture with wire nuts—white to white and black wire to black—unless you observe some different wiring arrangement. Put the new canopy in place and turn the power on.

Fluorescents

It makes sense to replace incandescent fixtures with fluorescent ones when you renovate, so long as they will not be turned on and off frequently.

Installation is easy. The channels of fluorescent fixtures have a number of knockouts; you can use any one for mounting. Take off the channel cover, tap the knockout with a hammer to break it free, then twist the knockout off with a pair of pliers.

Mount the fluorescent by placing the knockout over a threaded nipple and securing the fixture with a washer and locknut. Note that you can add a strap-mounted nipple to wall outlets, or a hickey and nipple to ceiling boxes that don't have nipples.

Run the black and white fluorescent power wires through the nipple and join them to the source-cable conductors with solderless connectors. The connections will be white to white, and black to black.

In large fixtures there is a mounting cutout. In order to mount these fixtures, place a metal strap inside the channel, across the cutout. Place the fixture and strap over the nipple. Hold the strap and fixture to the ceiling with a locknut.

Circular fluorescent fixtures are good replacements for the regular kitchen ceiling fixtures. With solderless connectors, connect the fluorescent fixture wires to the power wires in the box; black to black and white to white. If necessary, use a reducing nut or hickey to install a nipple long enough to project through the fixture. Fold the wires into the fixture canopy and secure to the ceiling by tightening the cap nut on the nipple.

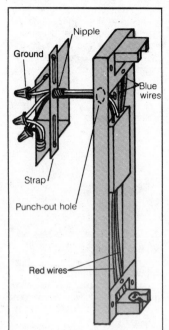

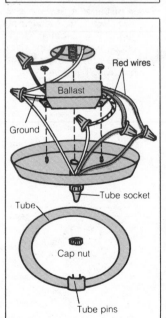

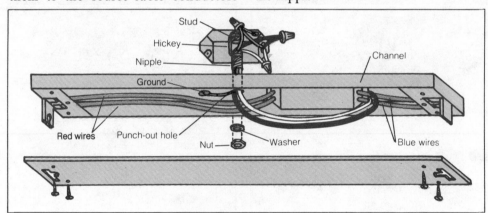

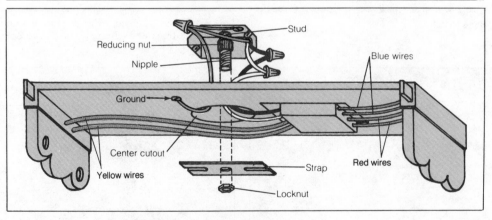

In bathrooms

Fluorescent lights in the bathroom are popular when it comes to putting on makeup, shaving, and so on. The fixtures can be mounted above, or on either side of bathroom cabinets.

As a rule, bathroom cabinets are recessed into the walls between studs, to which they are secured with wood screws. Sometimes they are on the outside edge of the studs. To remove the cabinet, just take out the screws on either side and lift the cabinet from the wall opening.

The opening offers easy entry to electrical connections on the interior wall. If you had an old incandescent fixture near the cabinet, the new fluorescent can be wired to the same box. Again, it is black to black and white to white.

If you find that you will need a new circuit for the fluorescent lights, install a junction box in the wall stud in back of the cabinet.

Power for a junction box is obtained by running a cable to an existing wall or ceiling box. Connect the leads from the fluorescent fixtures to the power cable in the junction box with solderless connectors.

Caution: Many local codes now require that GFIs (ground fault interrupters) be installed on bathroom circuits. If there already is a GFI on the bathroom

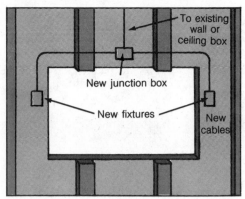

circuit in your home, be certain that you make the power connection for the junction box to a wall or ceiling box on the GFI-protected circuit. Remember that you must turn off power to the existing wall or ceiling box before you connect the new cable. Make sure that when the bathroom-circuit GFI is turned off, power is off in the box you are using for the new circuit.

Wiring cabinet lights

To prepare for the wiring, bring a cable from a nearby outlet box; but after you have first turned off the circuit. If there is a 2x4 header in the opening, drill a ½-inch hole through it to conform to the wiring access hole in the top of the cabinet. Lead the cable through the header hole.

To make the connections, place the bottom edge of the cabinet on the sill and draw the cable end through the opening in the top of the cabinet and into the wiring compartment. Anchor the cable with the cable clamp on the cabinet top. Fix the cabinet securely to the studs inside the opening. Using a wire nut, connect the cable's ground wire to a green wire from the cabinet. If there isn't any green wire, then connect the ground wire to a green grounding screw. Now connect the white wires from the cabinet and from the cable with a wire nut. Connect the black cabinet wire (it is sometimes red) to the black cable wire.

Installing a GFI

Wire leads instead of screw terminals are a feature of the GFI; and it is connected like an ordinary receptacle, with one big difference. The feed cable coming from the service panel must be joined to the leads marked "line," and the outgoing cable that leads to the rest of the circuit has to be hooked to the leads that are marked "load." If the GFI receptacle is the only fixture on the circuit, then connect the "line" leads in the usual way, but be sure to cap each of the "load" leads and fold them into the box. Use a wire nut for capping.

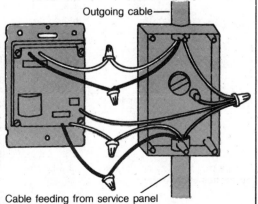

NEW CABINETS, COUNTERS & UTILITY SPACE

Single wall

What it takes

Approximate time: Allot your time in periods of no less than half a day.

Tools and materials: Hammer, saw, screwdriver, pliers, level, plumb line, electric drill and bits; screws, nails, grounds, 1x3 stock, wood shims.

First, locate the wall studs and grounds. Grounds serve the purpose of supplying an anchor to secure cabinets. They may be surface mounted or, like cleats, placed between studs. The best way is to notch them into studs. Because they will be covered by the cabinets, walls can be cut open for ground insertion without much concern about patching the wall. But level and plumb the grounds.

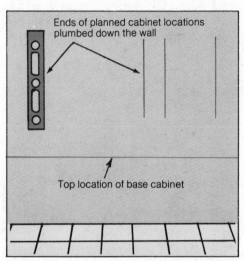

1. On the wall, lay out the left and right ends of the planned cabinet locations. Plumb these lines down the wall.

2. Lay out the top and bottom locations of the hanging cabinets. If you're planning on a soffit, or there is one already installed, then only the bottom location is necessary. Level the height locations laid out in Step 1.

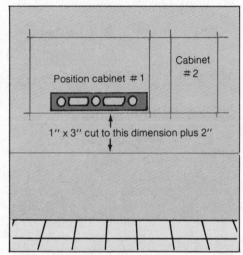

3. Measure the distance from the floor to the bottom of the cabinet. From 1x3 stock, cut two deadmen (support sticks) 2 inches longer than the measurement.

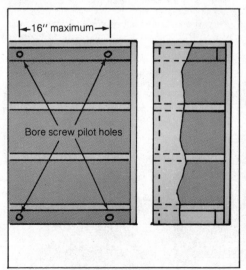

4. Bore pilot holes along the rear top and bottom cabinet framework every 16 inches (maximum).

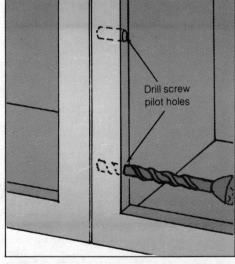

5. Bore holes so that when the two cabinets abut each other in a straight line the pilot holes will go through the edges of the abutting front vertical frames.

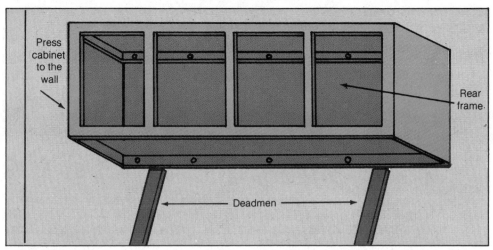

Press cabinet to the wall

Rear frame

Deadmen

6. Place the screws in the pilot holes. Raise the cabinet to the wall layout and place the deadmen under the rear framework. Of course, you will need a helper for this operation. Press the cabinet to the wall to provide friction and avoid slippage.

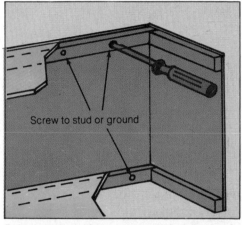

Screw to stud or ground

7. Anchor one top frame screw to a stud or ground. Check for level against the wall level lines previously laid out, then drive all screws into the studs and/or grounds.

8. Align the front faces of abutting cabinets and screw their front frames together.

The base cabinets

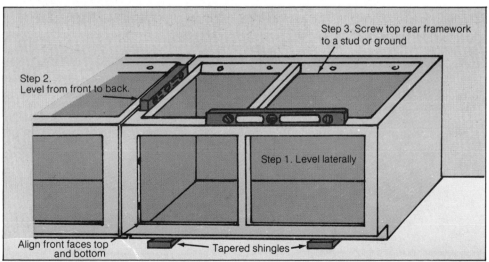

Step 3. Screw top rear framework to a stud or ground

Step 2. Level from front to back.

Step 1. Level laterally

Align front faces top and bottom

Tapered shingles

1. Place the cabinet against your marked line on the wall. Starting from the high side and working laterally, raise the cabinet until it is level. Do this by inserting tapered wood shingles underneath the cabinet, in line with the vertical frame members. Cut or break off all protruding shingles.

2. Check the cabinet for level from front to back. Shim if necessary.
3. As with the hanging cabinets, first screw the top rear framework to a stud or ground, then similarly align the front cabinet faces and screw the abutting vertical frames together.

The countertop

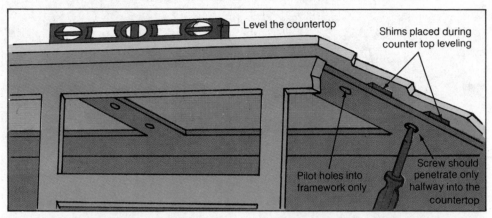

Level the countertop

Shims placed during counter top leveling

Pilot holes into framework only

Screw should penetrate only halfway into the countertop

1. Locate the high point of the countertop with a level. Place shims between the horizontal framework of the base cabinet and the underside of the countertop until it is level.
2. Secure the countertop by first boring pilot holes through the top horizontal framework which is lo-

cated between the front and the back frames.
3. Screw from the horizontal frame of the base cabinet into the bottom side of the countertop. But be careful to choose the right length of screw; long enough to grip, but not so long that it will penetrate the countertop.

Multi-wall installation

Individual steps for installation of L- and U-shaped cabinet lines are basically the same as for single wall cabinet installation. As a matter of fact, if all kitchens were living room size, it would be a simple matter, for kitchens of such size rarely require this type of installation. It is the small kitchen, where wall use has to be maximized, that needs the U- or L-shaped line.

The shape in itself, were it confined to the cabinets, would present no problem. The countertop is the culprit. Because it is

always desirable to have as few joints in the countertop as possible, it should be made in one piece even though U-shaped. Consequently, you will have the problem of installing a large, bulky item in a confined area.

Because of this problem, the procedure for multi-wall cabinet installation is slightly different. The countertop, though not secured first, has to be brought in first, to avoid maneuvering difficulties that would occur if the wall and base cabinets were already in place.

All a question of planning ahead

I found out the hard way—and I do mean hard! — when I did my multi-wall cabinet installation. I should have brought my countertop in *first,* even though it's put on *after* everything else has been installed.

Practical Pete

Completing the base units

The balance of the work on the base units is completed in the same manner as with the single-wall style. Level the cabinets while the countertop is resting on the deadmen. The top end of the sticks will be 6 inches higher than the cabinets and so will allow room to maneuver.

Fill in the missing cabinets, then level and align them with the others. Secure the top rear rail of framework of the cabinets to the wall. The countertop is the last item and is secured from the cabinet to the bottom of the countertop, the same as with single-wall units.

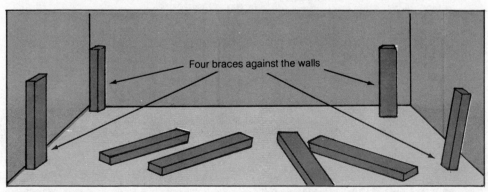

Four braces against the walls

1. Cut 8 deadmen 42 inches long. Place 4 against the wall; 1 at each corner and 1 at each end of the countertop location.

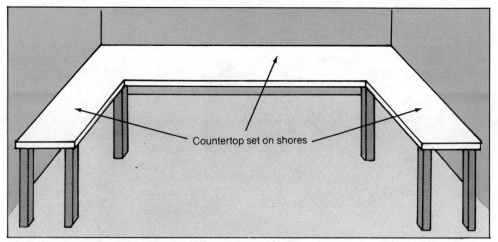

2. With the assistance of at least one person, carry the countertop in and set it on the deadmen sticks.

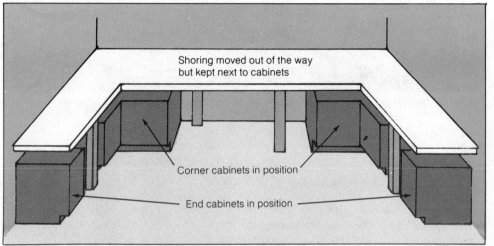

Shoring moved out of the way
but kept next to cabinets

Corner cabinets in position

End cabinets in position

3. Place the corner cabinets in their approximate positions. Move the deadmen to nearby locations adjacent to the corner cabinets. Place the end cabinets in position. Move the deadmen sticks out of the way but near the cabinets.

U and L hanging cabinets

As with single-wall application, guide lines have to be laid out for U- and L-shaped hanging wall cabinets. A change occurs, on the other hand, in the makeup of the deadmen (often called shores) and the positioning procedure. See page 76 in reference to temporary bracing; remember, sound bracing is half the work.

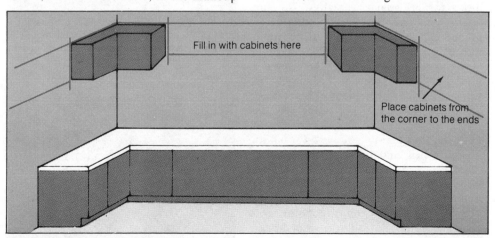

Fill in with cabinets here

Place cabinets from the corner to the ends

Cabinet placement starts in the corners as it does with the base units. The placement of the rest of the cabinets, however, is easier. The units are installed from the corners outward to the ends of the cabinet line, instead of placing the corner and end cabinets and then filling in between, as is done with the base units.

Readymades

Solid oak frames and doors give a real feeling of substance to this pair of base cabinet banks. Cathedral-shaped door dados would be difficult for even the experienced home carpenter to duplicate.

Constructing a cabinet from scratch can be a tough job. There are plenty of dado, rabbet, and lap joints to make, and precision is essential. Building special-design doors like those shown above is nearly impossible without an extensive (and expensive) assortment of shop equipment rarely found in home workshops. Even accomplished carpenters often choose to buy readymades rather than build comparable cabinets from the ground up. (If you're really eager to build your own, turn the page.)

Factory-made cabinets aren't just for use in a kitchen. Readymades like the ones shown here would add attractive new storage space anywhere in the house. And the basic installation techniques certainly don't vary from room to room.

If you do decide to invest in cabinets, ask your lumber dealer for brochures which describe the various cabinet lines he carries. There's such a range of sizes, styles, and prices to choose from that you shouldn't rely solely on display models when making your choice. One other thing to think about is that most base cabinets don't come with tops. If that's true of the model you've selected, you should decide on the color and composition of the top you want at the same time. **TIP:** Sales on cabinets or sets of cabinets aren't uncommon. Discontinued styles and slightly damaged cabinets are always sold at considerably lower prices. Shop around and you're sure to turn up a few bargains. *Unfinished* factory-made cabinets are available in certain styles at substantially lower prices than identical cabinets pre-finished.

Storage space dominates this kitchen design. Cabinet doors are made of melamine low pressure laminate. Cabinet ends are a matching wood grained embossed vinyl.

Slatted oak fronts give these cabinets a country feel. Note refrigerator, concealed at the right.

Cabinet installation

Installation is remarkably easy compared to the work involved in cabinet construction. Detailed manufacturer's instructions generally accompany each set of cabinets. Those specifics will supplement these general guidelines.

The most important part of the job is laying out the location of each cabinet before it is positioned and fastened in place. Use a tape measure, pencil, level, and chalk line to mark cabinet outlines on the wall as shown. You should also mark stud locations within cabinet areas before installation begins. That way you won't have to hunt for them at the last moment, just as the cabinet is ready to be fastened to the wall.

When putting up either wall or base cabinets, install the corner or end cabinet first. Adjoining cabinets should be bolted together through their corner stiles using 3/16-inch diameter round-head bolts. Fasten them together as they are being installed, but don't tighten the bolts fully until each cabinet has been leveled.

TIP: Another support suggestion is to temporarily nail a cleat along the lower side of the line where the back bottom edge of the cabinet will go. Use the cleat as you would dead men (see photo 6, this page) to support the cabinet while you level it. Then screw through the cabinet back and into a stud. Remove the cleat once all the cabinets have been secured to the wall and to each other.

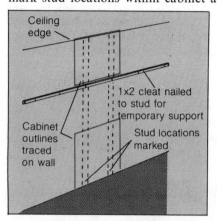

Ceiling edge

1x2 cleat nailed to stud for temporary support

Cabinet outlines traced on wall

Stud locations marked

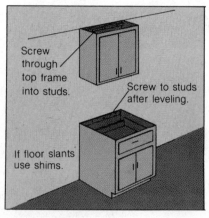

Screw through top frame into studs.

Screw to studs after leveling.

If floor slants use shims.

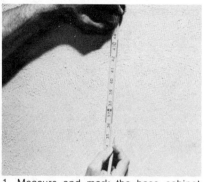

1. Measure and mark the base cabinet height from the floor. (The standard height is 36 inches.)

2. Use a level to mark a second point parallel to the first.

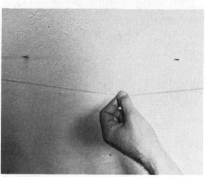

3. Aligning between your two measured markings, snap a chalk line across the wall.

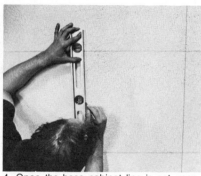

4. Once the base cabinet line is set, measure and mark for the height and width of the hanging cabinet, using the same technique. Hanging cabinets usually sit at a height of 18 inches above the countertop.

5. Move the base cabinet into place and check the leveling again. If necessary, shim to level with wood shingles. Once level, screw the cabinet to the back wall at the four corners.

6. Use two 19-inch dead men cut from 1x2 to prop your top cabinet while checking the alignment. Here the cabinet is supported on both sides, by the range on the left and the wall on the right. If your cabinet is going on a flat wall, have another pair of hands to hold it.

7. Once the top cabinet is leveled, screw through the back into wall studs at each upper and lower corner.

Custom construction

Cabinet-making involves more time, skill, and tools than other storage-related projects. The drawings below are *basic* designs for a wall and base cabinet appropriate for a kitchen, den, bedroom or bath. You can make design and dimension changes to fit your taste and space requirements. If you want a more elegant look and are willing to pay for it, an expensive hardwood-faced plywood can be used for cabinet sides. Doors or drawer fronts can be made from solid wood.

What it takes

Approximate time: 4-5 hours.

Tools and materials: Basic cutting and joining tools; router with dado, rabbeting, and rounding-over bits; plus the following materials: 6' length 1"x12" clear pine board, 4'x4' sheet ¼" hardboard, 2 drawer pulls, 2 offset semi-concealed hinges, 3'x3' sheet plastic laminate (optional), 2'x2' sheet ½" A/C plywood, 4'x8' sheet of ¾" hardwood faced plywood, 1 drawer guide assembly.

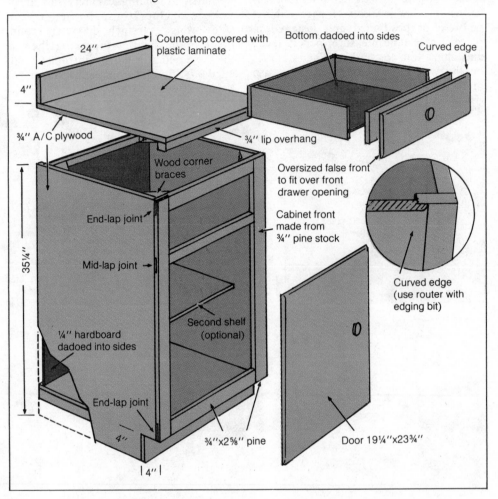

Countertop covered with plastic laminate
24"
4"
Bottom dadoed into sides
Curved edge
¾" A/C plywood
¾" lip overhang
Wood corner braces
Oversized false front to fit over front drawer opening
Cabinet front made from ¾" pine stock
End-lap joint
35¼"
Mid-lap joint
Curved edge (use router with edging bit)
Second shelf (optional)
¼" hardboard dadoed into sides
End-lap joint
4"
¾"x2⅝" pine
Door 19¼"x23¾"
4"

Building the base cabinet

1. Assemble the cabinet front from ¾" pine or birch stock. Use end-lap joints at the corners and a mid-lap joint for the middle divider (see page 20). Glue and clamp the pieces together and let the assembly stand until the glue has set.

2. Measure, mark, and cut the sides. Then join them together by installing the kickplate across the front and a brace across the back. Slide the hardboard back into dadoed grooves on each side.

3. Glue and nail the front frame in place, using 6d finishing nails. Notice here the kickplate assembly detail.

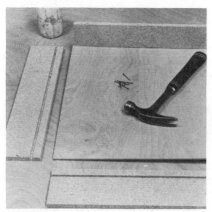

4. Construct the drawer, using ½" plywood or particle board for the sides, back and front. Use ¼" hardboard or plywood for the bottom. Dado for the bottom panel in front, back, and side pieces as shown. The drawer front can be made from two pieces of ½" plywood or a single ¾" piece that has been edged and rabbeted. **Note:** Buy a drawer guide assembly at your local hardware store. There are several varieties available, and all come complete with detailed installation instructions.

5. Reinforce the corners by gluing and screwing wood blocks in place at the top and bottom.

6. Cut doors to finished size. Use a router with a rounding over bit to put curve on the front edges. Then cut a lip along the inside of the door edges with a router or table saw. **TIP:** It is important to rout before rabbeting the door since the router needs a solid edge to guide it.

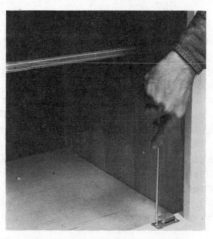

7. Attach offset, semi-concealed hinges to the door as shown. Then position the door in the front opening and screw the hinges to the front frame.

8. Attach a catch assembly to the door and the front frame of the cabinet. Then fasten a pull or handle to the door.

9. Construct a top and attach it to the top of the cabinet with glue and finishing nails. Use flat-head screws in the corners for extra holding strength.

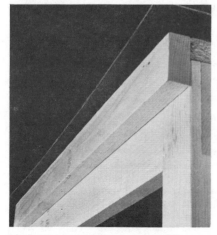

10. Cut the laminate for the top slightly oversize (¼"), then coat the back of the laminate and the plywood top with contact cement.

11. When the contact cement has dried to the touch, place kraft paper between the laminate and the top while aligning the laminate. Then slide the paper out and press the laminate against the top.

12. Trim the laminate overhang with a router and laminate trim bit.

Utility storage

Putting the space in your bathroom to work can really make life easier. By making more storage space, you can separate functionally different items that are now crowded together: shaving cream, make-up, dental floss, and band-aids, for example. The many small items you keep in the bathroom demand similarly small storage spaces so they can easily be grouped and identified. The shelves in your medicine cabinet are ideal for this type of storage. (For instructions on how to install a medicine cabinet, see page 131.) If your cabinet is overcrowded, transfer some

articles to a small set of shelves like the one below. You can gain extra wall space for shelves by removing wall-mounted towel racks and reinstalling them on the back of the bathroom door.

Larger articles like hair driers, cleansers, soap, and tissues can often be stored under the sink. If your under-sink space isn't being utilized, put it to work by building in some shelves or a cabinet, as detailed on the facing page. What about towels and dirty clothes? There's a good chance you might be able to find space for a hamper/shelving unit like the one on page 132.

Build a small set of shelves

A small set of shelves like this is always helpful for storing toiletries and other bath items. The dark mahogany sides contrast nicely with the pine top and bottom pieces. Any satin-style polyurethane or penetrating resin finish will work well here. Shelves of clear acrylic plastic will lend a unique and attractive appearance to your project.

Tools and materials: Basic cutting and joining tools; plus: one mahogany board (¾"x2'x8'); one pine board (¾"x18"x8"); 12 6d finishing nails; and 4 acrylic plastic shelves (¼"x18"x3⅞"). Have your glass dealer cut the plastic to size.

Approximate time: 2 hours, including finish coats.

Easy to make: 1) Measure, mark, and cut rabbets (¾" wide) and dados (¼" wide) in mahogany board, then rip board in half. Rip pine board into two identical pieces at the same time. 2) Glue and nail sides to top and bottom, square the frame up and brace it. 3) When glue has set, remove brace and finish as desired. 4) Insert acrylic plastic shelves and install.

Storage under the sink

Custom-made shelves. A quick, easy, and effective way to convert an empty undersink area to storage space is to build in some shelves. To get the most out of the existing space, measure carefully and custom-fit your design around the plumbing fixtures and corner leg supports.

Measure and cut the three side supports first, then cut shelves to size; each shelf is cut at a 45° angle at one end. Glue and nail shelves to center support, then add side supports. Offset shelves as shown above for easy nailing through center piece.

Cabinets. Building a cabinet under your bathroom sink isn't a difficult job. You should be able to make the entire cabinet from a single 4′x8′ sheet of ⅝″ or ¾″ plywood. If your sink has legs, try to remove them and use the cabinet sides to support the sink. Cut the sides and front first, then fasten the shelf supports to the sides and join the front to the sides. (Use white or yellow glue and 4d finishing nails.) Measure, mark, and cut the shelves, then install them. Cut the doors to size, then hinge them to the sides of the front opening. Before sanding and finishing, attach two magnetic catch assemblies to the doors and the front edges of the shelf, as shown in the final illustration. Finish knobs separately and install them when cabinet finish is dry.

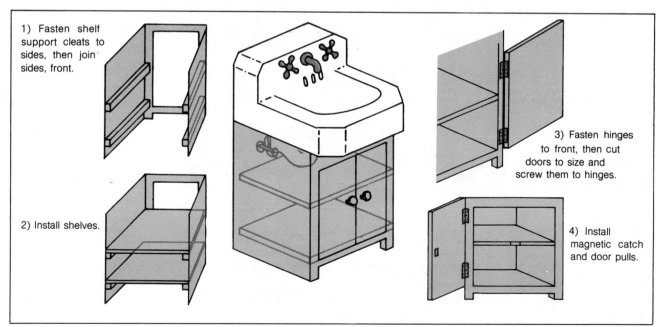

1) Fasten shelf support cleats to sides, then join sides, front.

2) Install shelves.

3) Fasten hinges to front, then cut doors to size and screw them to hinges.

4) Install magnetic catch and door pulls.

Medicine cabinets

The customary medicine chest for the bathroom is recessed into or mounted on the wall over the lavatory, and usually has a hinged, mirrored door. Other more elaborate cabinets have different styles of doors, built-in lighting fixtures, and electrical outlets. Cabinets are available in numerous sizes and styles. Of course, the medicine cabinet doesn't have to be located above the lavatory. You can hang a large mirror over the wash basin, and the medicine cabinet can be on another wall.

The inside of the cabinet consists of shelves, 4 to 6 inches apart, which hold tubes, bottles, and jars. You should allow one shelf to be taller so it can accommodate larger items.

Most homes built in the past quarter century have dry wall construction. If you have this type of wall in your bathroom, there is an easy way to install a medicine cabinet. Recessed medicine chests come ready-made to fit inside the 16-inch space between wall studs, making installation very simple. First, it is necessary to find the studs. This can be done by tapping the wall to find where it is solid, or by using a stud finder. The stud finder has a magnet that detects the hidden nails in the wall. Once you find the line of nails, you will know a stud is there.

- Locate two consecutive studs in the area where you want the cabinet to go. Hold the cabinet exactly where you want it, and draw its outline on the wall.
- Drill a hole inside the outline, and with a keyhole saw cut from the hole toward either stud. When you reach the stud, cut along the outline you drew on the wall.
- Now cut two 2x4s into 16-inch lengths. Toenail them into the top and bottom of the opening. These crosspieces should be behind the surface of the wall, but exactly at the edge of the opening. Make sure they are level.
- Place the cabinet in the opening, and drive screws into the 2x4s on all four sides. This will secure the cabinet.

Recessed cabinets are also available in greater widths which require special installation. You will have to saw out stud sections to accommodate these larger units. This installation also requires the addition of headers or crosspieces as replacement support for the missing stud sections.

However, if there's plumbing or wiring behind the wall at the place where you want to hang your medicine chest, it's better to install a surface-mounted cabinet.

What it takes

Approximate time: 1 afternoon.

Tools and materials: Stud finder, drill, keyhole saw, screwdriver; screws, nails, 2x4s, medicine cabinet.

After drilling a hole, saw in a curve toward the nearest stud. Then saw out the outline you have already drawn on the wall.

Toenail a 2x4 horizontal into the top and bottom of the opening. You can drive one or two nails into each of the vertical studs to hold the horizontal 2x4s in place while securing them.

Installing a medicine cabinet step-by-step

1. Locate the inside corner of the stud that will be the cabinet side support. You can use a stud-finder, drill exploratory holes, or use a keyhole saw as shown.

2. Once you've found the inside corner of the stud, use a level to mark a cut-line running along the inside edge.

Need more space than a normal-sized medicine cabinet can give you? National Recessed Cabinets (Miami, Florida) sells several different models of over-sized cabinets. They are installed just like conventional ones, but provide you with considerably more storage space.

3. Draw the outline of the cabinet box, starting from the line you've just marked. In a conventionally framed house, the opposite side of the box should line up pretty closely with the adjacent stud (see insert).

4. Cut out the hole for the box, using a saber saw or a keyhole saw.

On the wall, not in the wall
What if your bathroom wall is brick or plaster, or you don't have the time or energy to cut out a custom-fit recess between two studs for a medicine cabinet? Don't worry. With a little looking around, you can locate several types designed to be mounted on the wall using conventional wall fasteners. These cabinets can be installed in a few minutes, and are available in many different styles, some with built-in lights.

5. Install horizontal supports for top and bottom of box. Cut 2x4 stock to inside dimensions and *toenail* the two pieces in position as shown.

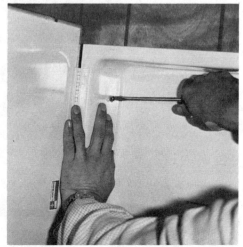

6. Position the cabinet and sink the screws through the holes in the side of the box into the support framing.

Build a hamper with shelves

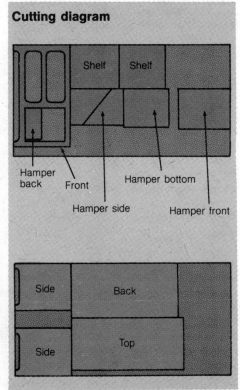

Cutting diagram

Shelf — Shelf

Hamper back — Front — Hamper bottom

Hamper side — Hamper front

Side — Back

Side — Top

Why keep dirty clothes in a corner or stuff them in a laundry bag when you can build a combination hamper/shelving unit like the one shown here? With its formica top, this combination storage unit can endure the spills and heavy traffic common to busy bath areas and still look like new. The enamel finish on the front, which is applied over one coat of primer-sealer, is also highly resistant to wear and staining and can be maintained with the swipe of a sponge.

The model you see above, only partly visible because of cramped bath space,

was designed to fit a particular bathroom niche, but you can adjust height, width and depth for the space you have available.

Note: You may also want to choose a patterned formica to give your project a more lively look; there is a large variety of colors and patterns available.

A **cutting diagram** can save both work and material. Arrange the elements from a scale drawing of your own design on 4x8-foot sheets of ⅝-inch and ½-inch plywood as shown top and bottom in the diagram above.

1. Cut out and label the parts to be assembled. A saber saw makes quick work of both curves and inside cuts. Start inside cuts by drilling out ⅜″ holes along the cut-line, as shown above.

2. Fasten shelf supports to left side and join both sides to front, using white or yellow glue with 4d finishing nails. Then square up corners with a carpenter's square, using two lengths of scrap lumber as diagonal braces.

3. Glue and nail shelves in place. You can get away with shelf supports on only one side by nailing through front and back panels into shelf edges. Now is a good time to seal, finish, or prime-coat the interior, before the top goes on.

4. Glue and clamp stops in place for hamper front in top corners of hamper opening, as shown. Use scrap lumber for these small pieces, and make sure they'll allow the hamper to open and close freely.

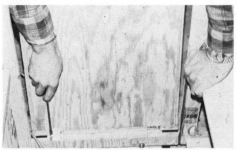

5. Put the hamper together. The easiest assembly sequence is to join back and sides first, nail in bottom, then attach front. When you've put the hamper together, square it up with a diagonal brace, and allow glue to set.

6. Install the hamper. First fasten hinges to bottom edge of hamper front, then position hamper as shown, drill out pilot holes, and screw hinges to front panel. Screws should be at least 1" long, and hinge plates no wider than ⅝".

Don't get unhinged over a simple problem.

What happens when you don't drill the pilot holes for your hinges directly on center? You end up with a door that won't close, like I did. The bit in my electric drill usually "dances" a little on the wood before taking hold, and this time it waltzed a bit too far off center and gave me a bad case of misaligned hinges. An old-time carpenter friend clued me in on a simple cure for the dancing drill: Use a sharp-pointed awl to make a small starter hole exactly where you want to drill. This keeps the bit in line just fine.

Practical Pete

7. Glue and nail top in place. Allow for an even overhang on sides and front; back should fit flush if it's going to be against the wall.

8. Set nails, then fill all exposed holes and cracks with wood dough. When dough dries, sand the wood smooth and remove sharp edges and corners. The final step before the first coat of paint is to remove sawdust with a tack rag or vacuum cleaner.

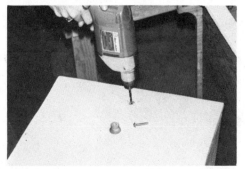

9. Paint on primer-sealer. You can varnish the inside shelves, as we've done here, or paint them the same color as the outside. Remove the hamper and paint it separately. For step-by-step instructions on how to put on the plastic laminate top, turn the page.

10. Almost forget the knob. Find the center of the hamper front and drill out a hole a couple of inches from the top for the screw-in knob. Finish the knob separately, then install it when final coat on hamper front has dried.

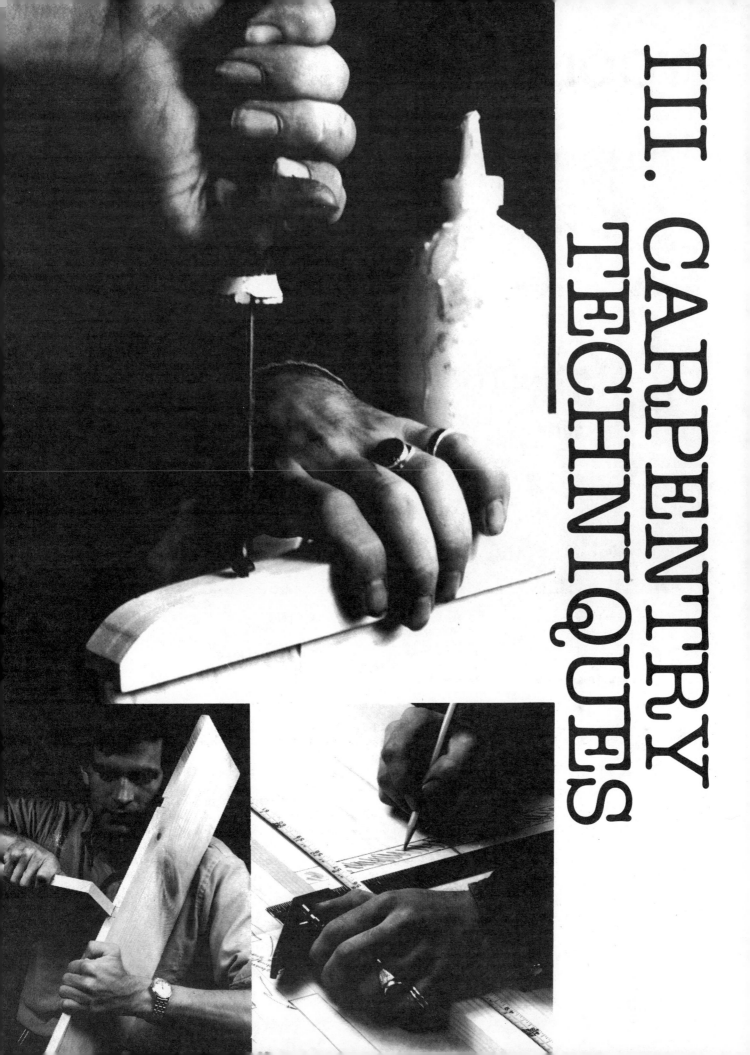

III. CARPENTRY TECHNIQUES

TOOLS & MATERIALS

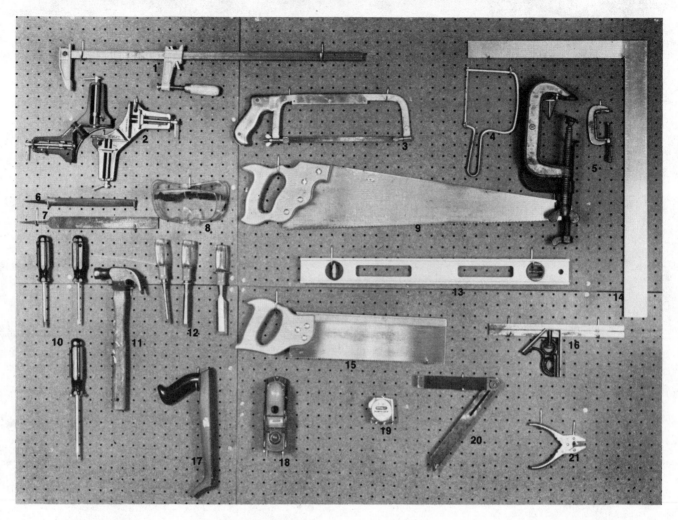

1. Bar or Pipe clamps (2' long)
2. Corner clamps
3. Hacksaw
4. Coping saw
5. C-clamps
6. Medium half-round file
7. Flat bastard file
8. Safety goggles
9. Crosscut saw
10. Screwdrivers
11. Hammer (16 oz. head)
12. Chisels
13. 2' Level
14. Carpenter's square
15. Backsaw
16. Combination square
17. Surform tool
18. Block plane
19. Steel tape measure
20. Sliding bevel
21. Slipjoint pliers

Basic toolkit

Great storage projects begin as well-planned ideas. Ideas then become designs; designs include specifications for materials as well as exact dimensions. Finally, after selecting the tools needed to do the job, work begins. This chapter describes the preliminary work, or first steps, involved in designing and building new storage space.

A good basic toolkit like the one described on the next few pages will see you through many projects, not just for storage, but for all kinds of home repairs and hobbies too. If you're just beginning to outfit your workshop, it's a good policy to buy quality tools. Initial savings on budget tools are usually offset when they wear out prematurely and must be re-

placed. With proper care good tools will last more than a lifetime. Detailed information on how to operate tools is included throughout this book as each tool is introduced; and you will also find descriptions of specialized equipment that can save time and effort.

An idea for new shelves, cabinets, closets, or other storage space becomes a design when you take measurements, make a scale drawing, and select the building materials you want to use. This sequence of events just about completes the preliminaries that help determine how smoothly the rest of the job will run. The only other first step is to estimate how long the job will take and what it's going to cost you.

Cutting and clamping tools

Saws are used for cutting material to size. They are among the most important tools in any workshop because they are used so often. With the five types of handsaws described below, you'll be able to handle just about any project.

The **crosscut saw** is for cutting across the grain of the wood; and for cutting plywood. Most crosscut saws have a 26-inch blade with 7 to 10 teeth per inch. The teeth-per-inch (TPI) count determines the speed and smoothness of the cut. Saws with fewer teeth per inch cut faster but leave a rough wood surface.

Use a **ripsaw** for making cuts that run with the grain. The TPI for most ripsaws is between 5 and 7; ripsaw teeth are larger and chisel-shaped. (Crosscut teeth look like little knives.)

Backsaws have a stiff metal spline which runs along the back of the blade. These saws have finer, denser (12-21) teeth and are used where smooth, accurate cuts are needed. Backsaws are often used with a miterbox (see page 146) for precise joinery work.

You'll need a **coping saw** to cut curves or contours in wood. It has a narrow blade which is pulled tight by a curved holder. These blades dull quickly and are liable to break when forced, so keep some replacements on hand.

If you're going to be cutting metal of any kind, you'll need a **hacksaw.** Hacksaw blades are available with different types of teeth for various metal-cutting jobs.

Keep your saws sharp, since dull blades cut less accurately and are dangerous because of the extra force required to make them work. Hacksaw and coping saw blades can simply be replaced when they dull, but all other handsaws must be re-sharpened and reset. Sharpening and setting requires a good deal of skill as well as special tools, so you're better off having a professional do the job. Prevent your saw blades from rusting by coating them with light machine oil once or twice a season.

The **plane** is a cutting tool with a chisel-like blade mounted at an angle in a wooden or metal body. Planes do the same fine shaping work as chisels, but over a wider, flatter area, since they are larger and can be used with more force. The blade is adjustable to control the depth of the cut. These tools can be costly as hand tools go, but the comparatively small and inexpensive **block plane** will handle most of your shaping and smoothing jobs. An effective and less expensive alternative to the conventional plane is sold under the name Surform. Shaped like a plane, Surform tools have a sharp, finely perforated cutting surface that works like super-rough sandpaper and can be easily replaced when it grows dull.

Files are for small shaping jobs like rounding off corners, softening a hard edge, or reaching into a tight or curved area which is too cramped for a chisel. A **medium-cut half-round file** and **flat bastard file** will suffice for just about all the woodworking you'll do.

Chisels are used for the fine cutting and shaping of wood. Unless you have a dado attachment for your circular saw (see page 148), you'll need a chisel for making rabbet, dado, and lap joints. A set of three chisels (¼-, ½-, and 1-inch blade widths) should be all you need for most woodworking projects. Keep them sharp. Careless handling and improper storage of these tools will dull the blade much faster than woodworking will. Protect your chisels between jobs by covering their blades with tape, and storing them individually in a separate case or holder.

Clamps are indispensable for holding different pieces of material together while glue is setting, or to hold stock firmly while you work on it. There are many different types of clamps, and each is usually available in different sizes, so choosing your first set could be a problem. These are the three most useful types:

Bar clamps are used where a long reach is needed. Two metal feet are attached to a bar or pipe (usually between 2 and 6 feet long) and the stock is clamped tightly between them. One of the feet is fixed at the end of the bar, and the other is adjustable, with a screw-in mechanism to provide clamping pressure.

C-clamps are by far the most common for medium-sized and small work. They come in sizes ranging from an inch to a foot or more and are the least expensive of all clamps, so you can add to your selection by purchasing them as they're needed.

Corner clamps are designed to hold two pieces of stock together at a 90° angle. Using a corner clamp is the best way to make sure a shelf, cabinet, or picture frame joint is perfectly square. (See page 152.) Keep a few on hand.

Handtool checklist

- ☑ 2 Corner clamps
- ☑ 2 Bar clamps (1'-3' long)
- ☑ 4 C-clamps (two 10″, two 3″)
- ☑ Block plane
- ☑ Surform tool
- ☑ 3 Chisels (¼″, ½″, 1″)
- ☑ Flat bastard file
- ☑ Medium cut ½-round file
- ☑ Hacksaw and blades
- ☑ Coping saw and blades
- ☑ Crosscut saw
- ☑ Rip saw
- ☑ 3 Screwdrivers (1 Phillips head)
- ☑ Hammer (16 oz. head)
- ☑ Slipjoint pliers
- ☑ Combination square
- ☑ Carpenter's square
- ☑ Level
- ☑ Steel tape measure
- ☑ Safety goggles

Measuring tools and how to use them

The amazing combination square

Here's a measuring tool that you'll always want to have close at hand because of its versatility. The combination square can be used for checking inside or outside square, marking from an edge, checking for true 45° angles, aligning shelf supports, or measuring, among other things. A better combination square will also contain a level and a scriber.

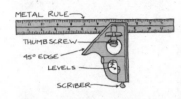

METAL RULE
THUMBSCREW
45° EDGE
LEVELS
SCRIBER

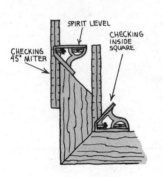

SPIRIT LEVEL
CHECKING 45° MITER
CHECKING INSIDE SQUARE

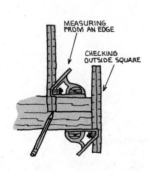

MEASURING FROM AN EDGE
CHECKING OUTSIDE SQUARE

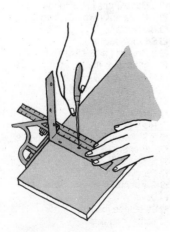

The level is an important tool whose name defines its function: to indicate whether or not a given surface is level. For putting up shelves, hanging cabinets, and other building projects around the home, you should have a level that's at least two feet long. Levels of this length contain at least two clear, calibrated tubes set at right angles to each other. Each tube is filled with liquid and contains a single air bubble. When the air bubble is centered exactly between the calibrations, you've got a level surface. The level will test for true horizontal (always read the horizontal tube, not the vertical one) or true vertical, more commonly called plumb. Don't drop, bang, or jar your level; it is a delicate instrument and rough use will make it inaccurate.

A square will tell you at a glance whether or not a square-looking corner measures a true 90°. Squares are also used for marking stock that has to be cut to smaller dimensions. The **steel or carpenter's square** is a sturdy, all-metal tool that is best used on large pieces like 4x8 panels. The **combination square** is a ruler attached to a metal edge which contains a 45° angle as well as a right angle (and sometimes a level bubble). The edge can be locked in place at any point along the length of the rule, or removed completely. It is a good first-purchase because it is compact, accurate, easy to use, and versatile enough to handle or help out on just about every measuring or marking job you do (see margin).

The sliding bevel is not an exotic animal, as some people may believe. To a carpenter, this is a tool that is used for transferring angle measurements. The sliding bevel consists of a metal straightedge (usually 1″ wide and 10″ long) which pivots and slides around a thumbscrew set in one end of a wooden handle. Tightening the thumbscrew locks the straightedge in place, "memorizing" the angle so you can transfer it to the stock. Easy to use and infinitely adjustable, the sliding bevel is an indispensable tool for custom-fit projects where odd angles are involved.

The tape measure is a compact and convenient invention that has largely replaced the folding rule as the carpenter's most frequently used measuring tool. Tape measures come in lengths as short as 6 feet, but you're better off with a 12-foot model, since measuring longer distances with a short rule is time-consuming and can cause inaccuracies. The metal tape, which comes in ½- or ¾-inch widths (¾-

inch tapes are usually easier to read), is rolled into a metal container that's small enough to fit in your pocket. Unrolling the tape puts a spring inside the container under tension, and unless your tape measure has a locking mechanism, the tape will recoil itself as soon as you release it. The tapelock, although more expensive, is a worthwhile feature if you're someone who does a lot of measuring. Make sure the tape measure you buy is graduated at least to 16ths of an inch; 32nds is better. The best tapes have inches on one side and centimeters on the other.

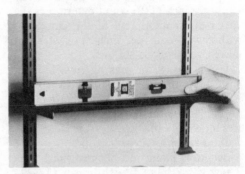

A level is an indispensable tool for hanging shelves. A true horizontal surface is indicated only when the bubble is centered exactly between the calibrations on the tube.

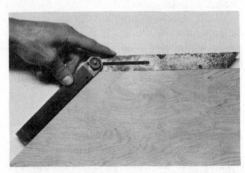

Use the sliding bevel for transferring odd angle measurements to your stock. Lock the adjustable metal straightedge in place after you've taken the angle by tightening the thumbscrew.

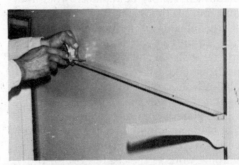

Your tape measure should be at least 12 feet long and calibrated to 16ths or 32nds of an inch. The metal lip at the beginning of the tape enables you to measure longer distances without the aid of a helper to hold one end. This model has a tapelock which will hold the tape at any given length instead of letting it recoil into the housing.

Choosing power tools

Power tools will usually enable you to work faster, more accurately, and with less effort than you could by hand. Below is a brief description of the most widely used power tools, including tips on what to look for when buying them. You'll find specific operating instructions on the pages ahead, as each tool is used.

The circular saw is a hand-held power tool that is used more often for cutting larger stock to manageable size than for precision work. With a good blade and a saw guide, however, the circular saw will do a great job of cutting wood to finished dimensions. If you're buying a circular saw, get one that will take a 7-inch blade; this will allow you to cut lumber up to 2 inches thick. Your saw should have a base that is calibrated and can be adjusted for both depth and angle of cut. Using a saw guide is the secret of straight, accurate cuts, so make sure your saw is equipped with one.

There are many types of blades available: one made especially for crosscutting, one strictly for ripping, a combination blade designed to do both (which usually comes with a new saw), special blades for plywood or for smooth finished cuts, and long-lasting carbide-tipped blades.

The saber saw, or portable jigsaw, has a thin blade that moves rapidly up and down. Saber saws are best suited for cutting curves and contours, and won't make straight cuts as true as those made with a table or circular saw. Most saber saws have a base that tilts and locks in position so you can cut at an angle.

Don't buy a cheap saber saw. They are usually underpowered and tend to vibrate at an alarming rate, which makes accurate cutting difficult. Plan to pay a little more for variable speed control, a calibrated beveling base, and a saw guide—extra features that are well worth the extra cost. Buy assorted blades.

Table saws are found less frequently in home workshops than other power tools because they are expensive and far from portable. The table saw is a real timesaver on projects where many pieces of the same size must be cut, since you can easily improvise a template or jig and thereby eliminate repetitive measuring and marking. The table saw uses the same blades as the circular saw, and the blade can be adjusted for angle and depth.

An electric drill is the least expensive and perhaps most versatile power tool you can own. With the right accessories, you can use your drill for sanding, polishing, grinding or sharpening, and driving screws, as well as for drilling holes. You can buy either a ¼- or ⅜-inch drill; this designation refers to the maximum diameter of the chuck, or bit-holder. Either model will work fine, although ⅜-inch drills are usually more powerful, especially at low speeds. Be sure the drill you buy has a variable speed trigger. Variable speed control means you can control the rpm simply by the pressure of your finger on the trigger.

Bits, like saw blades, come in several varieties. Get a set of common twist drills (bits are sometimes called drills) ranging in size from 1/16- to ¼-inch for starters, then buy them as you need them. Special bits for metal or masonry are also available.

The router is a specialized tool used for grooving and edging wood. The shape of the groove or edge is determined by the type of bit that is used. A router makes dado, rabbet, or lap joinery work a quick and accurate job, and is the best tool to use for trimming formica. Routers are adjustable for depth of cut, but not for angle.

The circular saw will make its most accurate cuts when you use it with a guide. A good circular saw has both depth and angle adjustments.

An electric drill makes holes in all kinds of material quickly and easily. Electric drills are the least expensive of the power tools, and can also be used (with different accessories) for sanding, polishing, and grinding.

Saber saws use a variety of thin blades and are designed for cutting curves. With a saw guide, however, you can also use this tool for straight cutting.

The router is used for making grooves and edges in wood. The bit you use determines the type of groove or edge effect. Using a guide is the best way to insure straight cuts.

Power tool safety checklist

☑ Keep power tools away from children and others who don't know how to use them.
☑ Read the owner's manual before using any unfamiliar tool.
☑ Never change a blade or bit, or try to repair a power tool that is plugged in.
☑ Before operating, check to make sure nuts and screws are secure; the motor's vibration will sometimes cause fittings to work loose.
☑ Make sure the blade or bit is *tightly* secured.
☑ Before you plug in, check the switch or trigger to make sure it's at "Off." As soon as you've finished using it, switch to "Off" and unplug your tool.
☑ Make sure your tool is grounded. Double-insulated power tools do not need to be grounded.
☑ Use only blades and bits that are sharp and in good condition.
☑ Exert moderate, controlled pressure; don't force the blade or bit.
☑ Examine the cut line and remove any nails, bolts, or other metal that might get in the way of the blade or bit.
☑ Clamp material securely.
☑ Wear eye protection. Under heavy dust conditions, wear a filter mask.

Selecting materials

Survey of common hardwoods

Birch is light-colored and similar to maple in appearance but not as strong or heavy. One of the easiest hardwoods to work, it is often used as a substitute for maple because of its lower cost. It can also be stained to look like cherry.

Cherry has a reddish brown color that grows deeper and warmer with age. It is dense, durable, and distinctive enough for the finest woodworking project. Never stain it. Finish it with oil, penetrating resin, or varnish.

Mahogany is tan in color and unusually light for a hardwood. Strong without being dense or hard, it is easy to work and should have a clear finish. The grain is open and requires filling.

Maple is white in color, with a tight, uniform grain. There are several varieties of this exceptionally strong, hard, and heavy wood: rock, curly, soft, and birdseye.

Oak has an open and irregular grain that makes it difficult to work but beautiful to look at when filled and given an oil or varnish finish. White and red oak are the two most popular types of oak lumber.

Walnut is dark in color, with a black and brown grain that gives the wood a rich, exciting look. Easier than oak or maple to work, it usually takes an oil finish.

Grain direction

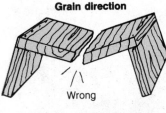

Wrong

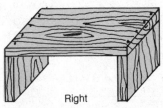

Right

In solid lumber the grain runs lengthwise.

If you cut even a short piece that must carry weight, be sure that the grain still runs lengthwise, in the direction of the legs supporting it.

Consider the materials you want to work with as you develop your design ideas. The standard thickness and rigidity of materials differ. This will effect your detailed plan for the project, as much as aesthetics and cost. For example, you wouldn't want to use expensive hardwood or acrylic for shelves that will be hidden from view most of the time. A low-grade softwood with knots will cost less and be easy to work with but it will sag and break under a load that plywood, hardwood, or glass of equal thickness could support. Metal shelving is also a possibility.

Lumber

There are two kinds of wood: hardwood and softwood. Although characteristics such as weight, knottiness, strength, coloring, grain pattern, and workability can vary from piece to piece regardless of species, the general distinctions between hardwood and softwood are important. **Hardwood** refers to lumber cut from deciduous trees. Oak, maple, birch, cherry, mahogany, and walnut are the popular hardwoods used for fine carpentry. Other hardwoods include teak, rosewood, ebony, and bubinga, but these *exotics* are extremely expensive, hard to find, and generally not used except as thin veneers covering less expensive wood.

Hardwoods are generally more expensive and more difficult to work with than softwoods. They are hard to cut, even with powertools. Don't try to nail or screw two pieces of hardwood together without pre-drilling the stock. Some lumberyards don't even carry hardwoods (cherry and walnut are much scarcer than maple and oak). All hardwoods are sold in random widths. The absence of standard lumber sizes for hardwoods means you may have trouble finding boards of matching widths and so you'll have more cutting and fitting to do.

In spite of the above shortcomings, the strength, durability, and beauty of these woods makes them ideal for certain building projects. (See margin for important characteristics of each species.) Oak or walnut shelves are set off beautifully by just about any kind of shelving hardware. Building a display cabinet or wine rack from maple or cherry will allow you to show off your woodworking talent and will also create a handsome focal point in your home.

Don't choose hardwood if you plan to paint or enamel your project; these woods are used almost exclusively where a clear, natural finish is desired to highlight the grain. Use hardwoods for projects and places in your home where you want storage space to be especially beautiful and on display.

Softwoods are used for every type of construction from rough framing to fine cabinetwork. Readily available, softwoods are a pleasure to work with because of their easy sawing and shaping characteristics. Pine and fir are the most common softwoods. Pine may have a slightly darker and more defined grain than fir, but otherwise the two are nearly indistinguishable. Construction lumber (2x4s, 2x12s, etc.), mouldings, and boards in varying dimensions are all made of softwood. For most storage projects, you'll want to use boards 4- to 10 inches wide and in ½-, ⅝-, ¾-, or 1-inch thicknesses.

Buying lumber. Lumber is sold in *board feet,* a number which you can calculate by multiplying length (in feet), width (inches), and thickness (inches) together and dividing the product by 12. You'll discover that the nominal dimensions of the stock, specifically width and thickness, differ slightly from the actual dimensions (see chart).

The grading system for lumber may vary depending on your dealer and the stock he has available. First and second grade hardwood stock is considered to be of highest quality. Select and #1 Common hardwood lumber will have slight surface defects. High quality softwood may be referred to as Select, Clear, or Supreme. To be sure you're getting the lumber you want at a price that's within your budget, do two things: (1) Describe your project to your lumber dealer. He will tell you what wood is available and may come up with some valid alternatives to your original lumber specifications. (2) Whenever possible, select the wood you buy yourself, piece by piece. Below are some important things to look for.

Make sure your wood has been fully seasoned. Green, or freshly cut lumber is full of sap and unsuitable for construction of any kind. Seasoning allows the sap and other moisture in the wood to dry out, reducing the chances of warpage, shrinking, or cracking. Wood that is sticky, white or slightly green in color, heavier than other pieces, or well-marked with pitch pockets or bubbles is not fully seasoned. Softwoods darken to a greyish tan as they season.

Examine the endgrain of each piece. If the growth rings appear as long curves across the end of the board, the stock is likely to warp (see illustration). The best pieces to buy are those that have a straight up-and-down endgrain. Plainsawn lumber, the most common, often has a circular endgrain, while quartersawn stock does not. Quartersawn lumber is more expensive, but if you want your shelves to be straight five years from now, go with the good endgrain.

Nominal vs. actual lumber dimensions

Nominal	Actual
1x2	¾"x1½"
1x3	¾"x2½"
1x4	¾"x3½"
1x6	¾"x5½"
1x8	¾"x7¼"
1x10	¾"x9¼"
1x12	¾"x11¼"
2x2	1½"x1½"
2x3	1½"x2½"
2x4	1½"x3½"
2x6	1½"x5½"
2x8	1½"x7¼"
2x10	1½"x9¼"

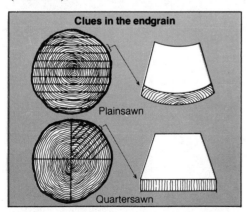

Clues in the endgrain

Plainsawn

Quartersawn

Plainsawn lumber, although economical and easily found, is highly susceptible to warpage because of the circular ring pattern that can be seen in the endgrain. Changes in temperature and humidity cause the wood to shrink or swell unevenly.

Quartersawn lumber has a vertical grain that reacts evenly to changing moisture conditions. The wood will still swell and shrink, but warpage is less likely to occur.

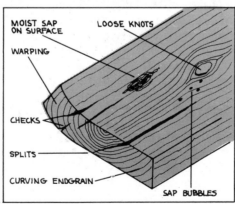

MOIST SAP ON SURFACE — LOOSE KNOTS — WARPING — CHECKS — SPLITS — CURVING ENDGRAIN — SAP BUBBLES

Characteristics of low-quality lumber. Don't buy wood that is knotty; it is difficult to cut and will split easily. Also be on the lookout for cracks and splits. Shallow, narrow cracks or *checks* in the wood are normal signs of seasoning, but deep splits that run with the grain are indicative of poor quality stock.

Plywood

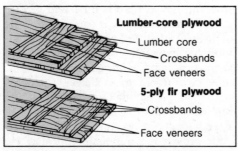

Lumber-core plywood
- Lumber core
- Crossbands
- Face veneers

5-ply fir plywood
- Crossbands
- Face veneers

Plywood is made from wood plies that are glued together so that alternating plies have their grains running at right angles to each other. This gives the material great strength in all directions.

Plywood is sold in 4x8-foot sheets, in the following thicknesses: ⅛-, ¼-, ⅜-, ½-, ⅝-, ¾-, 1-inch. The sheet on the left has an A grade face veneer, while face veneer on the right hand sheet is C grade.

How to cut at cross-purposes
A ripsaw is for cutting with the grain of the wood, right? Then how come my arm nearly fell off when I tried to make a lengthwise cut in a piece of ⅝-inch plywood? While resting my aching muscles, I realized that since alternating plies have their grains running at right angles, what I really needed was a crosscut saw. Sure enough, the job was not only faster and less strenuous, but more accurate too.

Practical Pete

Plywood is a popular alternative to solid lumber. It is stronger, less expensive, and virtually immune to warps or cracks because it is made from thin wood plies, or veneers, that are glued together under great pressure. It also has exceptional strength for its weight because adjacent veneers are laminated with their grains running at right angles to each other.

Plywood is sold in 4x8-foot sheets, in thicknesses from ⅛- to 1-inch. The type of glue used in manufacturing determines whether it is interior or exterior grade. It is graded according to the quality of its two face veneers. "A"-graded veneers are smooth and free of knotholes. A "B" grade means the veneer is solid but may have knots and plugs (plugs are boat-shaped patches used to fill holes). "C" veneers have a limited number of knotholes and splits. As an example of the grading system, a ⅝-inch A/C exterior designation would mean the plywood sheet is ⅝-inch thick, is made with waterproof glue, and has one clear, solid side and one side with knots and splits.

For most storage projects, you'll want at least one good side for painting or finishing. The lower, less expensive grades are used chiefly for tough construction, although they are great for raw shelving in garage, basement, or attic. You can also buy hardwood-faced plywood in different thicknesses. Use this more costly plywood for an especially smooth, hard surface that can take a natural finish.

Other building materials

Particle board is an economical lumber product made from wood chips that are bound in an adhesive matrix and compressed to form a hard composite material. Like plywood, particle board is sold in 4x8-foot sheets of different thicknesses. You may be able to find half sheets or particle board planks for smaller projects or "instant" shelving. Structurally weaker than plywood, this relatively new material tends to be brittle, hence more difficult to chisel and plane. It is used widely as shelving with track-and-bracket or other hardware shelving systems, but it is not suitable for general construction.

Acrylic plastic, popularly known by the brand names of Plexiglass or Lucite, is becoming a symbol of modern decor. It is unbreakable and can be cut, drilled, and smoothed much like lumber, using special blades and bits. It can also be bent to shape when heated. In clear form it is frequently used as display shelving, but is not rigid enough for large projects or heavy storage jobs. Acrylic is sold in sheet form (thicknesses: ⅛-, ¼-, ⅜-inch), and is comparable to hardwood in cost.

Particle board is a composite material made from wood chips. Warp-free because it has no grain, this material is comparable to plywood in price, but more difficult to work. It's sold in 4x8-foot sheets or in planks of different widths.

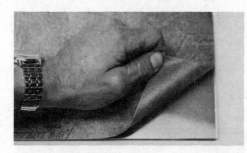

Acrylic plastic lends a modern, unique appearance for storage space that is decorative as well as functional.

Estimating costs and work time

Having to leave your work unfinished or rush through the job because you're pressed for time can take the fun out of any home craftsmanship. Changing specifications for materials in the middle of a project because of high costs is equally frustrating. To avoid these unfortunate circumstances, it's important to get an estimate of costs and work time before you begin the job.

If you have an accurate drawing of your project which includes a materials list, estimating cost is easy. Use the dimensions for each piece to determine how much lumber, plywood, or other material you'll need. When you've figured out how many board feet or sheets of plywood you require (and in what lengths, widths, and thicknesses, in the case of lumber), call up your dealer for a price quote. Remember, your cost estimate should include nails, glue, screws, sandpaper, finish, and any other tools or materials you'll need to complete the job.

Refer to the "What it takes" heading at the beginning of each project in this book for rough estimates of how much time you should allow. Even if you're planning a job not detailed on the pages ahead, you can probably find a project similar enough to yours to give you a rough idea of the time investment you'll have to make. If you have to figure out a time estimate from scratch, be generous. Remember to take drying times for glue, stain, and finish coats into account. Your estimate should also include time for cleaning up and (of course) coffee breaks.

Don't rule out readymades. If the anticipated expenses and time sap your ambition, there's a good chance you can find a set of put-together shelves that is less costly than the lumber required for a home-built unit.

Better hardware stores and home decorating centers have a variety of pre-fab shelves, cabinets and closets designed to fit a wide range of tastes. You can buy an expensive unit if your primary consideration is saving time or working with a minimum number of tools. On the other hand, there are plenty of economical alternatives to handcrafted storage space. Metal shelf supports are available at low cost, as well as track systems that require only a few wood planks to do the same job as a solid bookcase that would take more time and money to build by hand.

Consider a cutting diagram

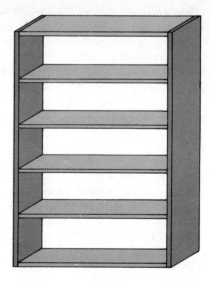 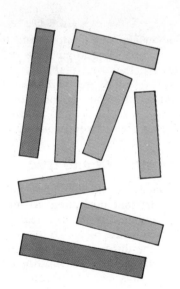 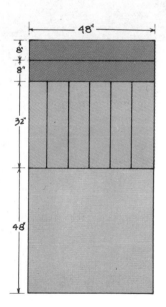

Measuring wisely before cutting larger stock to size saves money by minimizing waste material. A cutting diagram is especially important when working with hardwood, since these woods are expensive and often difficult to find. The easiest way to make a good cutting diagram is to make a scale drawing of each individual piece in your plan and cut them out. Then arrange the pieces by trial and error, like a jigsaw puzzle, edge to edge, until you get a cutting pattern that fits your stock. When transferring your dimensions to the stock, allow for the width of the saw blade; this is ⅛-inch for most power saws. A cutting diagram will also reduce the actual number of cuts you have to make. For pieces that will have to take stress in the middle, like shelving, be sure that the grain runs along the length, not across.

CUTTING & JOINING

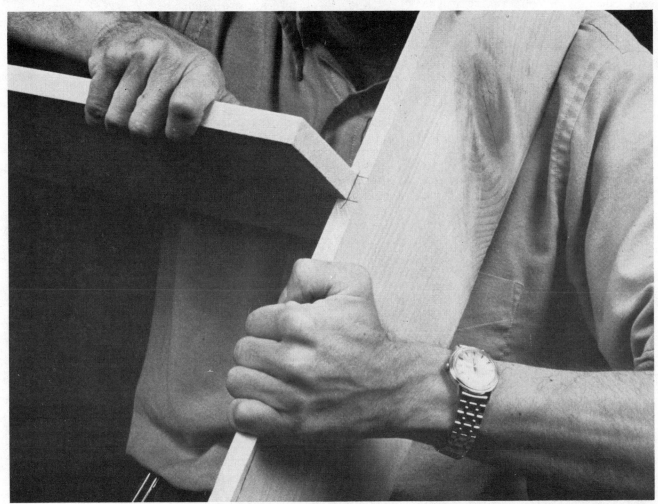

This chapter explains the tools and techniques you'll be using to put your project together. Whether your plans are simple or complex, good craftsmanship will make a big difference in the way your new storage space looks and works. Developing skill with woodworking tools takes time and patience, so take a good look at the sawing, smoothing, and joining techniques on the next few pages. The information on glues, nails, screws, and other fasteners will be necessary for just about any storage or home repair work you will want to do.

Sawing straight and true

Sawing wood and other building materials is an art that takes time to master. Making accurate cuts not only determines how easily separate pieces go together—it makes all the difference in the final appearance of your project. The tips below will give you a head start on sawing craftsmanship.

- **Measure and mark accurately.** If you're cutting small pieces from a larger sheet or board, plan your cuts in a sequence that will allow you to hold the stock in place and guide your saw as easily as possible. For example, when cutting pieces from a 4x8-foot plywood panel, make your longest cuts first to divide the sheet into smaller, more manageable sections. Be sure to allow for the width of the saw blade when marking and cutting.

- **Choose the right cutting tool.** Crosscut saws are for cutting across the grain of the wood; use a rip saw to cut with the grain. If the stock you're working with is delicate or if a smooth edge is important, use a backsaw with a TPI count of 14 or more. If you're cutting with a power saw, use a blade that is designed for the work you want to do (see page 148).Make sure all blades are sharp.

- **Hold the stock securely.** Smooth, straight, accurate cutting is difficult if the material is shifting or wobbling while you work on it. Use clamps to hold it in place, or recruit a helping hand or two.

- **Use a saw guide.** You may indeed have a steady hand, but a saw guide is more reliable. You can use the guide that was made for your saw, or improvise your own. A miter box (pages 146,7) is an absolutely reliable way of making precise handsawn cuts.

- **Don't force your tool.** Cut through the material at a speed that doesn't strain your arm or the motor of your power saw. Make allowances for stock that is thick, hard, or knotty; any of these characteristics will slow down a saw.

- **Prevent binding.** The weight or positioning of the stock can cause it to bind against your blade as you saw, making cutting difficult or impossible. Support the material in such a way that the cut will remain open and not clamp on your blade.

Preventing a rough edge

Saws and other cutting tools often leave a rough edge that is undesirable for precise joinery work. The blade leaves at least part of the cut-line jagged with small splinters and torn wood fibers; usually on only one side of the stock (see illustration below). Using a fine-toothed blade will produce a smoother surface. Smooth- or finish-cutting blades are available for both circular and saber saws, and of course a fine-toothed backsaw or hand saw (14 or more TPI) will also leave a smoother cut.

Even with the best possible blade or bit you may get some splintering, but there are some tricks you can use to prevent it or keep it at a minimum, as shown in the illustrations below.

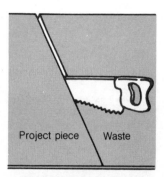

Account for the width of your saw blade. To cut your stock to exact dimensions, keep the "inside" edge of your blade on the outside edge of the cut-line. Centering the blade of the line will leave your piece too small.

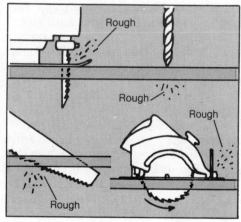

Masking tape placed along the cut-line will hold the surface of wood fibers together and so prevent a rough edge. It can also be marked clearly with a pencil if necessary.

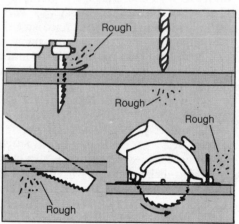

One surface or edge is always more susceptible to splintering than the other, depending on what tool or blade is used.

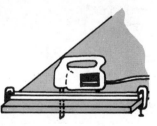

Make your own saw guide if you can't use the guide that goes with your power saw. All you need is a straight length of wood and a couple of clamps to hold it in place.

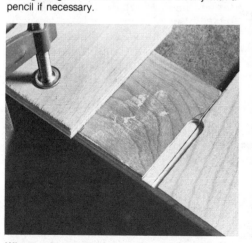

When making a rabbet joint with a router, prevent splintering by butting a scrap piece against the end of the stock.

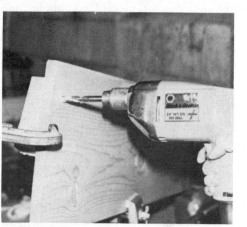

In drilling, you can avoid splintering if you clamp some scrap material to the stock, as shown. The point is not to drill straight through the stock but into the scrap wood.

Joint work

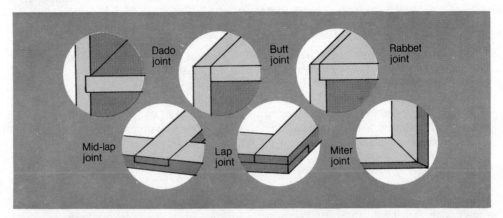

Dado joint

Butt joint

Rabbet joint

Mid-lap joint

Lap joint

Miter joint

Reinforcing joints

You can strengthen joints considerably by using one or more of the ideas illustrated below.

Use screws to pull the joint together.

Glue and nail a wood cleat in place; ¼-round stock looks better than square stock and works just as well.

Use metal braces; your hardware store will have different styles and sizes.

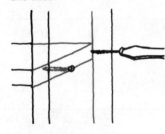

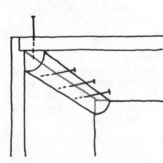

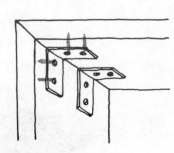

Fitting different pieces of wood together, commonly called joinery, is a crucial part of the craft of carpentry. The strength and final appearance of your work depends upon how well your joints are made.

The butt joint is the simplest joint you can make. Yet while its construction is a lot faster and easier than other joints, it is also a good bit weaker. Butt joints work well where strength or appearance isn't all that important, and you can use them if you don't have the time or tools for more complicated joints. Butt joints are always glued and are often reinforced with screws, wood blocks, or hardware for extra strength.

The rabbet joint is your best bet for corners. It is strong and has an attractive appearance. This type of joint is also fairly easy to make, especially if you have a miter box, router, and a circular or table saw. The rabbet should not be more than half the total thickness of the stock.

The dado joint is used most often for making built-in shelves. As with the rabbet joint, the depth of the groove, or dado, should not be more than half the thickness of the stock. Although most popular on projects where strength and permanence are primary considerations, dado joints add a special touch to small or delicate work, and can also be used for take-apart or adjustable shelving.

The lap and mid-lap joints are simply variations of the rabbet and dado joints, respectively.

The miter joint is nearly as weak as the butt joint and must be cut absolutely perfectly for the sake of strength and appearance. For this reason, it is used only on smaller projects, or where no corner joint may be seen.

The miter box

Here's a tool that's almost indispensable if you plan to work without a power saw. Miter boxes are really nothing more than sophisticated saw guides, but they enable you to make handsawn joints nearly as quickly and accurately as you might with power tools. There are many types, from simple wood or plastic ones that cost a few dollars to expensive metal units with calibrations for cutting any angle from 0-180°. A few of the inexpensive boxes can be used with conventional hand saws, but most require a backsaw. Generally, the more costly the miter box, the greater the number of angles you can cut.

The simplest, least expensive miter boxes are made of wood or plastic, with saw guide slots for cutting 45°and 90°angles.

If you do a lot of joinery by hand, get yourself a good quality miter box with a metal saw guide that can be adjusted to cut a variety of angles.

Making a rabbet joint

1. After you've marked off the depth and width of the rabbet, make the depth cut as shown above. Use a backsaw whenever possible for greater smoothness and precision.

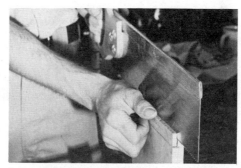

2. To make the second cut, clamp the stock firmly in place and saw along the line you've marked. Sawing "freehand" like this demands a great deal of skill, so work carefully.

3. Use a chisel to smooth the joint before fastening the two pieces together.

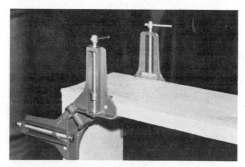

4. Corner clamps aren't absolutely necessary for making corners, but they do make gluing and nailing easier; you can also be certain that the corner is square.

Chisel tips

- For smoothing lap or rabbet joints, it's best to work with the bevel of your chisel facing up.

- Work with the bevel facing down when smoothing dado and mid-lap joints, or whenever the recess in the wood is completely enclosed.

- Try to work so the grain of the wood is running up and away from the blade, as shown in the top illustration. If the grain is running back towards you, the chisel blade will follow the grain down into the wood uncontrollably, leaving a rough, irregular surface.

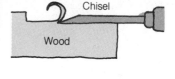

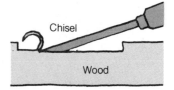

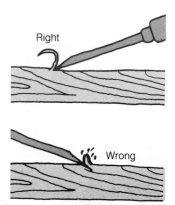

Dadoing step-by-step

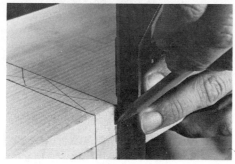

1. Use a square to measure and mark before cutting. Width of dado should match thickness of shelf. Since both sides or shelf supports will be identical, you can save work by marking them both at the same time.

2. Make the two outside cuts first, then make a series of inside cuts; the more you make, the easier your chisel work will be. Be sure to saw to the measured depth on every cut.

3. Use a chisel to remove the waste material and to smooth out the bottom of the groove before you assemble the work.

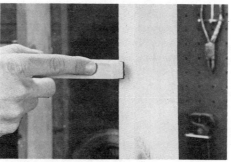

4. Dadoed shelves do not have to be nailed or glued in place, but if you want removable shelves, make the dado slightly wider than the thickness of the shelf.

Circular and table saw blades

Cross cut–for cutting across the grain of the wood.

Carbide-tipped–for cutting materials that are unusually brittle or hard: particle board, plastic laminate, masonite, hardwoods.

Plywood–also called finishing blades; for cutting plywood or making finish cuts in solid stock.

Hollow ground–for fine end grain cuts; good for fine-cutting thick, dense, or oversize stock.

Dado sets–for cutting dados in one operation. Most sets can be adjusted to cut different widths.

Router bits

Mortise–made especially for dadoing, but can also be used for rabbet joints.

Straight–for cutting slots and grooves; also for dadoing.

Rabbeting–for cutting rabbet joints.

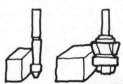

Laminate trimmers–one bit is for trimming the laminate flush; the other is used to bevel the corner where two laminated surfaces join.

Making joints the easy way with power tools

Power tools are your best bet for joint work. Cutting joints with hand tools often requires skilled chisel work in addition to careful sawing. With a circular saw or table saw, however, you can cut accurately enough so that smoothing the cut will be a quick, easy operation. Joints cut with a router hardly ever need additional work before assembly. Bear in mind that when you use a router or power saw for joinery, you must expect to spend more time on adjusting and aligning than on actual cutting. Cutting will be quick and precise, as long as you've adjusted the blade or bit and lined it up correctly with the marks on your stock. Use the guide that's right for your tool: for a circular saw, the adjustable metal guide or a straightedge clamped parallel to the cut-line; for a table saw, the miter gauge or rip fence; for a router, a straightedge clamped parallel to the cut-line. Some routers can be equipped with a special guide which is adjustable for straight or circular cuts.

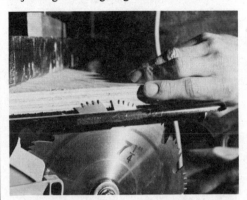

Circular saw. 1. Adjust the baseplate of your saw so that the depth of your cut is no greater than half the thickness of the stock.

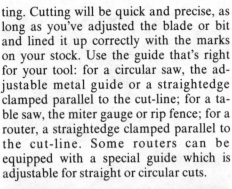

2. Adjust your saw guide and cut the dado. Saw the outside edges of the groove first, then remove waste material inside. Clean up the joint with a chisel before assembling.

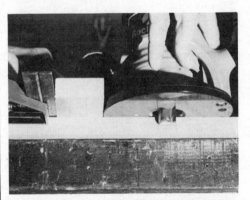

Router. 1. Line up the bit with the marks for the dado and clamp a straightedge to the stock to act as a guide. Use a square, as shown, to make sure the guide is parallel to the dado.

2. Turn the router on and let it reach full speed before applying the bit to the wood. Use steady, firm pressure. Routed joints rarely require smoothing with a chisel.

Table saw. 1. Adjust the height of the blade by turning the knob located near the on/off switch.

2. Hold the stock firmly against the *miter gauge*, making sure the gauge is set for a 90° cut, and feed it through the blade using even pressure.

How walls are constructed

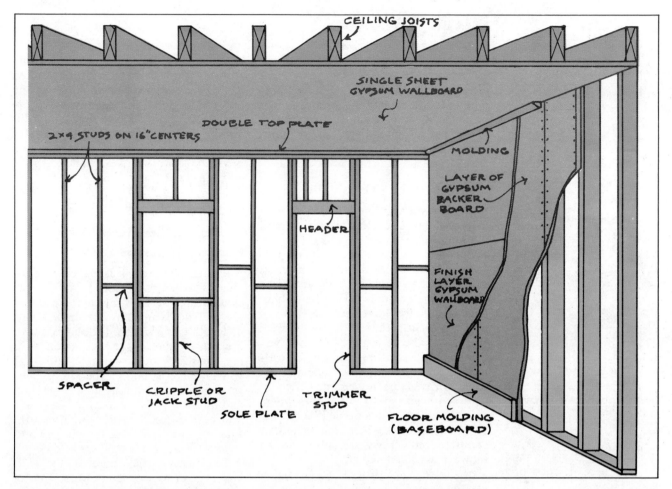

Knowing a little about how your house or apartment is built can be a big help in planning and constructing new storage space. For example, it's important to know how to locate studs if you plan to hang cabinets or shelves. Building a new closet, putting up a wall, installing hooks or hangers, and mounting pegboard are other projects that require some knowledge of the structure of your house.

Structurally, a house consists largely of a system of beams and joists joined to form a skeleton which supports both an outer and inner skin. The outer shell is of necessity thick and strong, usually consisting of several layers: plywood *sheathing*, asphalt-impregnated building felt, and exterior siding. Most interior walls are comparatively thin and delicate: sheetrock, paneling, or plaster.

Locating studs. Let's get back to our skeleton, or structural framework, known more commonly as *framing*. While you can't count on the wall itself to support a great deal of weight, the 2x4 framing joists, or *studs,* can really hold a load. The problem is to locate the studs in your wall so you can fasten into them. In conventionally framed homes, the studs run vertically on 16-inch centers (see illustration above), so if you locate one, finding others on the same wall is easy. Although you can use a stud-finder, or listen for a solid sound while knocking on the wall, the surest way to find your first stud is by drilling a small hole in the wall. If your bit stays in solid material and keeps turning out sawdust, you've found a stud. Only don't just drill randomly; measure 16 inches from a corner, door, or window frame. **Note:** An inconspicuous place for exploratory drilling is about 5 inches above the floor line; fill the hole later with spackling paste.

Old or unconventionally framed homes. Locating studs will be more difficult in these cases. It is not uncommon for builders to space studs on 24-inch centers in non-loadbearing walls for the sake of economy. In many old houses, post and beam construction was the rule: large beams set farther apart, and at random intervals. If you're having trouble locating studs and suspect unconventional framing, try removing the floor molding. Chances are you'll find an exposed nail or two which indicates solid wood underneath.

Screws, nails, and glues

Skillful cutting and fitting is only half the joinery story; choosing and using the right fasteners and adhesives is equally important. In fact, a poor-fitting joint can often be "rescued" with a good glue bond and a few screws to pull it tight. Screws, nails, and glue can be used separately or in combination, depending on the joining job you've got to do. The information on these two pages will help you to select and use the fasteners and adhesives that are best for your project. See page 26 for different types of fasteners available for mounting things on walls.

Screws

Screws are stronger and hold longer than nails, but are also more expensive and more time-consuming to "sink." For this reason, they're not used for rough carpentry such as framing a wall, or in cases where quick assembly is important. Used along with glue, screws will often eliminate the need for clamps because they can pull a joint together with great force. Screws can also be removed easily if you want to disassemble your project, although bolts are better for "take-aparts." (Bolts are available in the same variety of sizes and head types.) Use screws where an extra strong joint is needed, or on fine or traditional work where countersunk or counterbored screws are called for as shown in the diagrams, left.

Choose the length and gauge (shank diameter) of your screws according to the material you're joining. At least two-thirds of the screw's total length should extend into the base material, as shown at left. Select a gauge that's large enough for the holding power you want. If in doubt, use the smaller screw. Glue provides most of the bonding strength; screws pull the joint tight while the glue is curing.

You also have a variety of head types to choose from when selecting screws. Flat-head screws are used most often in woodworking because they are made for countersinking or counterboring, and are therefore less conspicuous.

Always sink screws in predrilled holes. Drill the pilot hole first, using a bit that's slightly smaller than the threaded section of the screw (see illustration at left). The pilot hole should be small enough so the threads bite firmly into the wood, and large enough so you don't have to strain while driving the screw in. Drill the shank clearance hole and the countersink depression next. (You'll need a *countersink bit* for this.) Special combination bits are available that drill pilot, shank, countersink, and counterbore holes in one operation without changing bits.

Nails

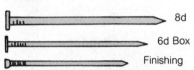

8d

6d Box

Finishing

Nails are the fastest, least expensive fasteners. The three types used most often for construction of all kinds are illustrated above. The *d* is an abbreviation for *penny*, or length classification. (The nails above are actual labeled size.) Common nails are for rough or large scale building; you'll need 8, 10, and maybe 12d nails for framing a wall or putting up a closet. Box and finishing nails are narrower in gauge and best-suited for finer joinery work. Finishing nails are made to be *set* and covered with wood dough (see below).

To determine the length of the nails you plan to use, remember that ⅔-¾ of the total length should extend into the base material. If you're nailing into hardwood or delicate stock, you may have to predrill your nail holes to prevent splitting or use a shorter, thinner nail. Use a bit that's half the diameter of the nail or less.

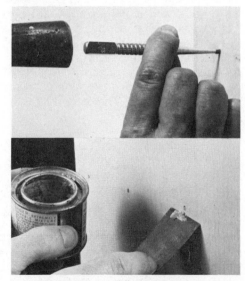

Use a special punch called a *nailset* to sink finishing nails slightly below the surface. Then fill holes with wood dough and sand the dough flush when it hardens.

Countersunk screw

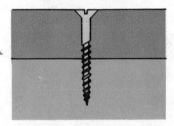

Counterbored screw

DOWEL PLUG

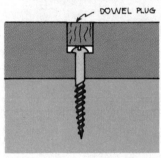

COUNTERSINK DEPRESSION

SHANK CLEARANCE HOLE

PILOT HOLE

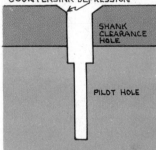

Types of screw heads

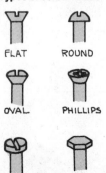

FLAT   ROUND

OVAL   PHILLIPS

PAN   LAG

Glue

Glue is a must for all permanent joints. Instead of forcing a joint together like screws or nails do, glue is a bonding agent that makes two separate pieces into one. The main types are described in the chart. *Setting time* is the time it takes for the glue to dry and form a bond. Maximum bond strength is achieved when the glue *cures*. When deciding what kind of glue you should use,

consider cost, ease of application, and the conditions which the glued joint will be exposed to.

Regardless of what glue you're using, be sure to read the manufacturer's description of the product and follow the directions for surface preparation and application closely.

Here are some general guidelines to good gluing. Clean the joint thoroughly before you glue; oil, dirt,

wax, and dust are all enemies of adhesion. Work the glue into the material; don't just bead it on. This is especially important when gluing porous surfaces like the endgrain of a pine or fir board. Last but not least, remove excess glue as soon as possible, using a damp rag. Glue allowed to stand even for a few minutes can leave a stain in the wood that's tough to remove.

Description/Setting time/Curing	Advantages/Limitations/Suggested use	Preparation and application
Polyvinyl acetate (PVA). Familiar white glue; usually comes in a clear squeeze bottle. Dries clear. Water soluble/3-4 hours/24 hours.	Inexpensive; sets quickly; no mixing/Poor moisture resistance; limited shelf life; discolors metal/For interior use on porous materials.	Apply generously to both surfaces; clamp securely; wipe away excess glue.
Aliphatic resin. Yellow glue similar to white glue in consistency. Dries clear or slightly amber. Water soluble/3-4 hours/24 hours.	More water-resistant than white glue; made especially for woodworking; no mixing; quick setting; economical for large jobs/Limited shelf life; not waterproof; will not bond non-porous materials/Use on wood-to-wood joints.	Apply generously to both surfaces; clamp securely; wipe away excess glue.
Resorcinol. Also known as waterproof glue; usually sold in cans, it comes in two parts/6-10 hours/24 hours.	Completely waterproof; excellent bonding strength on porous surfaces/Expensive; requires mixing; long setting time; leaves a dark glue line/Use on exterior wood-to-wood joints, or where a waterproof bond is needed.	Mix only amount needed, according to manufacturer's instructions; coat both surfaces; clamp. Heat will shorten setting time.
Epoxy. A two-part adhesive sold in cans or tubes; comes in several varieties, with differences based on setting time, opacity, and viscosity. Waterproof/¼-12 hours/24 hours.	Excellent bond strength; waterproof. (Short-setting epoxies are weaker.) Can be used as a filler/Expensive; requires mixing; offers no advantage over aliphatic resin on interior wood-to-wood joints/Use for small gluing jobs, or when joining dissimilar or nonporous materials.	Combine and mix *hardener* and *resin* according to manufacturer's directions. Use only as much as needed. Clamping is optional; avoid forcing epoxy out of the joint.
Contact cement. A specialized glue that bonds on contact; comes in cans and small tubes or bottles. There is no setting time/curing takes 24-48 hours.	Flexible; reaches 75% bond strength on contact; no clamping needed/Expensive; surfaces to be glued can't be realigned once they contact each other/Use for covering surfaces with veneer, plastic, and other laminates.	Apply generously and evenly to both surfaces (use a brush for large jobs). Allow to dry until slightly tacky. Align surfaces exactly and press together.

Tips from the gluing experts

A heat lamp can help you to cut down setting and curing times. Don't create a fire hazard by exposing the wood to dangerously high temperatures, and be sure the joint is heated evenly.

It's easy to make your own wood dough with some fine sawdust and a little white or yellow glue. Mix the sawdust into the glue gradually until you get a creamy, homogeneous paste.

Use scrap pieces of wood as clamping blocks; they will distribute clamp pressure more evenly and prevent the metal clamping feet from damaging the finished stock.

If you can't clamp your joint, use screws to pull the glued surfaces together and keep them under pressure while the glue sets. A few finishing nails will secure the joint while you drill screwholes.

The 007 bond
I got a great bond on my last glue job; so great that when I tried to remove my project from the workbench it wouldn't budge. Next time I'll use a little waxed paper to keep the glue where it belongs: in the joint and off the bench.

Practical Pete

Wall fasteners

Building new storage space often involves wall fasteners of one type or another. Whether you're hanging shelves, putting up pegboard, securing a built-in bookcase, or installing cabinets, you can be sure there's a wall fastener made for the job. Wall fasteners come in a confusing array of sizes and shapes, so if you're uncertain of size or design, ask your hardware dealer for advice. Tell him what kind of wall you're dealing with, and what you want to hang, secure, or support. **Note:** Don't make your wall-joining job more difficult than it needs to be. You may not need special fasteners at all if you can locate a stud or joist to nail or screw into. The wood framing behind your gypsum, panel, or plaster wall will always hold more weight than the wall material itself, so try locating studs before shopping around for wall fasteners.

If your wall is concrete, brick, tile, or some other solid, non-wooden material, or if you can't locate or utilize the framing, the information below can help you out. The most frequently used wall fasteners are listed below. Suitable wall types for each fastener are indicated in italics.

Installing standard fasteners

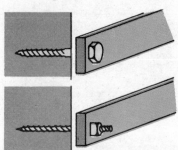

Lag screws and hanger bolts *for solid wood, studs, or other wood framing members.* Sink these heavy-duty hangers into studs or joists for holding loads of 20 pounds or more. (See hints on locating studs in a hollow wall, page 23.)

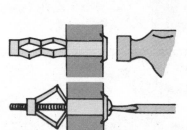

Mollies *for gypsum wallboard, wood paneling, plaster, and hollow walls.* Available in different sizes, these wall hangers consist of a threaded, collapsible metal housing and a matching bolt. To install a molly, first drill out a hole no larger than the molly's diameter. Then hammer the unit into the hole. Make sure the teeth on

Plastic expansion anchors *for gypsum wallboard, plaster, tile, hollow walls.* These inexpensive anchors come in several designs and sizes, but all operate on the same principle: driving a screw into the hole in the installed anchor forces

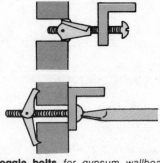

Toggle bolts *for gypsum wallboard, wood paneling, and hollow walls.* These fasteners come in a variety of different sizes, and are easy to install. Make sure the bolt is long enough for the spring-activated toggle to open up. The hole should be just large enough to accommodate the toggle assembly.

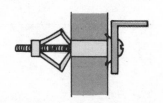

the lip of the molly are firmly embedded in the wall (first illustration). Turn the bolt clockwise with a screwdriver to collapse the molly and lock it in place. Make sure the lip doesn't turn with the bolt. Now you can remove and re-insert the bolt for mounting.

two plastic feet out against the hole, wedging the anchor in place. Most anchors are labeled with the correct bit diameter for installation; if not, use the bit that gives you the snuggest fit.

Metal expansion shields *for brick, concrete, stone, marble, and other solid walls.* These anchors expand as bolts or screws are turned into them, exerting pressure against the walls of the installation hole which wedges them in place. Although available in different styles and sizes, metal expansion shields are only suitable for use in hard, solid walls.

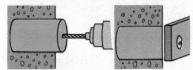

Wooden dowels *for brick, concrete, stone, marble, and other solid walls.* You can make your own wall anchors from wooden dowels. Your installation hole should be at least an inch deep and must match the diameter of the dowel so the wooden plug fits *very* snugly. **Hint:** A generous dab of epoxy glue will help hold the plug in place and compensate for an oversize hole. Drill out the pilot hole for the screw after you've hammered the dowel into the hole.

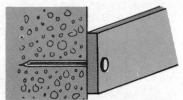

Masonry nails *for concrete and cinder block walls.* Because of the thick gauge of these nails and the shock transmitted to the stock, it's advisable to drill a pilot hole in the material you're fastening to the wall. Masonry nails are notorious for bending and won't penetrate concrete that is extremely hard or fine. ***Caution:*** *Always wear eye protection when nailing into hard materials like concrete or cinder block.*

Building the basic box

1. Working from a simple drawing like the one shown at right, transfer your measurements to the stock. Use a carpenter's square to make sure your cut-lines are true. Take the width of the saw blade into account when marking out adjacent pieces.

2. Use a saw guide to assure a straight cut. In this case a straight length of wood is clamped parallel to the cut line. To prevent binding, make sure the waste side of the stock is supported while you saw.

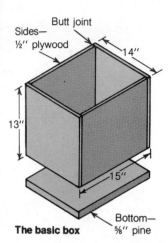

Sides— ½″ plywood

Butt joint

14″

13″

15″

Bottom— ⅝″ pine

The basic box

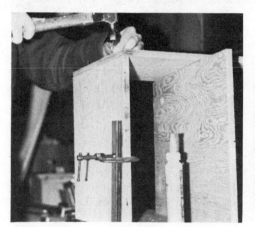

3. Glue and nail the sides together. For this box, a butt joint is used for the sake of speed and simplicity; a rabbet joint is stronger but takes longer to make. If you improvise a support like the one shown here, joining the sides is easier.

4. Square up the box using a square and a diagonal brace as shown. Nail one end of the brace to a side about midway between the corners. Then force the corner against the square and nail the free end of the brace to the adjacent side.

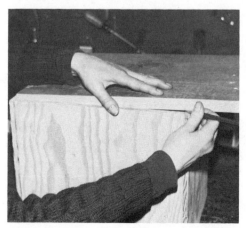

5. Measure and cut the base. For an exact fit, cut the stock to measured width, then fit it into the bottom and mark the length for final cutting.

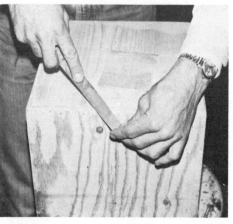

6. When bottom has been glued and nailed in, set all nails and fill the holes with wood dough. When wood dough dries, round corners with a file and smooth sides and bottom with sandpaper. Finish as desired.

7. Make a group of boxes and you can stack them as shown. An advantage of *modular* storage such as this is that it can be taken down, relocated, or rearranged quickly and easily.

FINISHING

Now that you've planned your new storage space, drawn up design details, selected materials, cut parts to size, and assembled the whole project, you're ready for finishing. Although the main function of finishing is to preserve and protect the wood or other material, a good finish really shows off the craftsmanship involved in the design and construction of your project for years to come.

Finishing means more than just applying paint or varnish. The three steps involved in surface preparation (to be described) are essential for a good finish. You may also decide that you want to stain the wood or apply wood filler before putting on the finish. Finishing decisions depend on a number of important factors: how much time and money you want to spend, the size of your project, the type of wood or other material you're dealing with, the surrounding decor, application details, drying time, and durability. Apply these considerations to the information on the following pages to determine how you want to finish your project, then do it!

Getting the surface set

Step 1: Fill holes

Fill all cracks and holes with wood dough. Clean up cracks or holes before you fill them by removing loose splinters and sawdust. Use a putty knife or any knife with a flexible blade to apply the dough. Always overfill depressions so they can be sanded flush. You can make your own wood dough by mixing sawdust with some white or yellow glue. Take some fine sawdust from the stock you're filling for the most inconspicuous patch. Mix in the sawdust gradually until the consistency is creamy, not stiff. Fill deep holes in stages, letting each layer of wood dough dry before applying the next.

Step 2: Make it smooth

Use sandpaper to smooth all surfaces to be finished. Sanding your project down before applying the finish is one of those jobs that is easy to neglect, but it really pays off, since any irregularities are always accentuated by finish coats. Sanding also improves absorption and adhesion by removing surface wood pores that may be clogged with dirt, wax, or oil.

Smoothing work will go faster and easier if you use sandpaper of the right abrasive strength (see chart below). Always work from coarse to fine grades. For example, a 100 grit followed by a 150 grit smoothing schedule works well on most lumber. Sandpaper will eventually wear out as abrasive particles become dull or clogged with sawdust, but you can get more "life" from each sheet if you use sanding blocks (see margin).

Don't forget to round off edges and soften corners slightly while you smooth to prevent chips and blemishes. You can use sandpaper for this job, but a *medium-cut bastard* file will work much faster.

Sandpaper

Grit	Classification	Common uses
600 500	super fine	wet or dry polishing
400 360 320	extra fine	
280 240 220	very fine	dry sanding between finish coats
180 150	fine	final sanding on bare wood before applying finish
120 100 80	medium	general wood sanding, preliminary sanding on rough wood
60 50 40	coarse	rough sanding, paint and finish removal

Always sand with the grain of the wood. Start with a medium grit and finish with a fine grit. The best way to sand flat surfaces is to use a sanding block, as shown above.

Round off sharp corners and edges with a file. For best results, keep the file at an angle to the edge, as shown. It's a good idea to give filed areas a once-over with some sandpaper.

Put power tools to work for you. Sanding discs are available as an accessory for your electric drill, and make quick work of sharp edges. An orbital sander is a good investment if you really want to speed up smoothing operations.

Sanding Blocks

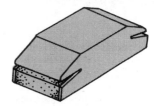

1. Commercial sanding blocks are easy to "load." You'll find them in most paint and hardware stores.

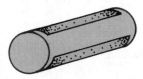

2. Use a length of dowel rod to make a sanding block for curved surfaces.

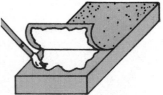

3. You can bond your sandpaper permanently to a wood block with some contact cement. Coat both surfaces, allow glue to get tacky, then press wood and paper together.

Step 3: Remove dust

Sanding leaves a thin layer of fine sawdust on the wood surface. Remove it with a tack rag. You can buy one at most paint and hardware stores, or make one by dampening a piece of cheesecloth in some varnish and allowing it to get tacky.

For large projects, save time and effort by using a vacuum to remove sawdust. Make sure the attachment you use has soft bristles, like the one shown, so there's no risk of scratching the wood.

Wood filler: how and when to use it

Open or coarse-grained woods like oak, hickory, mahogany, and teak will not take a smooth, even varnish or lacquer finish unless their large and irregularly spaced pores (see margin) are filled beforehand. To do this, you'll need some wood filler, a preparation made specifically for this job. Wood filler comes as a paste and usually requires thinning before application (check instructions on can). Most fillers work best on wood that has been sealed with a wash coat (thinned-down) of shellac or lacquer. When the sealer coat has dried completely, mix up your filler and brush a thick coat onto the stock. Work the filler into the pores of the wood with your brush.

Note: Wood filler comes in different colors, or it can be custom-colored by using a wiping stain as the thinning agent. When the filler begins to dry out or dull over (5-25 minutes), wipe it off with a coarse rag. Always wipe across the grain so you don't remove the filler that's lodged in the wood pores where it belongs. Don't stop until you have wiped it all off the surface. If it dries hard it is difficult to remove. You will have to soak a rag in turpentine or benzene to soften it enough to wipe away. Wait 24 hours for the filler to dry, smooth the surface with extra-fine sandpaper if necessary, and you're ready for stain and finish coats.

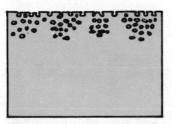

Coarse-grained woods have irregularly spaced pores.

Fine-grained woods have small, evenly distributed pores.

1) Thin wood filler according to manufacturer's instructions, then brush it onto the wood generously. Work the material into the pores of the wood with the bristles.

2) When the filler starts to dry out or dull over, wipe it off with a coarse rag. Always wipe across the grain to fill the pores and clean off excess.

Staining wood

There are three reasons for staining wood: to make it look like another type of wood, to give it an older appearance, and to make it blend in better with surrounding wood or decor. You may want to make a major tone change by staining a light-colored wood like birch to look like walnut. On the other hand, you may have several oak boards to use with track shelving that are slightly different in color. In a case like this, only a subtle stain is needed. It's even possible to spot-stain a piece of wood to make its color more uniform. Once the wood has been stained, the next step is to apply a clear finish to show off your work and to protect the wood from moisture, abrasion, undesirable stains, and general wear.

There are several different types of stains. Consult the chart at right to determine which one is best for the job you have in mind. Stains are available in a wide variety of wood tones. Don't rely on the name or color designation alone when choosing; all stain manufacturers have samples of each stain as it looks on different kinds of wood. You'll find these displays wherever stains are sold. As a final check, you should test your stain out on a scrap piece of wood identical to the stock in your project.

Staining wood is easy but very important as far as final appearance is concerned. Here are some tips that will help you to do a good job: If more than one can of stain is to be used, mix all the stain together in a large container before application to assure consistent color. When removing excess stain from the wood surface, dampen your cloth with stain first. A dry cloth is likely to remove pigmentation from the surface wood pores and leave lint behind. The end grain on any piece of wood is extra absorbent, and will "drink" enough stain to make it noticeably darker than the rest of the wood. Control end grain stain absorption by applying a limited amount of stain to these areas.

Stain samples

The grain-raising story

You've sanded the bare wood to a satin-smooth texture in preparation for staining and finishing. The stain goes on well and gives you just the color and highlights you'd hoped for. The only problem is that the stained wood surface seems to be rougher than it was before you applied the stain.

There's no need to be alarmed; the surface actually is rougher than it was after the final sanding. This is because the stain has caused the surface wood fibers to swell and stick out unevenly. Water-base and penetrating oil stains will always raise the grain to some degree, especially on softwoods. Wiping stains and non-grain-raising stains will not.

A raised grain can get in the way of a good finish, and should be smoothed "flat" when the stain has dried. Use a new piece of extra-fine steel wool for this job. Go over the wood lightly, so that you only remove the protruding wood fibers. **Note:** Some finishing experts raise the grain purposely *before* staining by wetting it down with a damp cloth. When the bare wood is smoothed again, it can be stained without raising the grain noticeably.

Comparing different kinds of stain		
Description	**Use**	**Application**
Non-grain-raising (NGR) stains. Also known as quick-drying or alcohol-base stains, these preparations are more expensive than other stains but do have several advantages: they dry quickly enough so that finish can be applied within 3 hours, and they can be sprayed on to save time with large projects.	Use NGR stains on hardwoods like oak, maple, or birch. These woods don't need a "transforming" stain to make them resemble some other wood type, but rather a slight shading to accent their already distinctive grain. NGR stains don't work well on softwoods.	Wipe or spray on; avoid brushing. Don't worry if the coloring isn't as dark as you want; just reapply the stain at 15 minute intervals for darker effects. Don't flood NGR stains onto the wood; additional tone is achieved by reapplication, not penetration.
Water-base stains. These stains are available in ready-to-use liquid form, or as a powder dye that must be dissolved in water before use. You can save money by mixing the stain yourself, adjusting the color simply by varying the concentration. Drying time: 24 hours.	Use these stains on hardwoods or softwoods, for either subtle or dramatic changes in tone. On absorbent woods like pine, water stains will raise the grain considerably, so don't use this type of stain if you want to avoid additional smoothing work before applying a finish.	Apply the stain generously, making sure to keep the surface wet until the wood is saturated. Wait a few minutes, then remove all excess stain with a cloth that has been slightly dampened in stain.
Nonpenetrating oil stains. Characteristically thick and paint-like, these stains have a linseed oil base and are heavily pigmented. Drying time: 24 hours.	Effective for darkening pine, fir, and other light woods; the best stain to use if you want to hide the grain of the wood rather than highlight it.	Apply generously, using a brush. Wait several minutes for the pigment to settle, then wipe the surface down, removing excess stain with an absorbent cloth. The harder you wipe, the lighter the final color of the wood will be.
Penetrating oil stains. These are the most popular stains for use on softwoods, and come in a wide variety of wood tones. Because of their mineral spirit or turpentine base, these stains penetrate deeply into the wood, and do a good job of sealing and protecting in addition to staining. Drying time: 24 hours.	Use mainly on softwoods, including plywood. Penetrating oil stains can be used effectively under a paste wax finish because of their protective quality.	Apply liberally, using a brush, sponge or rag. The intensity of the stain depends on how long it is allowed to penetrate into the wood, so wipe off early if you want a lighter shade. Reapply to achieve darker coloring or let the stain stand longer before wiping.

Using finishes

Putting a finish on your project serves two purposes: 1) to protect the wood or other material from general wear, and 2) to enhance the appearance of the project. Although there is a variety of wide finishes available, those described here offer a range of choices, and are more durable and easier to use than less popular finishes.

Paints and enamels, for sure results on any surface. Finishing with paint or enamel is a great way to transform a drab-looking project into something special. Compared to clear finishes, paints and enamels give more reliable, predictable results because they don't depend on the grain of the wood for good looks. Used as a cover-up, these finishes enable you to use inexpensive building materials (plywood, particle board) without worrying about the final appearance of your project. Use rustproof formulas on non-wooden materials like metal and gypsum wallboard.

Because of the confusing variety of products available, deciding what paint or enamel to use can be pretty frustrating. Choosing the right color, and deciding whether you want a flat, gloss, or semi-gloss finish are the first (and the easiest) decisions. Other considerations are cost, durability, drying time, and ease of application and clean-up. All this information is on the paint can, and your paint dealer can give you additional information and specific recommendations. Paint is less expensive than enamel, but enamel finishes are comparable to varnish as far as durability goes. Used often in high traffic zones like the kitchen and bathroom, enamel will stand up to hard use, won't stain or spot, and can be wiped clean with a damp cloth. If you're putting up a wall, constructing a built-in shelf or cabinet space, or finishing new storage space to blend in with the room, paint will give you the best results. Painted surfaces lack the hard brightness of enamel.

Whether you're painting over bare wood or wood that has been previously finished, at least two coats are required for a first-class job. The first coat, often referred to as the *base, primer,* or *undercoat,* must seal the wood, cover all stains or irregularities in the grain, and provide a smooth, uniform, and adherent surface for subsequent finish coats. Although the paint you use for finish coats can often serve as a primer (consult manufacturer's instructions), you're usually better off using a *primer-sealer.*

1. Use a primer-sealer as the base coat on bare wood or over an existing finish. Because of their short drying time and sealer/stain hiding qualities, commercial primer-sealers are ideal undercoaters.

2. Once the undercoat has dried, paint on the finish coat. Use a clean brush, dipping only the bottom third of the bristles into the paint. Always paint from the top down.

Combine oil and turpentine in a three-to-one mixture and soak this into the wood by pouring or brushing. Let finish penetrate for 15 minutes; remove excess; then buff wood surface with a clean, lint-free cloth.

Oil, for the traditional, hand-rubbed finish. Boiled linseed oil, turpentine, and elbow grease are all you need for this finish. One of the oldest and least expensive finishes, rubbed oil protects the wood from stains of all types and gives a warm, soft luster that is most beautiful on dark-grained hardwoods. Light woods like pine or maple can be stained before they are oil-finished, but never apply oil over filler or sealer coats.

Begin an oil finish by thinning your linseed oil with turpentine; one part turpentine to three parts oil is about right. (Later coats will be at full strength.) Flood the wood surface with this mixture, let it soak in for 15 minutes, then remove the excess and buff the wood until you get a dull glow. It's important to rub the surface vigorously, either with a lint-free cloth or your palm, to drive the oil deep into the pores of the wood. Additional applications (ten or so, no kidding) and rubdowns will produce an even deeper, richer glow. Wait at least 24 hours before reapplying the linseed oil, and rub in a little at a time, instead of flooding the whole surface.

The traditional rubbed-oil finish really takes a great deal of time and effort, and now there are several finishes available which will produce nearly the same results after one or two applications. Ask your dealer for "easy" oil finishes if the traditional method scares you off.

Varnish and polyurethane, for durability and beauty. These are far and away the most popular clear finishes. Available in either gloss or satin, these finishes will show the wood grain and protect against moisture, stains, and abrasions.

Old-fashioned varnishes took hours and sometimes days to dry completely—a major drawback, since dust and other particles would dry into the finish. Modern varnishes are made largely from synthetic resins (polyurethanes) and

will dry in 4-6 hours. When buying varnish, read the product description on the can to make sure you won't have to deal with extended drying times. All the synthetic varnishes (known by different brand names, but usually labeled as urethane or polyurethane) are quick-drying. Two coats of varnish are normally required for a complete finish. All varnishes are made to be used over bare wood, so check your finish for compatibility if you plan to use stain or wood filler.

Apply varnish generously, but avoid bending or slapping the bristles of your brush, since this can cause bubbles.

Spraying on a lacquer finish is usually easier if you hang up your project so that you can move around it freely. Keep the nozzle moving and build up at least three thin, even coats for a durable, good-looking finish.

Lacquer, the alternative to brush-on finishes. Lacquer is a fast-drying, multiple-coat finish which can be applied with an air compressor/spray gun unit, but is most often used in spray can form. Most hardware, paint, and home decorating centers have a wide selection of colors as well as clear lacquer. You'll also find *acrylic* finishes in spray cans; they apply and dry just like lacquer, but tend to be less durable.

Because of its quick-drying and spray-on application, lacquer is convenient and easy to use. It's great for

finishing curved, contoured, or large projects which would involve an undesirable amount of brushwork. (You won't have to clean any brushes either.) **Note:** Lacquer shouldn't be used over an oil-base stain. Follow the manufacturer's instructions pertaining to staining, sealing, and filling under a lacquer finish.

As far as spray finishing technique goes, just remember to keep the nozzle moving to avoid bubbles or runs. Build your finish up in thin layers, coat by coat.

Penetrating resin, for protection and durability without covering the wood. Unlike varnish, paint, or lacquer—surface finishes which protect the wood by covering it—penetrating resin is an in-the-wood finish that leaves the wood surface exposed. The synthetic resins that make up this finish penetrate deep into the wood and harden, making the wood surface strong and extremely resistant to water damage, stains, heat, and abrasion. A penetrating resin finish will darken the wood slightly and highlight the grain considerably, although in a softer, subtler way than varnish or lacquer. It is used

most often on walnut, mahogany, cherry, oak, and other hardwoods which have distinctive coloring or grain patterns. There are really only two drawbacks to penetrating resin finishes: They're expensive; and they won't do much for wood with an even, uninteresting, or light grain. Penetrating resin can be applied over a non-grain-raising stain.

This is one of the easiest finishes to apply; just let the liquid finish soak into the wood and wipe off the excess that remains on the surface. Most brands recommend two separate applications. Allow at least 4 hours between "coats."

Keep the wood surface horizontal, if possible, and pour the finish onto the wood, spreading it out with some extra-fine steel wool. The object is to saturate the wood pores, then wipe off excess finish with a rag.

Four clues to a fantastic finish

1) Study the information on the can or container before using the product. You'll find the manufacturer's recommendations for surface preparation, thinning agents, companion products (like stains, fillers, and sealers), application tools and techniques, and clean-up, to name a few.
2) Make sure the different preparations you use sequentially are compatible with one another. Never apply oil over sealer coats, for example. Compatibility infor-

mation should be on the can.
3) Prepare the surface. Any finish coat is only as good as the surface it covers. If you're working on bare wood, follow a filling, sanding, and sealing *schedule* that will really show off the finish. Wait for each coat to dry *completely* before applying another. You can speed up drying time by using a heat lamp.
4) Don't apply anything under damp or humid conditions, and make sure the surface you're treating is dry; otherwise absorption and adhesion are incomplete.

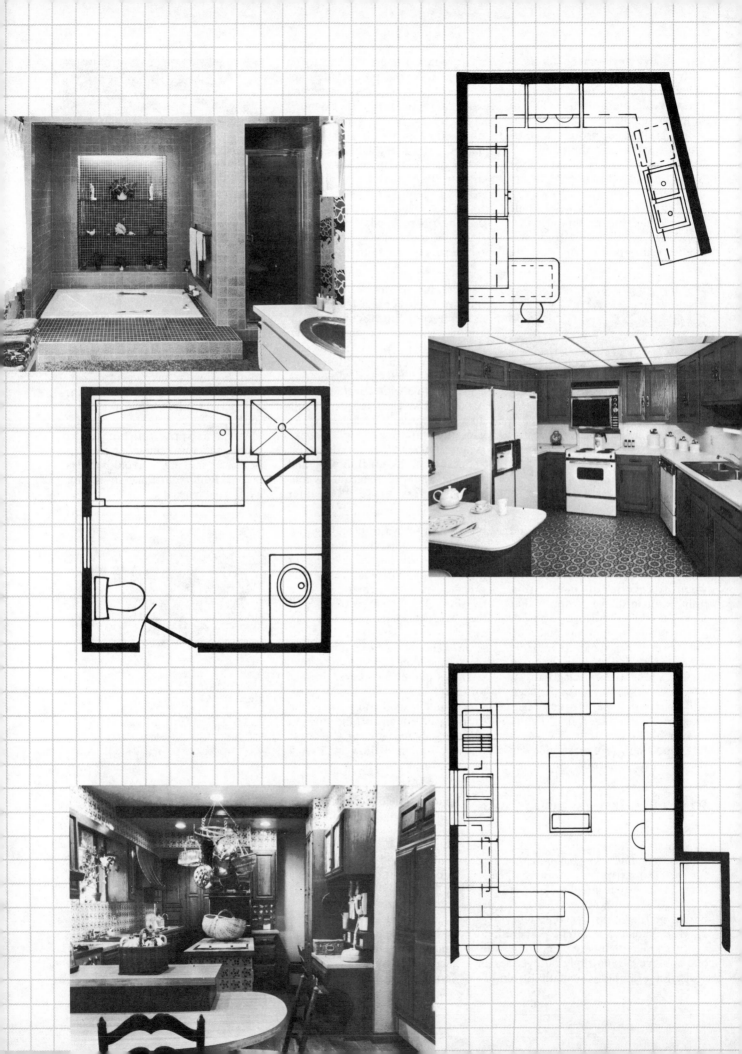

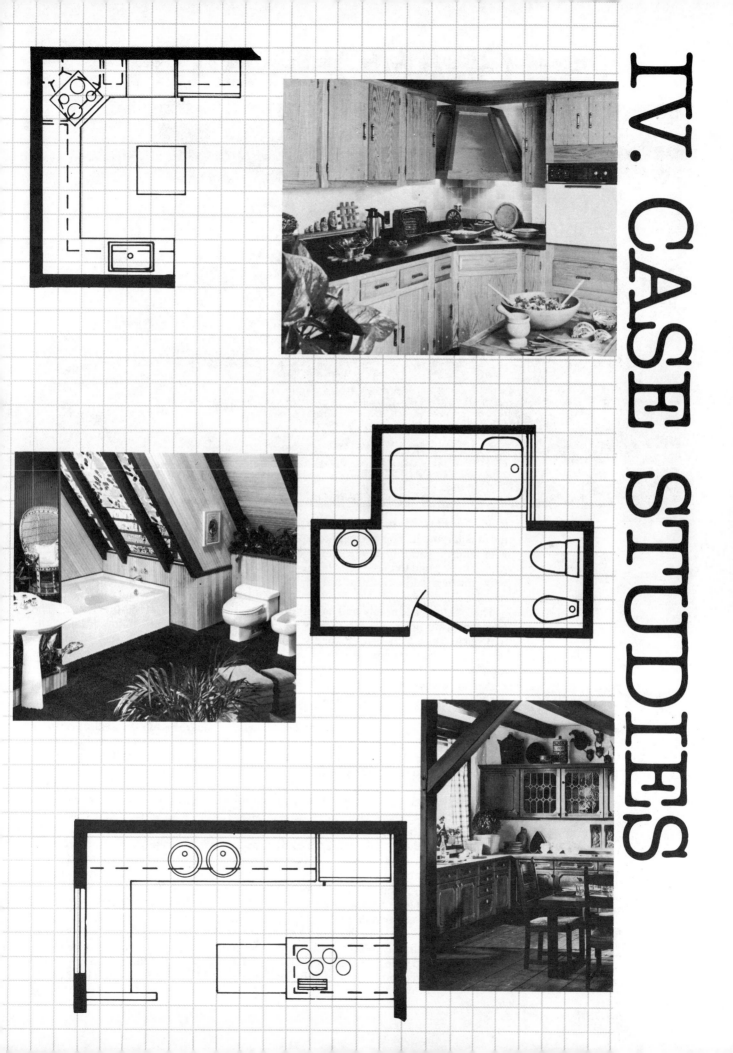

GLAMOUR BATH

After

Before

Compare this old bathroom with the way it looks above, after remodeling. Formerly, as you can see, unattractive fixtures crowded the room, while the walls and window were tacky, to say the least. On top of that, some of the pipes leaked. It was generally unattractive, and functioned poorly.

Remodeling your bathroom can also mean enlarging it. This project—complete with sunken bathtub—is an example of what can be done to make your home not only practical and beautiful, but luxurious as well.

The existing bathroom and adjoining bedroom were in an old farmhouse that had been allowed to become badly run down. By adding an extension on both bathroom and bedroom, the homeowners ended up with a much larger and more practical bathroom, as well as a master bedroom which connected to it directly.

The new portion of the bathroom features a sunken tub, natural stone for one complete wall, and mirror tile on the wall opposite the stone. A glass patio door opens onto a small sun deck surrounded by a stone wall—a second project you may or may not wish to tackle later on.

The old bathroom was narrow and dark, and the old tub took up a great deal of space. The old-style lavatory offered no storage space for bath items.

The original section of the room was remodeled to include a new 6-foot vanity with lots of storage area. The 9-foot ceiling height was kept, but the sides were "cambered" so that it would appear to be lower and would blend with the low ceiling in the new section. A new chandelier

also contributed to this effect. Ceramic tile, vinyl wallpaper, and an antique mirror set off by wall sconces completed the remodeling.

The trim wood for the bathroom was done in rough-sawn white cedar to match the trim of the rest of the house. The ceiling in the new added-on portion of the bathroom was 7½ feet, just enough to allow clearance for the sliding patio door and provide plenty of header support for the new roof. Lights were recessed into the ceiling in order to show off the wall, and a heat-light-fan combination unit was installed near the tub. Instead of running new duct work out to the bathroom, an electric baseboard floor heater was installed.

First step was to lay out the room addition. The complete size of the addition was 12x18 feet, which added 10′x6′8″ to the bathroom and 10x12 feet to the bedroom. The walls took up some floor space, which accounted for the difference in dimensions. This didn't include the outer rock wall or the deck.

Once the dimensions were laid out and stakes positioned to mark the outside of the walls, a back-hoe operator was called in to dig the footing trenches. The trench for the rock wall footing was 24 inches wide and 24 inches deep. The footing trench for the rest of the construction was 24 inches wide and 18 inches deep. From here on, you could follow the same steps as the couple who built the addition.

With the footing trench dug, your next step would be to figure the amount of concrete needed to fill the trench and to order it from a ready-mix concrete firm. Normally, if you give the concrete people the dimensions of the work, they can come pretty close to the amount; however, allow for a little extra because most companies will bring a bit more than you order to insure there being enough. It's a good idea to have a small project ready for a bit of concrete in case there is some left over.

Using a trowel, smooth the footing to provide a level working surface for both the stone wall and the concrete block foundation. Allow the footing to cure for a couple of days. While it is curing you can tear off the old siding from the wall where the addition will join the building.

If the building is also covered with some sort of sheathing, cut along the inside wall dimension of the addition to remove it. At the same time, cut 6 to 8 inches above the ceiling line, or where doors or archways will enter the addition, or around any areas where walls will be removed to join the old and the new sections. This provides for header supports.

After the footing has cured, you can start laying the concrete block foundation and the rock wall. It is necessary to exercise extra care in figuring the top of the concrete foundation footing so that the concrete blocks will come out at the right height, allowing you to join to the old portion of the building properly. And so, take care that the blocks are the same height as the foundation of the old building. Remember that a concrete block normally is 8 inches high (including a ⅜-inch mortar joint), and to this height must be added the joists, subfloor, and underlayment or finished floor. If the top of the foundation of the existing house is visible, it can be used to determine the proper height of the new foundation. It then is a case of measuring down to determine where the top of the footing should be located.

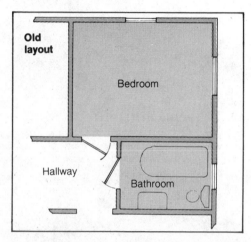

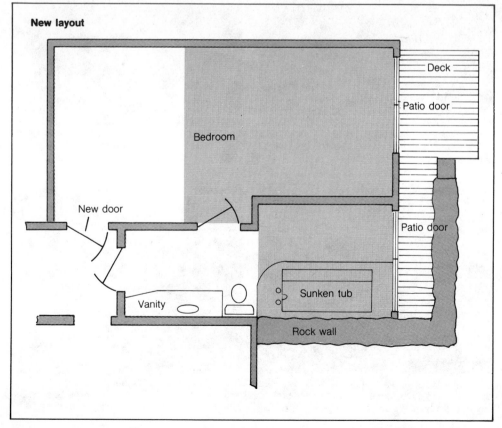

The important thing in your new layout is to avoid major plumbing work. Plan your new fixtures so that they fall within the same area as those they are replacing. This saves time and money.

Stone wall

What it takes

Approximate time: Depends on the weather, and if you have help; but allow a few weekends or a week if you're working by yourself, and are handy.

Tools and materials: Regular carpentry and masonry tools, plus shovel, wheel barrow, lumber for forms, mortar mix, metal reinforcing rods; finished lumber and regular building materials as needed.

Planning hints: Give plenty of time to planning your work, taking into account the weather, and the needs of members of the family. Be sure about the delivery dates of your materials; check that your order has been filled and that everything you will need is at hand *before* you start to work.

Mixing mortar

There are a number of good mixes. One of the best is as follows:
1 part portland cement
1 part lime
6 parts sand
Enough water to make the mixture smooth and creamy, yet allow it to stand up easily when placed in position.

A lot of money was saved on this project by using stone that was picked up in nearby fields. At the same time, you may not be so fortunate; you may have to buy stone. You can check local quarries to see what is available and at what cost.

Of course, you may decide simply to put up a regular stud wall with siding on the outside. Wallboard could be applied and taped inside, then covered with one of the several realistic imitation brick or stone materials; or you could put up one of the many types of wall paneling.

If you do decide on a stone wall, however, you will find that some of the best insulation you can get is provided by sandstone, soapstone, and even flintrock and marble; that is, you can save on heating as well as cooling cost.

Laying a stone wall such as this one is both difficult and easy. The hard part is the labor. The easy part is the skill. It

The wall for the room addition was built from stone that was picked up around the property. The alternative would have been a regular stud wall.

The secret of a sound stone wall is the correct mortar mix. It should be troweled on heavily to fill every irregularity in the stones.

After the mortar is applied, place the stone and force it well into place, allowing the excess to squeeze out. Clean off, and smooth the joints.

Know where you will place a stone before you lift it. Don't rely wholly on the mortar to make the fit, but select stones as much as possible according to contour.

The two sides of the wall run parallel and the space between should be kept even with fill—broken rocks and mortar—as the sides go up.

While the stone wall is being constructed, floor framing for the room addition can be built on the foundation of concrete block, if you have help.

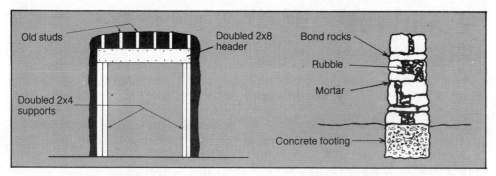

Old studs · Doubled 2x8 header · Doubled 2x4 supports

Bond rocks · Rubble · Mortar · Concrete footing

doesn't take long to learn how to find the right rock, flip mortar into place, position the rock, and then go on to the next one; but it does take some physical effort.

One of the secrets of good rock work is to mix the proper mortar. (See column at left.) Actually, the wall is two parallel walls constructed with rubble and mortar and cross-tie rocks between, as well as metal reinforcing rods.

The foundation wall of concrete block for the room addition had the top course of blocks plugged with mortar in which anchor bolts were set. The sill plate of the wall then was drilled to fit over the bolts. The anchor bolts should be about 4 to 6 feet apart, and high enough to allow you to fasten the sill plate securely in place.

Opening the wall. It was necessary to open the wall of the existing house in order to join the new addition. This operation took place in stages: first the siding was cut and removed, and then the sheathing was cut, but it was not removed until the addi-

tion had been framed and then closed in.

The opening was cut sufficiently high to allow for headers that were needed to support the wall and roof. For a span 10 feet or more, use floor jacks or shores to hold up the ceiling until the doubled 2x4 vertical supports and the doubled 2x6s, 2x8s, or 2x10s are installed for headers.

Tying in. The roof of the new structure can be tied to the roof of the existing house by first nailing a strip to the roof on which the new roof structure has been spiked. You must be sure to replace any broken or loosened shingles and install a metal or tarpaper valley at the intersection of the roofs.

The room can then be closed in, and a sliding glass door, with double-pane insulating glass, installed in the rough opening that may be sized according to the instructions that come with the door. It could take about an hour to fit the door into place, and it will be heavy enough to need at least one helper.

Bearing up under pressure

There's nothing to taking out a non-bearing partition. Removing a structural wall that's holding the house up is not an impossible job either, even for me. The problem is to find out *which* kind of wall it is before you start. All outside walls are usually bearing weight. So is an inside wall that runs down the middle of the length of the house. It usually is keeping the joists (that support the floor above) from bending or breaking in the middle. If you can't tell from the attic, cut a peep-hole in the ceiling right up against the wall. If you see a joist crossing over the wall, it's bearing. You have work on your hands—but not more than 14-feet-worth since you shouldn't remove more of a bearing wall than that anyway.

Practical Pete

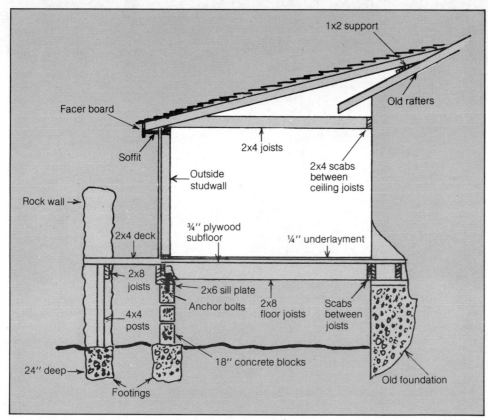

1x2 support · Old rafters · Facer board · 2x4 joists · 2x4 scabs between ceiling joists · Soffit · Outside studwall · Rock wall · 2x4 deck · ¾" plywood subfloor · ¼" underlayment · 2x8 joists · 2x6 sill plate · Anchor bolts · 2x8 floor joists · Scabs between joists · 4x4 posts · 24" deep · Footings · 18" concrete blocks · Old foundation

A sunken bathtub

What it takes

Approximate time: Allow 3 days, and try to have a helper.

Tools and materials: Hammer, power saw, electric drill and bits (including carbide-tipped bit), tile or glass cutter, tile nippers or pliers, screwdriver; lumber for forms, nails, screws, lag screws, anchors, mesh, sandpaper, concrete mix, shovel, trowel, caulking, grout, ceramic tile, alcohol and clean cloths; plumbing fixtures as required.

If your existing bathtub is in good condition you can install it in one of several ways to give it a "sunken" look. It can actually be recessed into the floor to project down into a basement or crawl space.

Another way to install a sunken tub would be to build a platform of 2x4s and plywood up around the existing tub, perhaps with steps; then cover it with tile.

Still one other way would be to partly recess the tub in the floor, with just a shallow platform built up around it. The method of installation would be determined by your personal preference, structural considerations, and the amount of time and money you want to spend on this particular part of the project.

The bathtub shown here is more like a swimming pool than the conventional sunken tub. However, construction is standard and will meet most building codes. If you decide to build a similar tub, check with your local code authorities to be sure you meet the requirements. One requirement, for instance, might be a waterproof membrane between the tub and the footing beneath.

The concrete tank shown here followed the detail of Fig. C.

Keep in mind that the tub was built in a room over a crawl space, which allowed it to rest on the ground.

First, a concrete footing was poured, 2 feet deep, and slightly larger than the dimensions of the tub. Because of the weight of the tub it would not be practical to set it over a basement or first floor.

With the footing poured you can start to assemble a form of 2-inch lumber. This can be built over the footing and is designed to create a wall 4 inches thick, and a bottom also 4 inches thick.

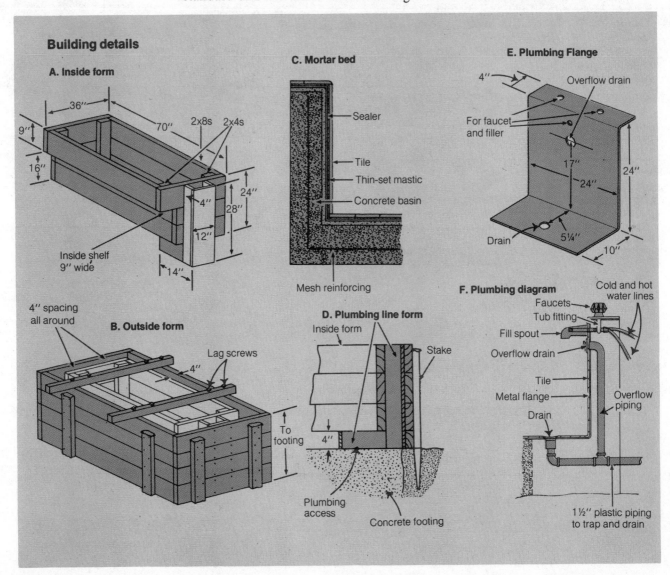

Building details

A. Inside form — 36″, 70″, 9″, 16″, 2x8s, 2x4s, 4″, 24″, 28″, 12″, 14″, Inside shelf 9″ wide

B. Outside form — 4″ spacing all around, Lag screws, 4″, To footing

C. Mortar bed — Sealer, Tile, Thin-set mastic, Concrete basin, Mesh reinforcing

D. Plumbing line form — Inside form, Stake, 4″, Plumbing access, Concrete footing

E. Plumbing Flange — 4″, Overflow drain, For faucet and filler, 17″, 24″, 24″, Drain, 5¼″, 10″

F. Plumbing diagram — Cold and hot water lines, Faucets, Tub fitting, Fill spout, Overflow drain, Tile, Metal flange, Drain, Overflow piping, 1½″ plastic piping to trap and drain

The inside form may be built as shown in Fig. A. The vertical and horizontal portions of the plumbing access form can be made from ¾-inch plywood, and centered on one end of the inside form.

The outside form was built of 2-inch lumber and made 4 inches higher than the inside form. Lengths of 2x4 were sharpened on one end and driven into the soil, then spiked to the form to brace and hold it.

The inside form can then be lowered into the outside form and positioned so that there is 4 inches of clearance all the way around. Lengths of 2x2 lumber are then lag-screwed to the inside form to support it 4 inches above the outside form at the bottom. The 2x2s are also lag-screwed to the outside form so the inside form will remain in position.

For further reinforcement, a 2x4 can be spiked across each end of the inside form and the outside form. Do not use metal ties, as you would between forms used for concrete basement walls, because of the potential for water leaks.

Pour the bottom of the tub just 2 inches deep, then position reinforcing mesh the full length and width, then pour 2 more inches of concrete and compact it. The bottom, of course, extends under the sides and ends (and step), except for the L-shape form in which the plumbing

later will be installed.

Trowel the exposed portion of the bottom smooth, then pour the step and trowel it. The walls are last, and they are reinforced with mesh and concrete tamped and compacted. After the concrete has set for a while (firm yet still workable) the tops of the walls are troweled smooth.

The concrete mix used here was 1 part cement, 2 sand, 3 parts pea-size gravel, water for a stiff mix.

After the concrete has seasoned for at least a week—kept damp during that time—remove the forms carefully. Any rough spots may be filled with latex patching plaster.

A sunken tub can be made any desired size. This one allows a depth of water up to 16 inches. The step was cast into the tub to make entry and exit easier. Because of the added depth, be sure to have firmly attached handholds or rails. The step and the area around the tub should have nonslip tub pads applied.

A drain must be built into the tub bottom, but the faucets and supply spout can be above and separate from the concrete form. You can locate your plumbing in an opening cast into the end of the tub. (See Fig. F). The opening can then be closed by a shaped piece of metal, as shown in Fig. E.

After the metal piece has been installed, the inside of the concrete tank may be sealed with four coats

of a special sealer. In this case, "Thoroseal" was used. Check your hardware dealer. When each coat has dried, it should be sanded before the next coat is applied.

Tile mastic for use on masonry surfaces that will be submerged in water is different from mastic used for surfaces such as in a tub or shower enclosure "Thin-set" mastic is sold at most tile and flooring stores, and is mixed like plaster. The mastic is quite viscous and sticky, and is applied in a coat ⅛ to ¼ inch thick. This thickness will permit adjusting any irregularities that might appear in the concrete.

The ceramic tiles which were used come in sheets 1 foot square, with each tile 4 inches square. The tiles are pre-grouted with silicone rubber, and grouting then is required only between sheets, and tiles that have to be cut.

The grout comes in cartridges that fit standard caulking guns, and excess caulk is easily removed with alcohol and a soft cloth.

After the tiles are applied, the mastic must be allowed to set for 24 hours before the grout is applied. Any mastic that squeezes out between the tiles can be removed with a damp cloth.

With the tub finished, you can then complete the floor of the bathroom, possibly using the same tile that was used for the tub.

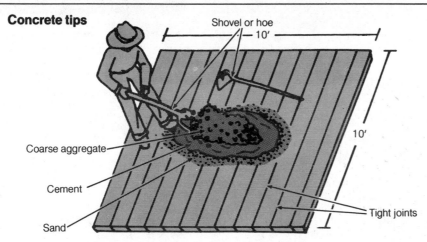

Concrete tips

Shovel or hoe
10'
10'
Coarse aggregate
Cement
Sand
Tight joints

For this project you will not be mixing a large amount of mortar, and so you will probably be mixing by hand. You will need a clean surface. This could be a wooden platform, or a mortar box, which will have sides to it. The platform or box should have tight joints to prevent loss of mortar. And it should be level.

The desired quantity of sand is placed on the bottom and the cement is spread on the sand,

and on top of this the coarse aggregate. To mix the materials—the dry first—you may use either a hoe or a square shovel with a D handle.

Turn the dry materials at least three times, or until the color of the mixture is uniform. Water is added slowly while the mixture is again turned at least three times. Add water gradually until you get the consistency you want.

Step by step

1. The first step in building a sunken tub, such as this one, is to construct a strong form. The outside edges of the inner form are the rough dimensions of the tub.

2. The bottom of the tub is poured, and it must be tamped solidly. The bottom is poured over a footing of concrete 2 feet deep, which sets before building the form.

3. The sides of the tub are poured next. It is important to tamp the mix thoroughly in order to remove all voids and to assure a continuous wall. Take time with this.

4. An opening should be formed in one end of the tub for fixtures. A metal plate was bent to shape, and then holes were drilled to accept the faucets and spout.

5. Latex caulking is now applied, the metal attached with screws driven into anchors set in holes that have been carefully drilled into the concrete.

6. The entire surface of the tub is then given several coats of mortar, sealer; and this includes the metal piece. This will provide a smooth surface for the tile.

7. Four coats of the special sealer were applied to the inside of the tub. Each coat was thoroughly sanded when it was dry. This takes time and care, but it's necessary.

8. After this, the tub was cleaned of debris, and vacuumed to get the dust out; then a thin-set mortar was mixed and applied with a trowel, over small areas at a time.

9. Tile mastic which is thin-set like this, is applied in a coat ⅛ to ¼ inch thick. This thickness also allows you to even out any irregularities in the concrete.

10. Sheets of tile are now pressed into the mortar, tapped smooth and flush with other sheets. Note the tile scraps; these are handy for spacing the tile.

11. Cut individual tiles free from the backing with a knife along the grout lines that are between the tiles. The tiles are 4x4 inches and come in sheets 1 foot square.

12. If you need to cut an individual tile, and you will probably have to for fitting, use a glass cutter or a tile cutter. Just score along the line as for window glass.

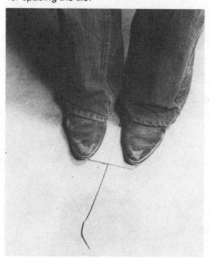

13. Place the tile with the scored line directly over a wire, then step on either side and break the tile along the line. It should break easily and cleanly.

14. To fit tile around plumbing trim, you will first have to mark it with a grease pencil, allowing some clearance that will be covered by the trim.

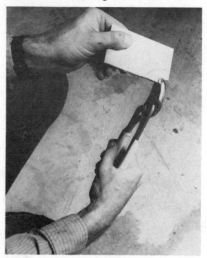

15. Some sizing of the tiles can be done by breaking away small pieces with a pliers. The water-pump type provides more leverage for this careful operation.

16. The best way to cut a hole in a tile is by drilling a ring of holes with a carbide-tip masonry bit in a power drill. Afterwards, file the rough edge smooth.

17. The tiles used here were pre-grouted with silicone rubber, and grouting then was only required between sheets and tiles that were cut. Mastic must set for 24 hours.

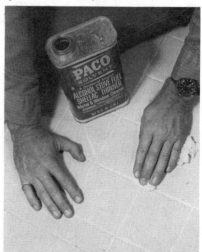

18. The way to clean up excess grout from the tiles is with alcohol and a soft, clean cloth. You can use the same tile for the floor of the bathroom as you did for the tub.

Vanity construction

The design shown in the drawing is a typical construction for an extended-cabinet vanity. Your first steps should be to decide upon the exact location of your unit. Take measurements to determine the precise amount of space available, and then establish a design.

It is necessary to decide in advance on the height of the vanity; and this will be based upon the personal preferences of those who will use the room most frequently. If children and adults are likely to share the bathroom, consider the possibility of a two-level, stepped-top setup with separate sinks installed at each level.

Mark out and cut the bottom, side, divider, back and frame pieces, then build the basic framework for your vanity, and install the bottom. Cut and fit the top, add laminate and trim the edges. Follow the drawing on this page.

Remember that it is important to avoid conflict with existing electrical, plumbing, heating, or structural elements. In order that no water or drain pipes would need to be moved the vanity should be designed so that the new basin will fall at roughly the same location as the old sink.

What it takes

Approximate time: A day for construction; at least an afternoon for installation.

Tools and materials: Power saw, pipe wrench, level, saber saw, screwdriver, file, punch, hammer, plane, trouble-light, electric drill and bits, sandpaper, screws, nails and hardware, patching compound, caulk, lumber, sink, and plumbing accessories.

Sink detail

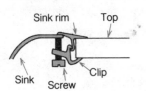

Sink rim — Top — Clip — Sink — Screw

Plumbing details

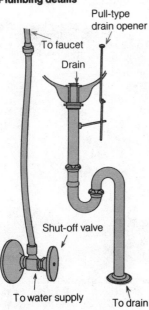

Pull-type drain opener — To faucet — Drain — Shut-off valve — To water supply — To drain

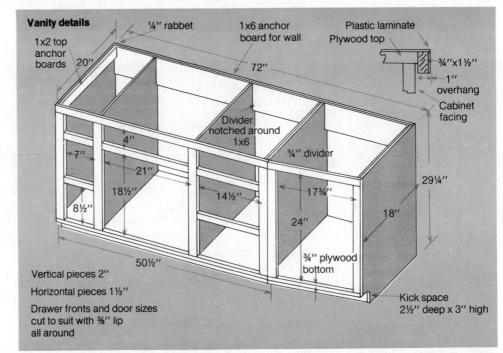

Vanity details

¼" rabbet · 1x6 anchor board for wall · Plastic laminate · Plywood top · ¾"x1½" · 1" overhang · Cabinet facing

1x2 top anchor boards · 20" · 72"

Divider notched around 1x6 · ¾" divider · 4" · 7" · 21" · 18½" · 8½" · 14½" · 17¾" · 24" · 29¼" · 18" · ¾" plywood bottom

50½"

Vertical pieces 2"

Horizontal pieces 1½"

Drawer fronts and door sizes cut to suit with ⅜" lip all around

Kick space 2½" deep x 3" high

Installation

1. Before you do anything else, shut the water off below the floor level. Then bleed and disconnect the hot and cold water lines. Disconnect the drain.

2. To remove the old wall-hung sink, lift up on the front edge and then lift the entire unit straight up and away from the wall. You may need a helper.

3. Next, remove the wall-mounting strip and all associated hardware; as well as any other projections. Remove electrical fixtures, reroute wiring. Fill holes, smooth the wall.

4. After the wall has been cleared and smoothed, place the vanity in position and level it. Make sure that it fits well against the wall, or walls. Use shingles or shims to level.

5. You may have to make a slight adjustment with certain pipes that project upward through the bottom of the cabinet. Best way to work here is with a trouble-light.

6. Now secure the vanity to the wall by driving nails, or large screws, through the cabinet into the studs behind the wall. Make sure that the vanity remains level.

7. Place lower part of new sink rim on vanity top, mark around lower part of rim, and then cut the sink opening with a saber saw; work slowly inside the line.

8. Punch out the holes for the clip-holding screws. Smooth with a file so that the screws will fit securely. Tighten screws no more than necessary; don't strip heads.

9. Now apply a bead of caulk to the sink rim. Don't try to scrimp here; use a quality product, because you will want years of watertight, troublefree service.

10. Place the sink and the trim ring in position, making sure they are properly aligned. Tighten the clips under the top to secure the sink in place.

11. Install the new faucets, connect the water and drain lines under the basin; and finally, clean off the caulk that was forced out around the metal trim ring.

After: A handsome marble-topped vanity provides hidden storage and requires no more floor space than the old steel legged sink.

Before: Neat and serviceable enough but a bit outdated. And not a single place to put bathroom cleaners or oversized toilet articles without tripping over them.

A bathroom renovation should be both functional and decorative. A full bath must be designed to include at the very least three major fixtures: sink, toilet, and shower or tub/shower combination. Maximum use of walls and floor for storage is crucial. These surfaces must additionally be water resistant and easy to clean. The range of decorative possibilities, beginning with color coordination of fixtures, goes on into almost limitless choices for mirrors, hardware, shower curtains, wallcovering, shelves, light fixtures, towel racks, bath mats, linens, soap dishes, etc.

The vanity and toilet shelf

The main reason for this renovation was to increase stowaway storage. Building a vanity below the sink was an obvious choice. The plastic laminate cabinet has double doors and a handy track-sliding drawer. No need to dodge sink pipes in

If your bath, as is frequently the case, has no window, you will want to make sure that a sturdy vented fan is in the plans. Shelf and storage space becomes increasingly important, as do electrical outlets, if you plan to use one or more of the electrical bathroom appliances available, including electric shavers, hair driers, heated rollers, and the electric toothbrush. This list of considerations becomes almost bewildering when the dimensions of an average bathroom are figured in. That's a lot of utility and style to arrange in a 5x8 room, no doubt the smallest in the house.

search of cleaning equipment.

The laminate is easy to maintain and plenty sturdy enough to support the molded marble sink unit above. A one-piece sink/counter is guaranteed to make cleaning easy.

A second narrower unit of molded marble extends from the edge of the sink over the toilet bowl to the wall. That's a handy resting place for any electrical appliances or toilet articles you'll be using. The join between sink and shelf units is plastered, then grouted, as is the wall/shelf join. To make tank repairs, the shelf unit can be removed, then replastered and grouted.

When installing a lighter weight counter, plastic laminate for instance, this section can be hinged to facilitate tank repairs.

The low backsplash is cast like a flange on each of the two counter sections and grouted across the top.

The overall effect of this marble topped vanity is one of elegant simplicity, easy on the eye and practical too.

The vanity and shelf unit looks like a single piece, and almost is.

The convenient roll-out shelf.

Updating—style and convenience

As is so often the case, renovating a single unit in this bath inspired additional touches. The toilet as a fixture was sound, but a colorful vinyl-covered foam rubber toilet seat was added, an improvement in appearance and comfort. A hand-held hygienic spray attachment makes a good shower better. The substitution of a light colored shower curtain gives the tiny room a brighter feeling. Flowered wallpaper on just two walls serves the same function, cheerful but not overwhelming.

TIP: To make a large bathroom cosier, use the opposite technique. A small print vinyl or treated paper on all available wall space and across the ceiling can really draw a room together.

A wall-mounted vanity shelf in tortoise plastic is handy for small items. The shelf is screwed to the wall. A matching trash basket and tissue holder complete this attractive accessory trio.

Handy over-sized plastic hooks on the back wall of the shower hold face cloths and rope soap conveniently. They are simple to mount, just peel off the protective paper over the self-adhesive and position on clean, dry tile.

The hand-held hygienic spray loops over the shower head when not in use.

Vanity shelf and flowered vinyl wallcover—designer touches.

Handy shower hangups.

A hinged laminate toilet shelf is a practical alternative.

TOWNHOUSE

The careful remodeling that produced this attractive result was designed to give a visually open effect, to increase the usable traffic area, and to add counter and storage space. The major changes involved removing the wall between the old kitchen and the larger dining-working area, and breaking through their low ceilings to the roof rafters above.

This kitchen renovation is designed to take advantage of open space, with emphasis on sharp lines and planes and a contrast of surfaces.

The unique aspect is the kitchen's location—on the top floor of a three-story townhouse. Built in the 1830s, the original structure was made of brick with wood support beams. Walls were plaster over lath that had been bound with plaster and horsehair. Later, the large original rooms were partitioned, using gypsum wallboard over studs, and the house was divided horizontally into two apartments. The upstairs kitchen was probably built at that time, with existing plumbing lines dictating the placement of the 2x5-foot 1920s porcelain sink. The modern stove and refrigerator would stay, but the cumbersome sink would have to be replaced.

Electricity had been installed by stapling wires along the baseboards and around the doors. Multiple extensions lay buried in enamel paint. New wiring for outlets and soffits to hide the cables would be required.

General Planning. The original kitchen layout, with a closet, stove, refrigerator, and oversized sink, limited workable floor space to less than 50 square feet—and no counter space! The central hall next to the kitchen was useful for transit only, with five doors and no windows. Through the trap door in another room, a good look at the attic above this area revealed a roof which continued over 4 feet above the ceiling.

Inspection showed that the two walls which separated the central hall from the kitchen and stairs could be taken out without affecting the building structure. With these walls removed, the new east wall would rise over 12 feet to the roof peak—perfect for a dramatic pine board cathedral ceiling. By opening the kitchen this way and cutting back the dormer storage closet, floor space would be more than doubled.

Removing the center room ceiling would expose the attic space above the small work room behind the hall. How best to employ this high sloped space? It would hardly be convenient as a pantry. The logical solution: a loft.

Designing the new kitchen. Ingenuity was required to turn the dormer area into useful space. Cutting back the storage closet would make space for the refrigerator. Repositioning the closet door would make it more convenient. Floor space under the other eave could be filled with useful counter space—a simple plywood surface supported by wood and finished with plastic laminate.

L-shaped floor cabinets (in the area where the wall had been) would define the cooking area and create work and storage space. The new sink, installed catercorner, could connect to existing plumbing.

Before final plans were made on the cabinets, a mock-up was built of wood scraps. The sink was put into place, to be sure there would be enough room for a splash back and to measure for the angle of the corner. The counter was specifically sized to accommodate the 6x6x½-inch terra-cotta tiles.

Other considerations. There is a dazzling variety of materials available for finishing surfaces. It takes some time to explore the possibilities, but it pays off when you use the best materials to fit the design at a price that sounds right.

When you sum up the cost of materials, it's important to consider durability, waste, error, and the time needed for installation. Don't forget those gallons of paint you may need! And don't cheat. Although you may want to keep costs down, be prepared to spend your entire budget—and maybe then some.

A showplace kitchen requires not only quality materials, but skilled labor as well. How much can you do yourself? Will you need an electrician, plumber, carpenter, or floor expert? Professional renovators may be the best investment for you. They have a variety of skills and are familiar with re-building. For this project, it took three renovators a total of 720 hours from the first blow of the sledgehammer to the last lighting fixture.

The following pages illustrate the special problems and solutions in this townhouse kitchen, with specific tips and on-the-spot photographs to show you the way to do it yourself.

Floor plans

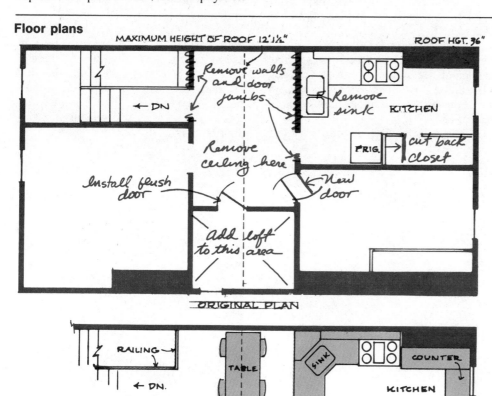

The original kitchen was 9½'x12½', but the sloping dormer cut heavily into usable floor space. The room next to the kitchen was a windowless 8'x12' box. Removing its north and south walls and ceiling created an additional 1400 cubic feet of usable space.

Removing the ceiling and wall

What it takes

Approximate time: At least 2-3 days, depending on how much is to be demolished.

Tools and materials: Straight bar, ripping bar, 20-ounce claw hammer, 8 pound long-handled sledgehammer (or a 2 pound short-handled sledgehammer), dust mask and filters, gloves, goggles, boxes to collect rubble, plastic sheet, and tape.

Removing a ceiling or wall is a major task requiring a lot of careful planning and a good deal of energy. You should be prepared to form your own demolition team and to take precautions to protect yourself and your home from a tremendous amount of dust.

The first step is to plan the cleanup. How will you get rid of debris? Collect enough boxes to hold chunks of broken wallboard, plaster, and lathing. You may need a truck or van to haul the debris to the dump, or you can hire a metal dumpster as used on construction sites.

Before you begin, find out where electrical, gas, and plumbing lines are and turn them off. Be careful not to damage the lines when you're working. You may have to use an extension cord to an outlet in another room to supply temporary power.

Close all doors to block the dust and cover exposed archways or open doorways with sheets of plastic, taped or tacked at the side. Put a portable fan at a window to blow the dust outdoors, or at least open all windows to ventilate the room. Be sure to wear gloves, goggles, and a dust mask to protect yourself from the dirt, and change the mask filters often.

If you're removing an entire ceiling, you'll find it easier to work in a team. One person pounds through the ceiling from the attic side with a sledgehammer; the other rips down the ceiling material from the underside with his hands. If there is no space above the ceiling, work from below using a ripping bar or straight bar and hammer. To separate the ceiling from the walls, perforate the corner bonds with the end of a straight bar hammered into the join.

A good way to crack a plaster wall is with a ripping bar. Hold the straight end, and take a long swing to whack the wall with the side of the hooked end. Once there's a large crack or hole, slip the hooked end in and pull the plaster down. But watch out! Half a wall of old plaster can come down at once. If you plan to remove only a part of a wall or if you're making a pass-through, you can use a circular saw for wallboard, or a power reciprocating saw to cut right through wallboard, plaster, and wood.

While working, always know where your partner is so no one gets hurt by falling debris. And when a large area of ceiling or wall has fallen, let the dust settle so you can see what you are doing. It's a good idea to clear away debris before it piles up, so you won't be stumbling over it.

1. "X" marks a spot where there is no ceiling joist. That's where to start a hole with the sledgehammer. Hold the head near the floor between your feet and swing upwards with both hands on the handle.

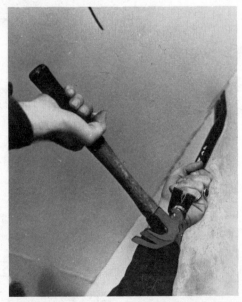

2. Place the end of the straight bar in the corner of the ceiling and side wall. Use a 20-ounce hammer to pound it into the corner, loosening old paint and wallboard. Continue to perforate the corners around the perimeter of the ceiling.

3. Both the ceiling and the wall have a layer of gypsum wallboard over plaster and lathing. You can rip down the wallboard with your hands. Use a crowbar or straight bar and hammer to pry the plaster loose.

4. Clear away the plasterboard and lathing to expose the wall studs or ceiling support beams. If there is attic space, pound the ceiling through with the sledgehammer from above. If not, work from below using a crowbar or straight bar and hammer.

5. A claw hammer will pry the lathing loose. In older buildings such as this one, the wood is bonded with plaster and horsehair.

6. Once the ceiling has been removed, there may be a rough edge at the top of a good wall. Use a straight bar and hammer to chisel away the edge; work carefully to avoid damaging the wall.

7. A power reciprocating saw will chew right through beams and wallboard. Wear goggles and a dust mask for protection, and have a partner hold the wood steady.

8. Work around electrical cables and plumbing fixtures when you tear down a wall or ceiling. The foreground of this photograph is only a portion of the square feet of floor space added to the original kitchen (shown beyond wall studs).

Boxed in again

The wall I wanted to remove *would* be the one with all those plumbing pipes and electrical wiring running inside it from floor to ceiling. I knew it was going to be trouble because the upstairs bathroom was right over it, and there were a lot of outlets and switches in it. I was not about to start re-routing water pipes myself, but I wanted to get started on the partition right away, and the plumber couldn't come for a week. He came up with the answer on the phone. "Pete," he said, "go ahead and tear out most of the old wall now, patch everything up, even paint if you want to—but leave just enough of the end of the wall standing so you don't disturb the pipes. I'll get there next Saturday and move 'em. Then you'll just have that tag end to finish up Sunday."
Sometimes I wonder why that guy doesn't run for president.

Practical Pete

Cathedral ceiling and walls

What it takes

Approximate time: Ceiling—It took two carpenters a total of four days to complete the ceiling. Walls—Three carpenters spent a total of three days installing the vertical wall planking.

Tools and materials: Insulation, plastic sheet, staple gun; saw protractor, power saw, electric sander, wood plane, bevel gauge, level to prepare planking; hammer, 8d and 10d cut nails, 6d galvanized finishing nails; 1x4s, 1x3 furring strips, cedar shims, 1x4 pine planking (for ceiling), 5-inch tongue and groove pine paneling (for wall).

With the removal of the old ceiling, roof joints and beams were exposed. Because the building was inexpensively constructed originally, the joists didn't form a uniform angle along the roof ridge and there was no main ridge beam. A new ridge would be needed to create a uniform ceiling angle.

The roof angle was 30°. The main wall sloped from the kitchen dormer, less than three feet from the floor, to the roof peak, 12 feet high. This wall area would help create a stunning cathedral ceiling.

The east wall was plaster to the height of the former ceiling and exposed brick to the roof. Usually, old brick can be restored with new mortar and cleaned up with carbon tetrachloride. But for this room it was decided that a new wall would be built over the brick.

The new townhouse kitchen ceiling was finished with 1x4 knotty pine boards nailed to a plywood base at random lengths. Random planking is less expensive than an even length design because it uses all the lumber. Also, the joins are scattered throughout and don't form an obvious line. The join lines form interesting verticals in the horizontal planking, adding to the overall effect.

The walls were covered with 5-inch tongue and groove pine boards in a vertical pattern, cut to fit the ceiling angle. The vertically planked walls make an attractive design complement to the horizontally planked cathedral ceiling.

The old crossbeams were replaced with handsome oak-veneered pine beams. These beams offer strong support for a snow-laden roof.

1. Here's how the ceiling looked before construction began. New plasterboard would be joined to old below the beam. Wood planking for the ceiling would begin above the exposed beam, rising from there to the roof ridge and extending down the far side of the ridge to the top of the north wall (see plans).

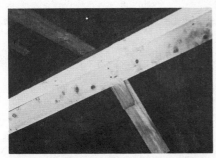

2. Lengths of 1x4 board are nailed at the ridge to form the ceiling angle. Shingles are used to shim the boards so they will make a flat support for the ceiling.

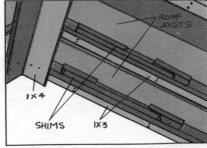

3. Strips of 1x3 furring are attached to the roof joists and shimmed to make a level nailing surface.

4. A staple gun is used to attach fiberglass insulation between the roof joists. Then the ceiling is covered with plastic sheeting.

5. Plywood is attached to the furring with 6d nails. The fit doesn't have to be perfect as long as the ceiling is covered and forms an even surface for the wood planking.

6. When preparing the wood planking, use a saw protractor to measure the boards for cutting. By taking time to measure and cut correctly you'll avoid a lot of problems when it comes to nailing up the boards.

7. The boards are butted tightly against each other and fastened to the plywood with 6d galvanized finishing nails.

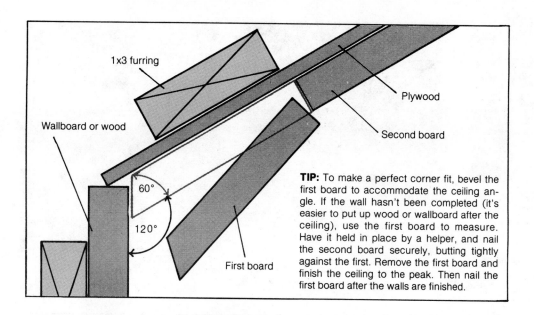

1x3 furring

Wallboard or wood

Plywood

Second board

60°

120°

First board

TIP: To make a perfect corner fit, bevel the first board to accommodate the ceiling angle. If the wall hasn't been completed (it's easier to put up wood or wallboard after the ceiling), use the first board to measure. Have it held in place by a helper, and nail the second board securely, butting tightly against the first. Remove the first board and finish the ceiling to the peak. Then nail the first board after the walls are finished.

Covering the walls

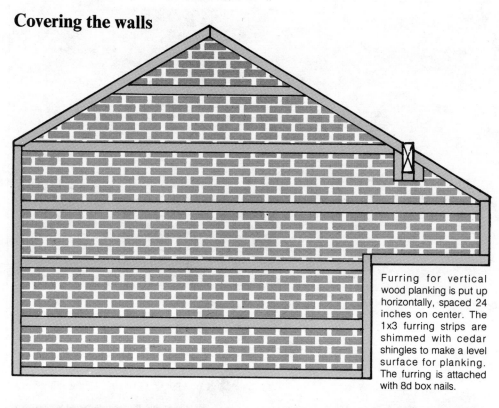

Furring for vertical wood planking is put up horizontally, spaced 24 inches on center. The 1x3 furring strips are shimmed with cedar shingles to make a level surface for planking. The furring is attached with 8d box nails.

8. Tongue and groove pine, used for the walls, comes in a variety of widths. The notched edges slip into each other to make a strong, snug fit.

9. Furring strips are attached at the base of the ceiling to form a level surface for wall framing. A bevel gauge is used to measure and cut the boards to fit snugly at the lower edge of the ceiling. Boards are then nailed to the furring with 6d finishing nails.

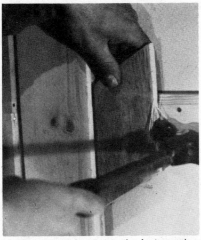

10. To prevent damage to the factory edge, a scrap piece of pine is used to hammer against when fitting one edge into the next.

11. One door is covered with planking and attached with a length of continuous hinge. The boards are matched to give the impression that the door is part of the wall.

12. Wall planking is cut to accommodate electric outlets and switches.

A

B

C

D

A. The expanse of pine board which climbs the east wall gives the room a feeling of grace. It's easy to maintain after applying a coat of varnish.

B. This photograph, taken after work had been completed, shows the east wall planking which extends into the work area, stopping just short of the stove space.

C. Ceiling planking stops just short of the beam. Plasterboard continues below the beam to the dormer wall.

D. The cathedral ceiling, so vast in feeling that it's hard to believe the roof peak is only 12 feet high.

Plastic laminate counter

Plastic laminate makes an excellent surface for kitchen counters. Laminates are easy to clean and are durable under normal use. Some laminates, however, can be damaged by bleaches or cleaners, and may be sensitive to extreme heat. Be sure to observe the manufacturer's recommendations for maintenance.

Sheets of laminate are available in standard sizes from 2x5 feet to 5x12 feet, the more durable 1/16-inch for horizontal surfaces and 1/32-inch for vertical surfaces. They come in a wide range of designs—from solid colors to abstract patterns and wood grain—and are available in matte or gloss finish.

1. Here's the difficult dormer area for which a plastic laminate counter was planned. A high, unusable shelf built previously has already been removed. The new counter took about two days to build.

2. To make a support for the countertop, fasten 1x3 boards to the wall with panel adhesive and wallboard screws. Frame out to the width of the counter and use braces for additional strength. Level carefully.

3. Use 8d nails to secure ⅝-inch plywood to the framing, fitting it to the contour of the wall. Laminates can be glued to most flat surfaces, but plywood and chipboard are the most commonly used bases.

4. A power saw with a fine-toothed blade is the quickest way to cut the laminate. It can also be cut with a fine-toothed hand saw or scored with a special laminate-cutting blade and snapped apart. Cut from the decorative side, and make the pieces slightly oversize for trimming.

5. Apply contact adhesive to the back of the laminate and the plywood top. Let it dry for about 15 minutes. Work carefully when putting the laminate in place, because the adhesive sticks instantly.

6. Clamp the edges with C-clamps. Use pieces of wood between the clamp and the laminate to protect the surface. Let the work dry in the clamps for half an hour before removing.

7. You can trim the edge with a saw and file, but the neatest edge is made with a router and a special bit made specifically for trimming laminate. Gaps between the laminate and the wall should be filled with latex caulking compound. Run your finger along the seam to smooth the caulking.

8. Clean, smooth lines define the new counter area, which adds 10 feet of working space. You can install shelves beneath the countertop and finish them the same way. The shelf here adds 18 inches of storage.

TIP: Care must be taken when laying down large sheets of laminate to which adhesive has been applied so that they will not adhere before you are ready. Lay small strips of wood between the laminate and the plywood surface. Press down, starting at an edge, moving the wood strips as you go along.

Custom cabinets

What it takes

Approximate time: Three days.

Tools and materials: Saw, hammer, screwdriver, level, sander, 8d box nails, wallboard screws, finishing nails, wood putty; 1x3s, 4x3s, ⅝-inch birch plywood.

In order to create an L-shaped area for sink and counter space, it was necessary to design and build custom cabinets. Two important considerations in figuring dimensions were the size of the sink to be installed and the height of the stove which was already in place. For ease and efficiency, the sink would be positioned catercorner, with counter space on both sides.

One potential problem was the water that would splash behind the sink (thus over the edge and down the side of the cabinet). The solution: a boxed surface of tile recessed an inch behind the sink lip, high enough to stop water. The width of the counter and height of the backsplash (which continues along the wall to hide pipes and gas lines) were determined by the size of the counter tiles (6x6x½-inch) and the space required for grout.

Storage space beneath the counter would be divided into three cabinet areas: a door and shelves next to the stove; a door beneath the sink; and a drawer, door and shelves on the end. The last 12 inches of the counter would be open beneath.

1. The base frame is made with 2x4s, nailed together with 8d box nails and covered with ¾-inch birch plywood. Notice how the bottom is recessed for a kick board.

2. The cabinets are framed with 4x3s, 1x3s, and ⅝-inch birch plywood, nailed with 8d box nails and fastened to the wall with wallboard screws. Horizontal boards are level; verticals are plumb.

3. The top is cut from a single piece of plywood, with a cutout for the sink. The edge is trimmed with 1x3 pine, attached flush to the top surface with finishing nails.

4. A box is framed and covered with plywood for the backsplash. Notice how the angle is cut back so it doesn't form a point. The side piece of plywood is cut from a single sheet.

5. Doors are attached flush to the front surface with lengths of continuous hinge. For a natural finish, nails are recessed and filled with wood putty. Hardware goes on after the cabinets are painted or varnished.

Tile countertop. Ceramic or terra-cotta tiles add a nice design touch to a countertop and sink backsplash. Available in 4- or 6-inch sizes, they are laid the same way as for floors or walls. Bull-nose end pieces are rounded to fit corners and sides.

For best results, plan the way the tiles will fit even before you buy them. You may want to place the dry tiles on the counter and tape them to the wall to be certain of the design. In this case, full 6x6x½-inch terra-cotta tiles fit perfectly because the counter was custom built to accommodate the width of four full tiles (plus grout).

The tile for this counter took about eight hours to install. The sink was put in shortly thereafter. Allow grout at least 24 hours to dry.

Vinyl tile floor

Choosing from the dozens of floor vinyl designs on the market can be overwhelming. One-piece vinyl may need expert fitting, but tiles are easy for anyone to put in. Some are backed with adhesive—you pull off the protective paper and stick the tile to the floor. Though less messy, it is not necessarily easier or faster to put down adhesive tile than to spread floor cement and lay the tiles in place.

Preparing the surface. Check to see that the subfloor is firmly attached. Renail loose boards and drive all nails flush. On an old tiled surface, replace missing tiles with new ones to fill the space. Larger areas can be filled with ¼-inch plywood. Smooth small gaps with floor grout or wall compound.

For best results, the subfloor should be smooth, dry, and free of dust and grease. Scrape off splatters of spackle, wax, or other material that might form a bulge.

Lining up the tiles. The placement of the tiles depends on the design and the shape of the room. Some designs combine four or more tiles to form a pattern, others don't need special attention. Rarely are rooms exactly rectilinear, and the edge pieces which are cut to fit often show the slant of a wall.

The key to laying tile so that it looks straight is to mark off the center of the room. Snap chalk lines from the center of opposite walls to determine where the room center intersects. Measure the intersecting lines. How will the tiles fit? Lay dry tiles down along the lines to check; you may need to adjust the lines.

Oddly shaped areas are more difficult to set straight. Sometimes you should go by what the eye sees as straight—even if it doesn't measure that way. For example, in this renovation, the tile at the top of the stairs can be seen first, because it opens up into the room. The tile was not laid so it would be in the middle of the top step; rather, it was done so there would be two full 12-inch tiles and an even line of trim on the wall side. Since the other side is the bannister and spindles, it is not as noticeable that the tile is not parallel to the edge at that spot.

What it takes

Approximate time: A couple of hours for a small room, up to two full days if there are repairs and a lot of special fitting.

Tools and materials: Spackling compound, wallboard compound, commercial floor grout, ¼-inch plywood to fix a bad floor, floor cement, notched trowel, tiles, utility knife.

TIP: Professionals use a grout that comes in powder form and mixes with water. Troweled onto a broken subfloor, the grout provides a strong, smooth bond for the tiles.

1. Large areas of missing tile can be patched with ¼-inch plywood. Fill the gaps between the wood and tile with spackling compound or wallboard compound applied with a taping knife. Let it dry for 24 hours.

2. Patch small areas with a new tile cut to size. Use a taping knife to apply floor cement to the back and stick it in place.

3. Spread floor cement with a notched trowel. Take large sweeping movements with the tool to spread the adhesive. Let it dry until it is tacky to touch before you lay the tiles.

4. Lay each tile in place, doing a quarter of the room at a time. Press tiles down gently; don't slide them, or the adhesive will ooze at the seam. Run your finger along the seams to pick up excess cement.

5. To fit the areas next to the wall, place a new tile over the first full tile from the wall. Take another full tile and butt it against the wall. Cut along the edge. The piece cut off will fit the area next to the wall.

6. Vinyl flooring is extremely durable, resists damage by spirit solvents, grease, and alkalis, and has high resiliency. The tiles are easy to lay and look great.

COMPACT KITCHEN

What it takes

Approximate time: Three days.

Tools and materials: Hammer, screwdriver, level, electric handsaw, hack saw; screws, nails, wood shims, stain, putty, cabinets and hardware.

Before: Here's how the kitchen looked before renovation began.

After: This kitchen renovation is designed to update and organize a very limited work area. The new fixtures and countertops make the fullest practical use of space.

The basic work involved is carpentry and the installation of new fixtures. The range, refrigerator, sink, and dishwasher seen in these photos are new, but they are replacements for original appliances, not additions. Thus, no additional electrical lines were required, though several outlets were added or repositioned.

For guidelines to follow when removing old cabinets and fixtures, see the pertinent chapters in the front of this book.

The work sequence described in this case study begins with the installation of base cabinets. Preparation for the reconstruction involved removal of the old fixtures, roughing in plumbing and electrical lines, and basic plastering to even out damaged walls.

Setting base cabinets

Base cabinets go in first. Leveling and setting the base or floor cabinets is the key to the entire job. If the base cabinets are not level, the entire job will be misaligned, since the splashback and top cabinets are leveled on the base installation.

If the floor is fairly level, the base cabinets can be set and shimmed. If shimming is not sufficient, lay down ¼-inch Masonite and level that. Shim the Masonite if necessary, and tack it down.

Once the cabinets are in place, they should be secured to the rear wall with four screws. To secure cabinets to each other, first countersink through the corner stiles; then drive screws through them.

1. Base cabinets should be carefully leveled, both front-to-back and side-to-side.

2. Cabinets are shimmed with angled wood shingles until they are perfectly level.

3. It was three days before the new sink and countertop could be installed. The old sink was hooked up for temporary use.

The countertop

The pre-cut, pre-finished plastic laminate countertop is installed next. It is set on the cabinets and secured by drilling through cabinet corner blocks into the countertop deck. When drilling into the underside of the countertop, be careful not to go through the laminate surface.

Once counter is secured, sink can be installed.

Appliances

With the counter and base cabinets in place, all appliances can be installed and hooked up.

Here the dishwasher fits under the counter and hooks into the plumbing beneath the sink. The refrigerator, which opens toward the kitchen, fits snugly at the end of the sink counter. On the opposite wall, the edges of the range are leveled to exactly match the adjacent 36-inch countertop.

Backsplash

There are two types of backsplash popular for use in the kitchen. The standard backsplash extends 4 inches up the wall behind the countertop and sink area. The second type covers the entire wall from the top of the counter to the bottom back edge of the hanging cabinets. If installing a standard low backsplash, the wall cabinets must be leveled before hanging. Begin the installation with an end or corner cupboard and shim to the wall until it is

level. The standard measurement for the height of hanging cabinets is 18 inches from the countertop deck. The high backsplash measures 18 inches, so the cabinets rest on top, automatically level if the base cabinets have been properly leveled.

Soffits

If you are not installing top cabinets, you may want to construct a ceiling soffit even with the top front cabinet edge. Furring strips (1x3) are secured to and leveled on the top of the wall cabinet at a distance from the front edge which measures the thickness of your soffit material: ¼ inch for ¼-inch Masonite, or ⅜ inch for ⅜-inch Sheetrock, for example. Carefully measure and secure corresponding furring on the ceiling above. Furring can be a continuous vertical strip or short (2-inch) strips spaced 16 inches apart. Nail fitted Masonite or Sheetrock to the furring. What is most important is that the finished soffit be even and level with the cabinet fronts. The finished soffit can be painted or wallpapered as desired.

Hanging cabinets

The first cabinet is screwed to the back wall with four screws. When working from a corner, hang the corner cabinet first. Any shimming is done between the first cabinet and the wall, not between cabinets. The next cabinets are also screwed to the wall, and then attached to each other.

1. The corner cabinet is positioned and screwed hand tight to the wall while aligning.

2. Standing at eye level in front of the cabinet, you can check the work with a level.

3. When working on hanging cabinets, it is easiest to stand on the countertop, but be sure to protect the surface from scratches.

4. Slender wood shims are driven between cabinet edge and wall.

A second bank of cabinets

If you are putting up a second bank of cabinets rather than a soffit, the second tier will be leveled and secured on the first bank. Installing a second row of cabi-nets is not much more difficult than building a soffit. The extra expense translates into a lot more storage.

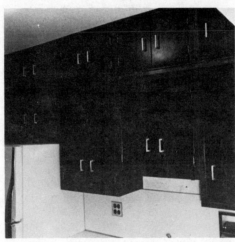

1. A second bank of cabinets here rises to the ceiling. To reduce weight and expense, the upper bank is in fact a skeleton, hinged doors on a frame, not full boxes.

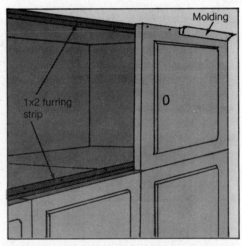

2. The door frame is aligned with and secured on two lengths of 1x2 furring. One strip is nailed across the top front edge of the lower bank of cabinets, just far enough back to accommodate the depth of the skeleton frame. The second furring strip is carefully aligned parallel to the first and nailed to the ceiling.

3. A right angle panel L on each end frame makes alignment easier and gives additional vertical support.

4. Here's how it looks when the work is in progress. When the installation is completed, however, it will appear as solid as a real cabinet. Those skeletons are useful for storing infrequently used items.

Molding

Molding gives a finished look to your cabinet installation. While measuring and leveling your work carefully is imperative, molding will disguise any minor join flaws and smooth the whole cabinet area into its setting.

1. Matching molding, available from your cabinet manufacturer, should be installed at all wall, soffit, and double bank intersections.

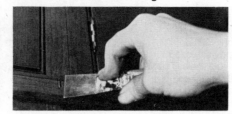

2. Countersink nail heads with nail set and touch them up with crayon or wood putty and stain mixed to match the wood.

Details and additional features

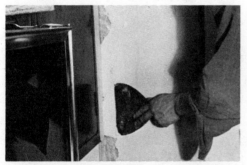

1. The cabinet-wall intersection is carefully spackled prior to wallpapering.

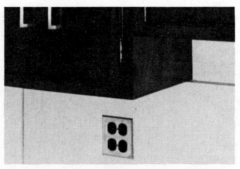

2. Cutouts for electrical outlets in a high backsplash must be made prior to installing the laminate.

TIP: Bear in mind the resale value of your home when you're planning a renovation. For instance, low counters of around 32 inches, and high ones of 39, may really limit the number of prospective buyers for your home.

3. A built-in paper towel and plastic wrap dispenser is available as a unit from various manufacturers. The backsplash cutout required, as for outlets, must be made before installation.

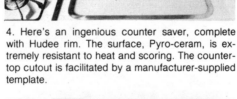

4. Here's an ingenious counter saver, complete with Hudee rim. The surface, Pyro-ceram, is extremely resistant to heat and scoring. The countertop cutout is facilitated by a manufacturer-supplied template.

5. A convenient ready-made rack for can storage. Available pre-assembled, the rack is screwed to the back of a cabinet door.

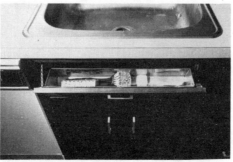

6. A bottom-hinged sponge and brush drawer in front of the sink. A drawer such as this can only be installed where cabinet doors hang flush with their frames.